Helion & Company Limited
Unit 8 Amherst Business Centre
Budbrooke Road
Warwick
CV34 5WE
England
Tel. 01926 499 619
Email: info@helion.co.uk
Website: www.helion.co.uk
Twitter: @helionbooks
https://helionbooks.wordpress.com/

Text © Joseph Mathers 2025
Photographs © as individually credited
Colour Profiles: Giorgio Albertini, David Bocquelet, Luca Canossa, Tom Cooper, Goran Sudar
Maps: Tom Cooper

Cover image: At around 1830hrs on 3 March 2022, the Russian paratroopers of the 5th Air Assault Company, 2nd BTG, 31st Guards Air Assault Brigade, ran straight into a waiting Ukrainian ambush inside central Hostomel. In the ensuing chaos, a pair of badly wounded paratroopers were loaded into a BMD-4M in an attempt to evacuate them. Unfortunately, the BMD had only travelled a short distance when it crashed into a concrete block and turned vertical, becoming hopelessly stuck. The crew abandoned the vehicle, leaving one Corporal Ponomarev alone in the rear passenger compartment with the two casualties. Outside, intense gunfire sounded as several Russians were shot just metres away, but no Ukrainian advanced to check inside the BMD itself. Apparently unaware of how closely death was passing, Ponomarev busied himself with tending to the two wounded, one already dying, the other begging for water. Eventually, when the sound of firing had fallen away, he ventured outside to search for help. By now, night had descended, and he found the streets deserted beyond the wreckage and corpses of the rest of the company. When he returned to check on the wounded, they too were gone. At a loss, Ponomarev took shelter from ensuing shelling in a garage, where he fell asleep. He was found the next morning by Ukrainian soldiers and taken prisoner, ending his ordeal. (Ukrainian GUR)

Designed and typeset by Mach 3 Solutions (www.mach3solutions.co.uk)
Cover design Paul Hewitt, Battlefield Design (www.battlefield-design.co.uk)

Every reasonable effort has been made to trace copyright holders and to obtain their permission for the use of copyright material. The author and publisher apologise for any errors or omissions in this work, and would be grateful if notified of any corrections that should be incorporated in future reprints or editions of this book.

ISBN: 978-1-804517-20-8

British Library Cataloguing-in-Publication Data
A catalogue record for this book is available from the British Library

All rights reserved. No part of this publication may be reproduced, stored in a retrieval system, or transmitted, in any form, or by any means, electronic, mechanical, photocopying, recording or otherwise, without the express written consent of Helion & Company Limited.

We always welcome receiving book proposals from prospective authors.

CONTENTS

Abbreviations and Acronyms		2
Acknowledgements		2
Note		2
Introduction		3
1	Unchecked Hubris	3
2	The Ukrainian Prelude	8
3	The Battle Begins	13
4	The Race to Kyiv	15
5	The Tipping Point	24
6	Reinforcing Failure	29
7	The Battle of Moschun	35
8	The End in the West	39
9	Eastern Axes	45
10	The Breakthroughs of the 2nd GCAA and 41st CAA	53
11	The Tide Turns in the East	63
Appendix		72
Select Bibliography		75
Endnotes		75
About the Author		86

Note: In order to simplify the use of this book, all names, locations and geographic designations are as provided in *The Times World Atlas*, or other traditionally accepted major sources of reference, as of the time of described events.

ABBREVIATIONS AND ACRONYMS

AB	Air Base
AFV	armoured fighting vehicle
APC	armoured personnel carrier
APFSDS	armour-piercing fin-stabilised discarding sabot
ATGM	anti-tank guided missile
BMD	*Boyevaya Mashina Desanta* (airborne combat vehicle)
BMP	*Boyevaya Mashina Pyekhoty* (infantry combat vehicle)
Bort	two-digit identification number on Russian and Ukrainian military aircraft
BRDM	*Boyevaya Razvedyvatelnaya Dozornaya Mashina* (combat reconnaissance/patrol vehicle)
BTG	battalion tactical group
C2	command and control
CAA	Combined Arms Army
CB	Covering Brigade
CTG	company tactical group
EW	electronic warfare
FSB	*Federalnaya Sluzhba Bezopasnosti* (Federal Security Service)(Russian)
GAAB	Guards Air Assault Brigade
GAAD	Guards Air Assault Division
GAD	Guards Airborne Division
GCAA	Guards Combined Arms Army
GMRB	Guards Motor Rifle Brigade
GRU	*Glavnoye Razvedyatelnoye Upravleniye* (Main Intelligence Directorate) (Russian)
GSB	Guards Spetsnaz Brigade
GTA	Guards Tank Army
GTB	Guards Tank Brigade
GTD	Guards Tank Division
HEAT	high-explosive anti-tank
IAP	International Airport
IFV	infantry fighting vehicle
KORD	*Korpus Operatyvno-Raptovoyi Diyi* (Rapid Operational Response Unit) (Ukrainian national police special forces)
MANPAD	man-portable air-defence (system)
MMRB	Mountain Motor Rifle Brigade
MRAP	mine-resistant ambush protected (vehicle)
MRB	Motor Rifle Brigade
MRLS	multiple rocket launcher system
MT-LB	*Mnogotselevoy Tyagach Legky Bronirovanny* (multi-purpose towing vehicle light armoured)
MTO	material-technical support
NATO	North Atlantic Treaty Organization
NBC	nuclear, chemical, biological
NIB	Naval Infantry Brigade
NLAW	Next Generation Light Anti-Tank Weapon
OPFOR	opposing force
OSK	Operational Strategic Commands
POW	prisoner of war
PSZSU	*Povitriyani syly Zbroiynyh syl Ukrayini* (Ukrainian Air Force)
Rosgvardia	Russian National Guard
RUK	*razveyvatelno-udarnnyy komplekx* (Reconnaissance-Strike Complex)
SAM	surface-to-air missile
SOF	special operations forces
SRG	sabotage and reconnaissance group
SV	*Sukhoputnyje voyska* (Russian ground forces)
SVR	*Sluzhba Vneshney Razvedki* (Foreign Intelligence Service)(Russian)
TDF	Territorial Defence Forces
UAV	unmanned aerial vehicle
VDV	*Vozdushno-desantnye voyska* (Russian airborne forces)
VKS	*Vozdushno-kosmicheskiye sily* (Russian Aerospace Force)
VOG	Russian and Ukrainian designation for a grenade used by grenade launchers
VSRF	*Vooruzhonnije Síly Rossíyskoj Federátsii* (Armed Forces of the Russian Federation)
ZSU	*Zbroini syly Ukrainy* (Armed Forces of Ukraine)

ACKNOWLEDGEMENTS

The author must first thank his family and friends for their enthusiastic support, without which this project would have been impossible. The author also wishes to express his earnest gratitude to Christopher Lawrence, Sasho Todorov, Milos Sipos, Stanislav Gurak, and Max Schönhausen, whose shared insights, materials, and expertise regarding the battle contributed greatly to this book.

The author wishes to also thank Sandra Andersen Eira, Andrii Kulish, and Vlad Podol for their generous permission to use their photographs for the book. To the same end, he thanks Inna Gadzynska (Texty.org), Marian Kushnir (Radio Liberty), and Dmytro Dzhulay (Radio Liberty). The author also expresses his gratitude for the invaluable translation help provided by Eric Golub, Lubov Nikolaevna Golub, and Emilia Scobbie, and the support and guidance of Dr Sarah Bulmer, who supervised the dissertation underlying this work. Finally, the author gives his greatest thanks to Tom Cooper, for the unexpected opportunity to write and publish this book in the first place.

NOTE

To minimise confusion, the Russo-Ukrainian term for an artillery or air defence battalion (*divizion*) is not used in this book. In the same vein, to prevent confusion between *Oblasts* and *Raions* (both frequently translated as 'region'), only the latter are referred to as regions in this work. Likewise, to help the reader distinguish between Russian and Ukrainian units, the former are abbreviated (e.g. 15th Motor Rifle Brigade becomes 15th MRB) whilst the latter are not.

INTRODUCTION

This book, the eighth in the War in Ukraine mini-series, was born from Volume 2's opening invocation for additional research into the events of the Russo-Ukrainian war. Its focus is Ukraine's successful defence of Kyiv during the opening campaign of Russia's full-scale invasion. In just over a month of bitter fighting at the gates of the capital, Putin's hope for a swift *coupe de main* was extinguished and the two decades he spent rebuilding and modernising the Russian military essentially squandered. By contrast, Ukraine's victory secured its survival as an independent nation, although was not enough to decide the ultimate outcome of the war, which continues to rage on at the time of writing in summer 2024, predominately in the east of the country.

Despite its historic significance, comparatively little has been written on the Battle of Kyiv which could be considered operational military history. Many of the current popular works on the war are chiefly journalistic in character and pay only anecdotal attention to the course of the fighting itself.[1] There is also a growing body of academic and analytical literature, but this is often more interested in generating applicable lessons for Western militaries than studying the events themselves in detail.[2] Nevertheless, a small core of military history work is emerging. Volumes 2, 5, and 6 of the War in Ukraine mini-series provide some of the first operational histories to be published, covering the opening two weeks of the invasion, the Battle of Chernihiv (a city northeast of the capital), and the early air war respectively.[3] Other notable works include the British Army Review's special edition on the Battle of the Irpin River and Christopher Lawrence's *The Battle of Kyiv*.[4] This small but formidable collection provides much of the secondary evidence used in the book and the author owes its writers greatly.

For primary evidence, the book depends upon the wealth of open-source material on the war accumulated across mainstream and social media. It is no exaggeration to say that the Russo-Ukrainian war is the best-documented conflict in human history thanks to this body of evidence, and the author has relied upon it constantly to cross-examine other primary and secondary sources. Inevitably, mysteries persist, even with such powerful tools of investigation, and this remains far from a comprehensive history. Nevertheless, as one of the first efforts to tell the complete story of the Battle of Kyiv from beginning to end, the author hopes it will still advance the historical understanding of the war. He also hopes this book may inspire others to take up research in the field, as Volume 2 inspired himself.

Lastly, it is important to note that a full coverage of the geopolitical context of the war has been omitted, as this has already been described at length in previous volumes. Instead, the first chapters of this book concern themselves chiefly with the immediate context of the invasion, the institutional contexts of the Russian and Ukrainian militaries, and how these factors together shaped the fighting around the capital.

1
UNCHECKED HUBRIS

Regarding Putin's decision to invade, much has been said of whether he acted according to a 'rational' logic of preventing Ukraine's entry to NATO and protecting the pro-Russian separatists in the country's east or else according to an irrational desire of restoring the Russian empire.[1] Regardless of his underlying rationale though, there is little doubt that Putin's decision was not made with accurate information. Fatally, his intelligence apparatus informed him that Ukraine would put up little resistance in the event of war. Indeed, the invasion was termed as a Special Military Operation (SVO) not only because the euphemism was more digestible to the Russian public, but because Putin earnestly believed the undertaking would be less than a full-scale war, rather a lighting operation over in a matter of days, akin to his 2014 seizure of Crimea. This fundamental miscalculation at the highest level of Russian decision making would subsequently stunt the strategic, operational, and tactical performance of the Armed Forces of the Russian Federation (*Vooruzhonnije Síly Rossíyskoj Federátsii*, VSRF) as they went into a war they were neither psychologically nor practically prepared to fight.[2]

Understanding why the Russian intelligence assessment of Ukraine was so flawed reveals something of the true character of Putin's regime. Like most authoritarians, Putin feared an internal *coup d'état* or, still worse, a democratic revolution above all other threats to his rule.[3] Accordingly, the security apparatus of the Russian state was structured first and foremost with internal threats in mind, often at the expense of their efficacy in prosecuting external threats. Russia's intelligence machinery reflected this situation exactly. Unlike Western nations which typically divide their intelligence agencies into domestic and foreign branches, the three main Russian intelligence agencies of the Federal Security Service (*Federalnaya Sluzhba Bezopasnosti*, FSB), the Foreign Intelligence Service (*Sluzhba Vneshney Razvedki*, SVR), and the Main Intelligence Directorate (*Glavnoye Razvedyatelnoye Upravleniye*, GRU) all shared overlapping domestic and foreign responsibilities and were often in direct competition with one another. By keeping his intelligence machinery so divided, Putin ensured each agency hung on his approval, diminishing the chance of any one plotting against his regime. Crucially, however, this arrangement of divide-and-rule compromised the 'true' purpose of the FSB, SVR, and GRU: effective intelligence gathering. Lack of clear accountability meant their intelligence operations were frequently uncoordinated and occasionally even duplicated each other, whilst strong incentives existed against reporting any unwelcome news to Putin, which could disadvantage an agency vis-à-vis its competitors.[4]

These factors proved disastrous for Moscow's pre-war intelligence gathering inside Ukraine. Lack of accountability led to carelessness, with Russian intelligence networks reportedly relying almost entirely on Russian-speaking informants and even embezzling the funding they received.[5] This carelessness was married to an optimistic view that the Ukrainian population was apathetic and would not resist, seemingly confirmed by FSB polling which revealed extremely low levels of popular confidence in the Ukrainian government. The same polling also revealed high levels of confidence in the Armed Forces of Ukraine (*Zbroini syly Ukrainy*, ZSU) and a strong popular will to fight in the event of invasion, but these less welcome facts were overlooked.[6] Choosing from the intelligence 'platter' of FSB, GRU, and SVR operations inside Ukraine, Putin heard only what he wanted to hear and ignored the rest, including the warnings of some senior officials that the conditions for success were not yet met and that the invasion should be delayed. Indeed, the efforts of Russian intelligence to destabilise Ukraine in the run up to the invasion proved largely unsuccessful. Attempts to simultaneously foster a false-flag Ukrainian nationalist uprising and a pro-Russian uprising both failed,[7] whilst other provocations staged along the eastern border were repeatedly exposed as manufactured.[8] Nevertheless, Putin pressed along with the invasion, having convinced himself that Ukraine was a non-entity.

Planning to Fail

The same optimism and carelessness which had compromised the Russian intelligence operation soon bled into the military planning of the invasion too.[9] According to Russian doctrine, the planning should have been masterminded by the Russian General Staff (*GenStab*), specifically its Main Operations Directorate, which contains the *GenStab*'s most talented officers. The directorate would establish a Combat Management Group (*Gruppa Boevogo Upravleniya*, GBU) months in advance, which would provide oversight over the entire campaign's planning and help translate political objectives into strategic-operational ones. Such a process had already been demonstrated with at least some success during the Russian intervention in Syria of 2015–2019, when, following a few adaptations, it managed to isolate the anti-Assad insurgency from its supporters abroad, and then nearly defeat it on the battlefield. However, in the case of Ukraine of 2021–2022, Putin dispensed with this process entirely. The *GenStab* was kept largely in the dark as to his intentions, with some deputy heads of branches finding out about the invasion only days before it began. Meanwhile, the GBU managing the campaign was established just a day before Russian troops crossed the border, resulting in organisational chaos.[10] In fact, besides Putin himself, the only people entirely privy to the invasion plans were a select handful of his Security Council members.[11] Chief among them was Minister of Defence Sergey Shoigu and head of the *GenStab*, Army General Valery Gerasimov, who together conducted the majority of the strategic planning.[12]

Two key reasons for this break in doctrine can be identified. In part, the move was born out of Putin's fear that the invasion plans would be revealed if too many were in the know. Ironically, this concern proved well-founded if ultimately futile, as American intelligence had obtained the plans by November 2021 anyway, although their warnings went initially unheeded by the Ukrainian government.[13] The second reason for the break from doctrine was Putin's own hubris. It appears he was so sure of success that he shunned the expertise of the Main Operations Directorate altogether. In fairness, success was all he had known in his previous military campaigns in Chechnya, Georgia, Syria, and Ukraine, even if the latter had only been a partial victory. Needless to say, this record gave Putin an inflated idea of his own capabilities as a strategist, with or without the assistance of the *GenStab*.

As a result of these factors, the planning of the invasion was conducted in a largely haphazard fashion, with the junior planners that were enlisted often unaware of the wider context behind their taskings. The notion that the campaign might not succeed was apparently never seriously considered either and no contingencies were made. The final plan born out of this context was not necessarily doomed to failure on its own terms, even with its underlying assumption of Ukrainian weakness. Russian troops following it did enjoy initial success in the south of Ukraine where a series of contextual factors aligned in their advantage.[14] However, the extraordinary decision to brief the operational level commanders of the plan only a week or two before the invasion started, together with the existing shortcomings of the VSRF itself, almost guaranteed some form of disaster.

Seizing Kyiv

At the heart of the plan was the encirclement and capture of Kyiv.[15] Sitting astride the western and eastern banks of the Dnipro River, in many ways the capital represented Ukraine's centre of gravity: it was the seat of President Volodymyr Zelensky's government, the headquarters of the country's military and intelligence machinery, and the nexus of much of its transport infrastructure. As far as the Russian plan hinged on dislocating Ukrainian society, the fall of Kyiv and the removal of Zelensky would go a long way toward its success, if not decide the war outright. Accordingly, the seizure of the capital became the main Russian effort, in obedience with Clausewitz's principle of striking the enemy's centre of gravity to bring about their complete collapse.[16] Thus, at Kyiv, the stage was set for the invasion's decisive battle.

In essence, Putin hoped to seize the capital in a shock-and-awe operation. First, cyberattacks would knock out the communications networks of the Ukrainian government and armed forces. Then, a brief but fierce aerial bombardment would target the air defence sites, airfields, and military bases arrayed around Kyiv. With the way cleared, helicopter-borne elements of the Russian Airborne Forces (*Vozdushno-desantnye voyska*, VDV) would seize Antonov International Airport (IAP), located 30 kilometres north-west of the city centre. This would provide an airhead into which further VDV units would land via transport aircraft,[17] along with their infantry fighting vehicles (IFVs), which were too heavy to lift by helicopter. Once disembarked, the force assembled would drive the short distance to central Kyiv and neutralise Zelensky and his cabinet, a mission they had previously rehearsed with the FSB. In this task, the VDV would be assisted by the various Russian sabotage and reconnaissance groups (SRGs) already infiltrated into the city, consisting mostly of GRU Spetsnaz.[18] Whilst this decapitation operation was proceeding, VSRF mechanised forces would strike toward Kyiv from the north-west, north-east, and east, bypassing population centres and sweeping aside what resistance they encountered on their way. These forces would meet south of the city, completing its encirclement, and dig in to meet expected Ukrainian counterattacks. The entire sequence of events was expected to take less than 24 hours to complete.[19]

Once Kyiv was encircled and Zelensky removed, Russian special operations forces (SOF) and VDV would begin gradually securing the city by seizing key infrastructure and isolating areas of resistance. The Russian National Guard (Rosgvardia) would help quell the inevitable protests, whilst the Chechen National Guard would hunt down the protests' organisers and dispose of them, a task for which they were well suited with their reputation for brutality and ruthlessly effective counter-insurgency operations.[20] Finally, a pro-Russian puppet regime would be installed, likely lead by Ukraine's most prominent pro-Russian politician: Viktor Medvedchuk. Ironically, it was these stabilisation operations which were the focus of the Russian planning, rather than the task of fighting through to Kyiv itself.

Forces and Means

Volume 2 has already covered the organisation and equipment of the pre-invasion VSRF in considerable detail, but the subject is worth revisiting briefly in specific attention to the forces tasked against Kyiv. The bulk of the mechanised elements striking from the border were drawn from the Russian Ground Forces (*Sukhoputnyje voyska*, SV), which committed four Combined Arms Armies (CAAs) for the purpose. The backbone of the operation, these were arrayed clockwise around Kyiv as follows:

- 35th CAA, deployed on the north-western axis in the Mazyr area of Belarus, reinforced with elements of the 29th, 36th, and 5th CAAs.
- 41st CAA, deployed on the north-eastern axis in the Gomel area of Belarus, elements of the 90th Guards Tank Division (90th GTD) attached.
- 2nd Guards Combined Arms Army (GCAA), deployed on an east north-east axis in the Khomutovka area of Russia.
- 1st Guards Tank Army (GTA), deployed on an easterly axis in the Sudzha area of Russia.

The exact chain of command for these armies remains murky as between them they covered three of Russia's four Operational Strategic Commands (OSKs) (the largest administrative unit of the VSRF): the 35th CAA was from OSK East, the 41st CAA and 2nd GCAA from OSK Centre, and the 1st GTA from OSK West. However, it seems all four armies were subordinated to OSK East for the operation, nominally placing them under the control of its commander: Colonel General Aleksandr Yuryevich Chaiko.[21] Nominal is important to emphasise, as Putin himself frequently bypassed Chaiko and his army commanders to micromanage their units directly, even down to the tactical level.[22] Exactly how much control Chaiko was actually able to exert amongst this meddling is still undetermined.

Each army was itself composed of several divisions and brigades, including dedicated artillery, rocket artillery, and missile brigades, alongside other support assets. Perhaps most important among them was the single material-technical support (MTO) brigade each army possessed, responsible for providing truck-borne sustainment to its constituent units. The allocation of only one MTO brigade per army reflected Russia's doctrinal preference for rail-borne rather than truck-borne logistics. Indeed, the VSRF had largely been constructed around a strategy of 'active defence', which envisioned it fighting a future war against NATO largely from inside Russia, where it would be able to rely on Russia's extensive internal rail infrastructure for resupply.[23] In such a conflict, an MTO brigade would be more than capable of keeping an army supplied over the 20–40 kilometre distances expected between the nearest railheads and the front. For the invasion, however, armies were tasked with operating at distances of 100–200 kilometres from the nearest railheads, a range their MTO brigades physically could not sustain them over, even assuming no Ukrainian resistance.[24] This logistical overreach was not considered an issue by Russian planners, who expected to seize a rail link to Kyiv via Chernihiv almost immediately,[25] whilst the airhead at Antonov IAP would make up for any shortfall. As it happened, neither of these silver bullets came to pass, and the MTO brigades ended up shouldering an impossible burden, leading to a logistics disaster as Russian troops outside Kyiv ran short of all conceivable supplies.

Just as the VSRF's logistics doctrine was misaligned for the war it was about to fight, its tactical organisation also left much to be desired. The core tactical unit of the VSRF was the Battalion Tactical Group (BTG), a battalion sized battlegroup drawn from the best personnel and equipment of a parent unit. Typically, a brigade was expected to generate at least two BTGs, whilst a division would generate around six, two BTGs per each regiment. The rationale behind this system was twofold. Firstly, Russia's hybrid recruitment policy meant most brigades and divisions were staffed at ratios of roughly 70 percent professional contract soldiers to 30 percent conscripts.[26] The BTG system provided a way of concentrating all a unit's contract soldiers together to produce a combat capable force at short notice. This was particularly significant for the invasion, as conscripts were not legally allowed to participate in combat operations outside Russia without a declaration of war, which the SVO did not amount to,[27] although, in practice, some conscripts were pressed into combat regardless.[28]

The second reason for the use of BTGs were their own merits as small, modular, and relatively nimble formations with disproportionately heavy firepower. The core of a BTG drawn from a motor rifle unit would usually consist of a motor rifle battalion mounted on BMP or BTR IFVs, with an attached tank company. A BTG drawn from a tank unit would invert this ratio, possessing a tank battalion with an attached motor rifle company. Brigade or divisional level fire-support would then be attached, usually including a self-propelled howitzer battalion, a battery of multiple rocket launch systems (MRLSs), and an air defence battery. Lastly, the BTG would be rounded off with a variety of logistics, engineering, reconnaissance, and electronic warfare (EW) assets.[29] In total, a nominal motor rifle BTG would number roughly 700–900 personnel

Russian infantry seen during a pre-war exercise. (Russian Ministry of Defence)

strong, 200–300 of whom were dismounted infantry. The result was a formation ideally suited for the expeditionary 'hybrid' conflicts Russia fought in eastern Ukraine and Syria. These wars demanded compact formations which could be rapidly deployed abroad to meet crises, a role the BTG filled well. The fighting was broadly conducted at arm's length, with BTGs leveraging their indirect-fire capabilities behind a screen of local proxy forces, avoiding losses among their precious cores of dismounts.[30] Indeed, it was not uncommon in the 2014–15 fighting in eastern Ukraine for a BTG to deploy with all its fire-support assets but just one tank company and one motor rifle company.[31]

For the 2022 invasion, however, the BTG concept was stretched far beyond its limits. As the VSRF would soon discover, this was no hybrid conflict, but a full-scale conventional war. Dismounted Russian infantry had to shoulder the brunt of the fighting themselves, and BTGs were frequently rendered combat ineffective when they ran out of dismounts as a result, even if they still possessed most of their heavy equipment. Exacerbating this problem, the average BTG had shrunk from around 700–900 personnel strong in the mid-2010s to 400–600 strong by February 2022, making them even more fragile. This was because of the *GenStab*'s extraordinary decision to generate as many BTGs as possible in the run up to the war, regardless of not having enough contract personnel to actually man them all. This led to bizarre skeletal BTGs being fielded, with fully crewed vehicles and artillery systems but few if any dismounts.[32] Admittedly, a few Russian divisions and brigades did deploy more as complete units than as BTGs, such as the 55th Mountain Motor Rifle Brigade (55th MMRB), part of the 41st CAA, and the 155th Naval Infantry Brigade (155th NIB), attached to the 35th CAA.[33] However, these formations remained severely undermanned without their conscripts. For example, the 155th NIB, though possessing a paper strength of 3,100 personnel, deployed to Belarus with only 1,600 or so.[34] Ironically, this was the exact problem BTGs had been adopted to address in the first place. In the end, both the VSRF's 'complete' units and those organised around BTGs entered the invasion significantly undersized for the intensity of combat they were about to face.

Putin's Chosen

If the SV's mechanised units were the backbone of the force arrayed against Kyiv, the VDV was its spearhead.[35] At the very tip was a joint BTG drawn from the 31st Guards Air Assault Brigade (31st GAAB) and 45th Guards Spetsnaz Brigade (45th GSB), responsible for securing Antonov IAP. This would be followed by the 98th Guards Airborne Division (98th GAD), embarked on Ilyushin Il-76 transport aircraft. Meanwhile, attached to the 35th CAA on the ground, the 76th Guards Air Assault Division (76th GAAD) and 106th Guards Airborne Division (106th GAD) would cross the border on their vehicles, along with a second BTG of the 31st GAAB.[36] This assignment of both conventional airborne tasks and mechanised tasks to the VDV reflected its unique ability to perform in either role, thanks to its fleet of specialised air transportable BMD IFVs. In fact, Putin had actually guided the VDV towards a more exclusively mechanised role in the years before the war, overseeing reforms which had equipped several VDV formations with T-72B3 tanks, increasing their firepower at the expense of their air mobility.

An orthodox priest blesses new BMD-4M IFVs and BTR-MDM APCs assigned to the 76th GAAD in 2019. The twenty-first century replacement to the aging but more numerous BMD-2, the BMD-4 continues the same trade-off between survivability and light weight as its predecessor. Concerns regarding this issue were raised early in its procurement, but Putin overruled them. (Russian Ministry of Defence)

Whilst this might seem anachronistic to Western eyes, cultivating the VDV as an alternate source of mechanised power to the SV was perfectly rational for Putin, fearing a *coup d'état* as he did. Because of its position as an independent combat arm, the VDV was administratively under direct presidential control, unlike the SV which answered to the *GenStab* first. This made it an ideal organisation to counterbalance the SV in the event of a military coup, a capacity Putin carefully developed by favouring the VDV with investments, protecting it from the *GenStab*'s attempts to absorb it into the SV, and orientating it toward a mechanised role. The result was a classic example of divide-and-rule, with the VDV duplicating many of the SV's capabilities and competing with it for resources.

Whilst rational from an internal security perspective, this mechanised role for the VDV made little military sense. To save weight, BMDs were far more lightly armoured than BMPs, leaving them vulnerable even to rifle-calibre machine gun fire at close range. They were also significantly smaller, meaning the size of a nominal VDV dismount squad was only five strong in comparison to the SV's seven. These sacrifices had been justified for the sake of air mobility, but now VDV formations were confined to a more exclusively mechanised role, they became only disadvantages. Unfortunately for the Russian paratroopers, it would take several tactical disasters outside Kyiv for these vulnerabilities to be fully understood.

Russian Airpower

Supporting the advance on Kyiv from the air, the Russian Aerospace Forces (*Vozdushno-kosmicheskiye sily*, VKS) deployed around 220 combat aircraft for the operation, grouped together under the command of the 6th Air Force and Air Defence Army, which was likely subordinated to OSK East.[37] This was a formidable concentration of airpower, larger than the entire Ukrainian Air Force (*Povitriyani syly Zbroiynyh syl Ukrayini*, PSZSU), which fielded just 125 operational combat aircraft in February 2022. As detailed in Volume 6, Russian aircraft were also qualitatively superior to their Ukrainian counterparts, possessing better avionics, missiles, and radars, and enabled by A-50U airborne early warning and control aircraft and Il-22PP EW aircraft, capabilities the PSZSU entirely lacked.

Nevertheless, whilst enjoying superiority in the 'hard' factors, the VKS was handicapped by a series of deficiencies in the equally critical 'soft' factors. As with the SV, the VKS had not been organised nor trained for concerted offensive operations. Instead, Russian airpower thinking had largely focused on parrying a future NATO 'massed missile-aviation strike', a threat which emphasised rigid cooperation between Russian interceptors and air defences.[38] Accordingly, individual initiative in pilot training was not emphasised, with decision making expected to be conducted at the level of the command post rather than the level of the cockpit. This left the VKS essentially incapable of running a proactive strategic strike campaign in the manner of a Western air force, where pilot initiative would be vital for surviving raids deep into enemy airspace. Instead, VKS sorties were highly scripted and generally flown in a close air support role against targets on the frontline, limiting the impact of Russian airpower during the invasion.

In lieu of aircraft, Russian long-range strikes were predominantly conducted with ground-launched Iskander-M ballistic and Iskander-K cruise missiles, contained within the missile brigade(s) of each CAA. These were highly effective weapons, especially because Ukraine fielded few surface-to-air missile (SAM) systems capable of intercepting ballistic missiles. The VSRF had also developed a sophisticated doctrine for their employment, termed the Reconnaissance-Strike-Complex (*razveyvatelno-udarnnyy komplekx*, RUK). This concept saw Iskanders integrated into a network of intelligence and targeting sensors, allowing strikes to be planned and executed almost as soon as targets could appear for them. In practice during the invasion, however, this ideal proved far from fully realised, with actual Iskander targeting cycles frequently taking hours to complete. This problem, together with the limited stocks of available missiles, prevented Iskanders from having a decisive impact in the war's opening months.

A Su-34 tactical bomber lands after a training sortie in mid-February 2022. The type would carry out the bulk of Russian airstrikes during the invasion, usually with unguided bombs. (Russian Ministry of Defence)

2
THE UKRAINIAN PRELUDE

Though the storm clouds of the approaching war were visible gathering several months before the invasion actually began, uncertainty reigned within Ukraine and across the West as to when the storm would break or, as all hoped, whether it might in fact peacefully disperse. An initial Russian military build-up around the Ukrainian border in April 2021 had raised some alarm, but this dissipated after most of the units involved returned to their garrisons. In fact, it was only during a second larger build-up for Russia's Zapad 2021 exercise that September when American intelligence officials began to realise preparations for war were underway.[1] Unlike the previous Zapad exercises, Zapad 2021 was held at an unprecedented scale, involving units from all four OSKs.[2] More ominously, the conclusion of the exercise did not see Russian units return to garrison. Instead, still more Russian formations arrived throughout October and November to join those already deployed.[3] The growing fears of the American intelligence community were confirmed when a high-level source inside Russia allegedly leaked them details of the invasion plan itself.[4] Still smarting after being caught off guard in 2014, Washington was determined that Ukraine, and the West, would not be surprised again.

On 2 November 2021, Zelensky was personally briefed by the American Secretary of State Antony Blinken of Russia's intention to invade. The meeting took place in the unlikely setting of the United Nations Climate Change Conference in Glasgow, as Blinken recalled later: '[It was] the two of us, sitting almost knee-to-knee in a room on the margins of the summit meeting. It was very stark, very palpable. [Zelensky] took the information very stoically'.[5]

The following weeks and months would see similar warnings repeated constantly by American and British officials visiting Kyiv. Though the Ukrainians listened, they remained sceptical, believing that Putin was only attempting to apply diplomatic pressure. Instead, Zelensky took pains to downplay the fears of war until the very eve of the invasion, causing frustration in both Washington and London. Whilst bewildering to Western officials, this public show of scepticism was well-founded on private fears. Zelensky knew mobilising the ZSU would incur immense political and economic costs for his administration, something he could ill-afford with the low public approval ratings he was suffering. Zelensky also feared that the Russians would exploit the resulting unrest to sow insurrection or even use it as an excuse to invade. Ultimately, this decision to remain outwardly calm likely went a long way in thwarting the destabilisation operations Russian intelligence actually did have planned. However, it also came at a steep cost for Ukraine's military readiness.[6]

Like the VSRF, the ZSU consisted of both contract soldiers and conscripts. Accordingly, it also used the BTG system to pool together brigades' contract personnel, although these were generally fielded less consistently than in Russian practice. A more fundamental difference was the ZSU's use of the Operational Reserve system, which saw active brigades staffed at only 30–60 percent of their paper strength to save costs, the remaining strength being made up of reservists who would be called up in the event of war.[7] The brigades of the ZSU's Reserve Corps were organised on the same principle, but maintained at only 5–10 percent of their paper strength, providing a 'true' operational reserve in the sense that these were separate reserve units.[8]

Whilst this Operational Reserve system allowed Ukraine to maintain a much larger military than it might otherwise have been able to, it was predicated on the timely call up of reservists to bring brigades up to combat strength. Unfortunately, Zelensky's decision not to mobilise meant many brigades remained only as skeletons even as the invasion began. Some sources indicate that a first wave of mobilisation was clandestinely ordered on 18 February 2022,[9] but clearly its effects were not felt everywhere. The 72nd Mechanised Brigade, which would play a pivotal role in the defence of Kyiv, began the war severely understrength; its 2nd Mechanised Battalion numbering only 150 strong when it should have possessed around 500 soldiers. Nevertheless, the ZSU was able to rapidly make up for this manpower shortage after the invasion began, with tens of thousands of reservists and civilian volunteers flocking to enlist.[10] By contrast, Russian units appear to have been only as strong as the number of contract personnel in their BTGs when they crossed the border. Little evidence exists of any deployed Russian unit receiving fresh personnel (at least in the invasion's first months). Instead, most reinforcements seemingly came at the operational level, with entire fresh units arriving to fight alongside those already engaged. As a result, Russian units would frequently 'bleed out' whilst their Ukrainian counterparts continued fighting, despite enduring equivalent casualties.

The late mobilisation also affected Ukraine's Territorial Defence Forces (TDF). The TDF was organised in January 2022 as a separate branch of the ZSU, providing a corps of static light infantry brigades to defend the regions they were stood up in. Small cadres of contract personnel provided a nucleus for each brigade, with civilian volunteers and reservists expected to bring them to full-strength in the event of war. Unfortunately, the short intervening time between the TDF's official establishment and the invasion meant most brigades had not even completed training their contract personnel when the war started, let alone registered and trained their reservists. Despite being caught unprepared, the TDF would go on to play a crucial role during the invasion. As an organisational skeleton, it was perfectly placed to absorb and organise the huge numbers joining up in the war's opening days, relieving some pressure from the army's overburdened recruiting centres. It also provided a legal structure around which civilian volunteers organised their own TDF formations, even if these were not technically part of any brigade. Together, these grassroots formations and the pre-existing brigades became major obstacles to the Russian advance, holding out in urban terrain even as regular ZSU units were forced to retreat. In this manner, several major settlements east of Kyiv were able to continue fighting, despite being encircled well behind the Russian frontline.[11]

Another source of auxiliary combat power was provided by the Ukrainian National Guard. Administratively part of Ukraine's Ministry of Internal Affairs, in practice National Guard units were subordinated to the ZSU for combat operations. This reflected their dual role as both an internal security force and a conventional military branch, with some National Guard formations possessing similar tables of organisation and equipment to ZSU mechanised brigades. For example, the elite 4th Rapid Reaction Brigade, garrisoned at Antonov IAP, fielded two infantry battalions mounted on BTR-3 IFVs, a battalion of T-64BV tanks, a battalion of D-30 towed 122mm howitzers, and several ZU-23-2 23mm anti-aircraft guns. However, as with the TDF and army, the National Guard was hampered by Zelensky's decision to mobilise at the last possible moment. For instance, the 4th Rapid Reaction Brigade did receive a complement of some 200 conscripts prior to February 2022, but they still arrived far too late to be fully trained before the eve of the invasion. As a result, they were left behind at Antonov as a company tactical group (CTG) whilst the rest of the brigade was deployed away from Kyiv on 20 February. Ironically, far from protecting them, this fateful decision placed the conscripts right in the path of Putin's *coup de maine*.[12]

A convoy of 4th Rapid Reaction Brigade vehicles seen during pre-war exercises. The column consists of several BTR-3E infantry fighting vehicles, intermingled with KrAZ and MAZ trucks. A pair of Ukrainian Mi-8 helicopters are visible overflying the procession. (Ukrainian National Guard)

Organising the Defence of Kyiv

Descending from the strategic context of Ukraine's preparations for the invasion to the organisation of Kyiv's defences themselves, it is worth bearing in mind that a great deal of mystery still surrounds this subject, as much because of the accusations of incompetence and even treason that follow in its wake as the plain lack of information.[13] On 12 January, Central Intelligence Agency (CIA) director William Burns visited Kyiv to warn Zelensky that the Russian invasion would strike toward the capital from Belarus, beginning with an air assault against Antonov IAP.[14] At a time when there was only a burgeoning acceptance that Russia might launch a limited invasion in Ukraine's east, this notion of Russian forces storming Kyiv remained almost unthinkable to Zelensky. His scepticism was supported by Ukraine's Main Intelligence Directorate (*Holovne Upravlinnia Rozvidky*, GUR), which assessed the Russian forces north of Kyiv as too small to have a reasonable chance of taking a city populated by over three million people; the 35th and 41st CAA's together numbering just some 30,000 strong.[15] Accordingly, the majority of the Ukrainian military was deployed in the east, leaving the north only thinly defended. Among the units sent east was the 4th Rapid Reaction Brigade, departing the very place Burns had warned the invasion would fall first.[16]

Despite Zelensky misjudging the scope and scale of Russia's intentions, the Ukrainian General Staff (*GenStab-U*) still made contingency preparations for the defence of Kyiv, although its own generals shared the prevailing view that the invasion would come from the east. The equivalent of a Russian OSK, the ground units across the north of Ukraine were grouped together under Operational Command North (OC North), led by Major General Viktor Nikoliuk. However, responsibility for organising the defence of Kyiv itself was assigned to Colonel General Oleksandr Syrskyi, leaving Nikoliuk to command the defence of the Chernihiv and Sumy oblasts. Supported by the Commander-in-Chief of the ZSU, General Valerii Zaluzhnyi, the two generals began dispersing their units from garrison as early as 8 February, using the Blizzard-2022 military exercises as a cover. The movement was so sensitive that Zelensky and his own ministers were kept only loosely informed, in part out of fears of Russian informants, in part because the *GenStab-U* knew they were stretching Zelensky's directive not to mobilise. This dispersal would save many units from being caught by airstrikes at the outset of the invasion, although it was at best only partially completed, with some brigades strung out between their garrisons and deployment points and others still inside their bases when the first Russian missiles landed.

One unit only semi-dispersed on the eve of the war was the 72nd Mechanised Brigade, commanded by Colonel Oleksandr Vdovychenko. On 22 February, the brigade's 1st and 3rd Mechanised Battalions had been deployed to Kyiv's eastern flank from the brigade's garrison in the city of Bila Tserkva, located 85 kilometres south of the capital. Most of the brigade's tank battalion (T-64BVs), 1st Artillery Battalion (equipped with 2S1 Gvozdika self-propelled 122mm howitzers), 3rd Artillery Battalion (equipped with BM-21 Grad 122mm MRLS), and 4th Artillery Battalion (equipped with MT-12 Rapira 100mm towed anti-tank guns) were earmarked to follow. By contrast, the brigade's 2nd Mechanised Battalion and 2nd Artillery Battalion (equipped with 2S3 Akatsyia self-propelled 152mm howitzers) remained at Bila Tserkva, still awaiting their orders to deploy on the western flank of Kyiv. This uneven posture

Humvees and paratroopers of the 80th Air Assault Brigade on exercise circa 31 January 2022. Note the Humvees are equipped with DShK heavy machine guns. (80th Air Assault Brigade)

COMPANY TACTICAL GROUPS

One level below BTGs, company tactical groups (CTGs) represented the same principles functioning at the company scale.[17] Like BTGs, CTGs were task-organised formations designed to bring together various sub-units into one cohesive combined arms task force, typically using a tank company or a motor rifle company as a core. For example, a CTG formed by the VSRF 36th Motorised Rifle Brigade in 2015 consisted of a motor rifle company, an air defence group, a self-propelled howitzer battery, and a platoon each of mortars, tanks, and engineers, along with various supporting elements.[18] In pre-war Russian doctrine, such formations (commonly referred to as reinforced companies) would be used as vanguard detachments in front of their parent formations. This was the role Russian CTGs were often seen employed in during the Battle of Kyiv. By contrast, at the time of writing, CTGs and even platoon tactical groups have largely replaced BTGs altogether as the primary tactical unit used in Ukraine, in part because of the increasing need for dispersion, in part because the VSRF has lost much of the institutional expertise needed to perform combined arms warfare at battalion scale.

The ZSU also employs CTGs, although these were usually tasked as independent raiding and assault groups early in the invasion rather than as vanguards for larger units, reflecting the massive frontages Ukrainian brigades often had to cover. Ukrainian CTGs were also seen employed in purely defensive roles, such as the force organised by the 4th Rapid Reaction Brigade for the garrison of Antonov IAP. This unit was a CTG only in a nominal sense, consisting of just an infantry company, an air defence platoon, and two D-30 howitzers located nearby in the suburb of Horenka, reflecting the arbitrary way in which the term can be employed. Posing further problems for clarity, Russian and Ukrainian companies will usually have attachments from other arms as a matter of course (e.g. a tank company with a mechanised infantry platoon), making the delineation between a CTG and a usual company group murky at best. This same problem afflicts the distinction of a BTG from a reinforced battalion. To provide as much clarity as possible, this book refers to BTGs and CTGs for VSRF units as a matter of course, reflecting their more established role in Russian doctrine, whilst ZSU units are referred to as BTGs and CTGs only when named as such in primary sources.

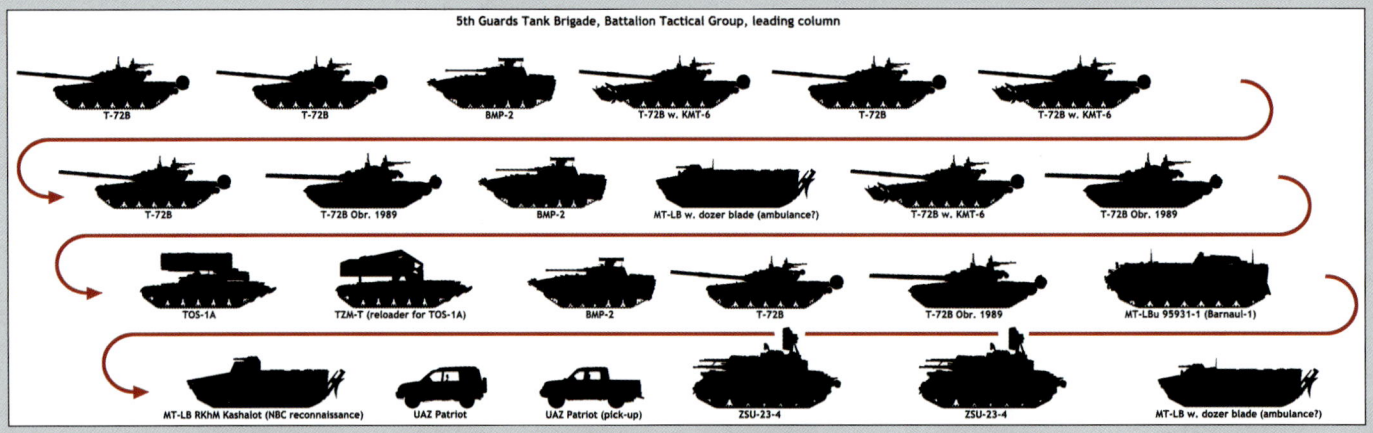

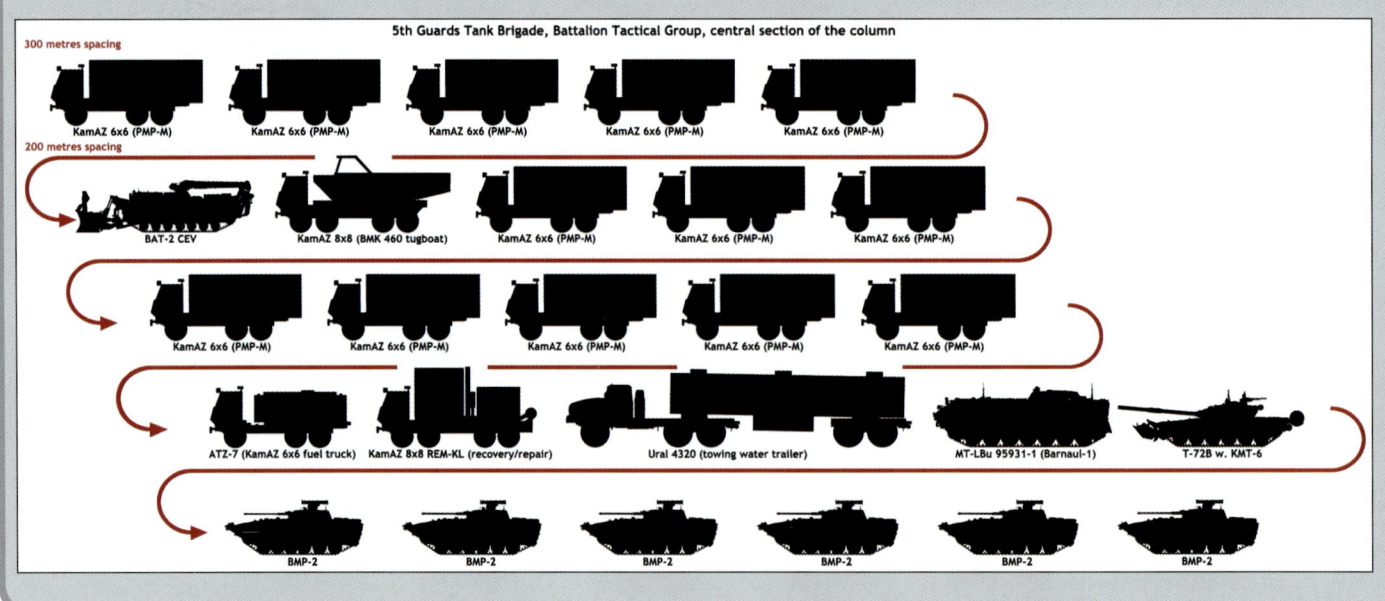

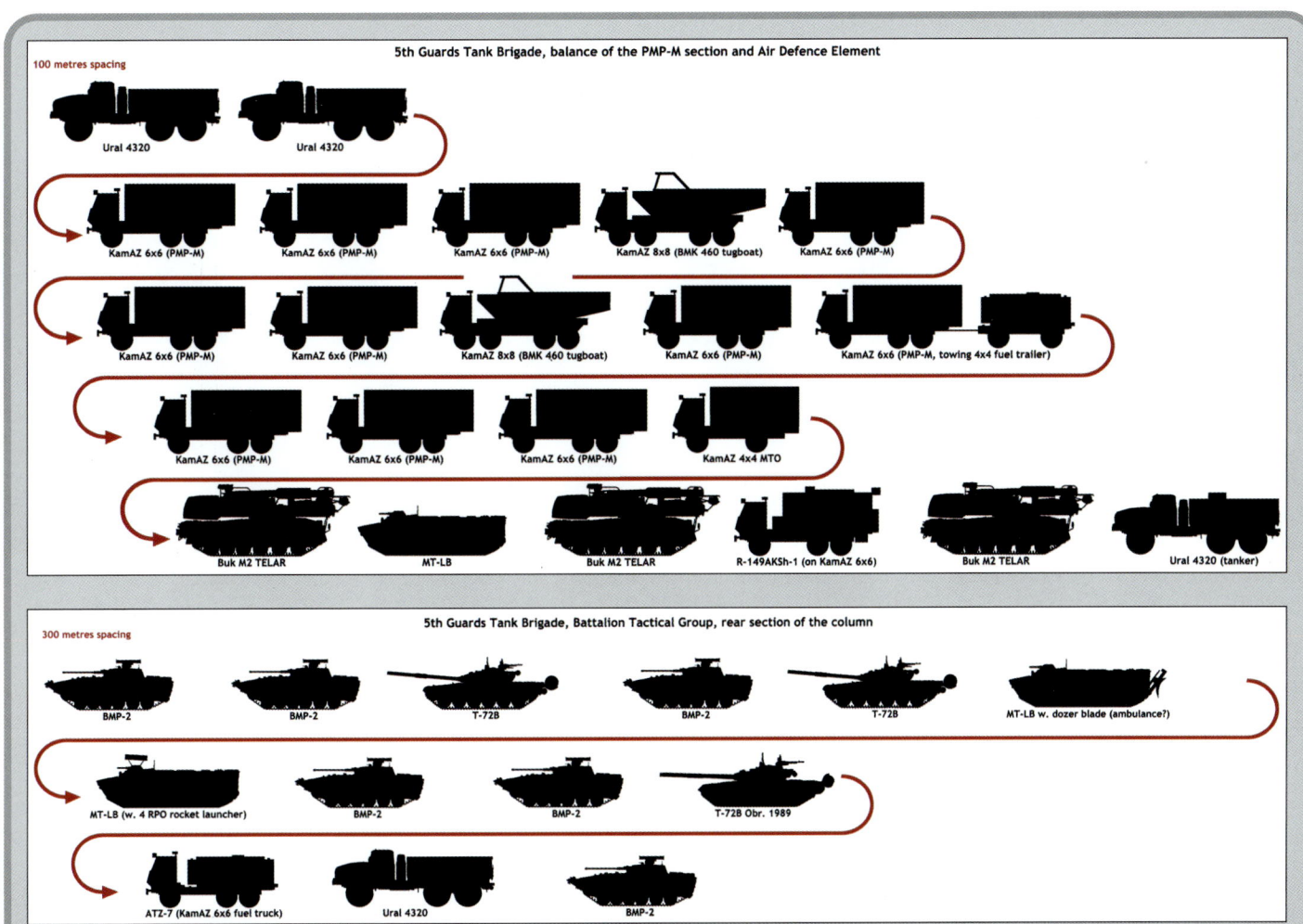

Diagrams reconstructing the vanguard CTG of the 5th Guards Tank Brigade captured on traffic cameras whilst travelling south in the Chernobyl Exclusion Zone on 24 February 2022.[19] The core of the formation was comprised of roughly one and a half tank companies, one and a half motor rifle companies mounted on BMP-2s, a substantial air defence section (including a Buk M2 medium SAM battery), and almost the entirety of the brigade engineering battalion's PMP-M pontoon bridge company. The formation was likely task-organised around this latter element, acting as an escort for its vulnerable transport trucks and engineering vehicles. The leading section of the column presents a complete example of a CTG, in this case comprised of a T-72B company, a BMP-2 platoon, a TOS-1A heavy flamethrower section, a section of ZSU-23-4 Shilka self-propelled 23mm anti-aircraft guns, and an attached section of Rosgvardia or Spetsnaz riding in UAZ Patriot utility vehicles. Also of note is the MT-LB APC in the rear of the column with a rack of four RPO-A Shmel thermobaric rocket launchers fixed to its turret; an improvised modification seen occasionally in VSRF service in 2022. Another unusual vehicle amongst the BTG's complement is the single RKhM Kashalot nuclear, biological, chemical (NBC) reconnaissance vehicle based on an MT-LB chassis. Entering service in the 1970s, the Kashalot contains advanced sensors for detecting contaminants and a variety of markers to denote danger areas. The type was pictured a handful of times among Russian columns during the initial invasion, although whether any were actually employed to assess radiation levels in the Zone can only be speculated. (Diagrams by Tom Cooper)

reflected OC North's contingency planning, which believed a Russian attack toward Kyiv would come from the north-east rather than the north-west. Accordingly, the bulk of the 72nd Mechanised Brigade was orientated east, and its sub-units headed in that direction given priority for rail transport.[20] As a result, the only significant Ukrainian formation deployed forward on the north-western side of Kyiv at the time the war began was a single BTG from the 80th Air Assault Brigade, on exercise in the Chernobyl Exclusion Zone.[21] Alone, this formation would have to delay the advance of the entire 35th CAA long enough for the 2nd Mechanised Battalion to be railed into place.

Whilst Kyiv was thinly held by regular ZSU units, Syrskyi could also call upon a plethora of reserve, TDF, and National Guard formations garrisoned inside the city, including the 101st Guard Brigade of the General Staff, the 112th and 114th TDF Brigades, and the 1st Presidential Operational Brigade (National Guard). Aware that this was still far from enough, Syrskyi set about organising combat units from the local 184th and 169th Training Centres, generating several infantry battalions, two batteries of 2S7 Pion self-propelled 203mm howitzers, and a battery of D-30 howitzers (previously used for ceremonial salutes).[22] This example would later be followed by the students of the National Defence University of Ukraine, located in western Kyiv, who created their own battlegroup from the handful of BMPs and tanks stored on campus.[23] Nonetheless, even with these scratch-built formations, the capital remained distinctly exposed on the eve of the invasion. Without the timely arrival of reinforcements from the west of Ukraine, Kyiv would be easily isolated by Russian armies passing its flanks.

The situation of Nikoliuk's command was even more vulnerable than Syrskyi's. Although defending a border frontage with Russia approximately 700 kilometres long across the Chernihiv and Sumy oblasts, Nikoliuk initially had only two manoeuvre brigades assigned to him: the 1st Tank Brigade, based out of Honcharivske

A platoon of T-64BVs from the 93rd Mechanised Brigade on the move on the eve of the war, 22 February 2022. Aside from airborne assault units equipped with T-80s and reserve units equipped with T-72s, the T-64 was the primary workhorse of the ZSU. (93rd Mechanised Brigade)

but already dispersed on exercises north of Chernihiv city, and the 58th Motorised Brigade, dispersed across the Sumy Oblast. He could also draw upon the 119th and 117th TDF Brigades, based in Chernihiv and Sumy respectively, along with a scattering of National Guard and support units. Needless to say, this force was dwarfed by the three combined armies it faced. In the final days before the invasion, the *GenStab-U* appeared to recognise the vulnerability of Nikoliuk's position and rushed to reinforce him with elements of the 27th Rocket Artillery Brigade (equipped with BM-27 Uragan self-propelled 270mm multiple rocket launchers) and the 19th Missile Brigade (equipped with OTR-21 Tochka-U tactical ballistic missiles), the first of which arrived around 23 February. Also dispatched at the last moment was the 93rd Mechanised Brigade, which received its movement orders to the southern Sumy Oblast that same day.[24] Only its 3rd Mechanised Battalion would be in position when the war began, the rest of the brigade having to unload from transport trains almost straight into combat.[25]

Air Command Centre

The overall unit responsible for protecting the airspace over OC North was the PSZSU's Air Command Centre (AC Centre), grouping together one anti-aircraft missile brigade, three anti-aircraft missile regiments, and three brigades of interceptors, along with several other supporting units.[26] Unlike OC North, most of AC Centre's units had not dispersed prior to the invasion, despite the efforts of its commander Lieutenant General Anatoily Kryvonozkho. This mystery is deepened by the fact that the PSZSU had observed VKS Su-24MR and Il-20M reconnaissance aircraft mapping the positions of its air defences in the months before the war yet still neglected to move them. This failure is in part explained by the general lack of funding and effective training which had afflicted the PSZSU in the years prior to 2022, leading to a number of Ukrainian SAM systems being left in such a state of disrepair that they were unable to move, a particularly acute problem for the units equipped with S-300 heavy SAM systems. The fact that Kryvonozkho was managing his command remotely from a Kyiv hospital at the time due to a

In addition to its organic interceptors, AC Centre could also count on Su-24 bombers from the 7th Tactical Aviation Brigade and Su-25 attack aircraft from the 299th Tactical Aviation Brigade. Photo of a Su-24M undergoing servicing in mid-January 2022. (PSZSU)

coronavirus infection likely did not help matters either. Nevertheless, whilst AC Centre was unprepared at an organisational level for the approaching storm, individually its pilots, SAM crews, and support staff had no shortage of moral courage, a trait which would keep them fighting even in the face of the VKS's overwhelming quantitative and qualitative superiority.

The Lamps Go Out

On 23 February, the day before the calamity, the mood in Kyiv was one of an uncanny calm.[27] Bars and playgrounds remained busy that afternoon as Zelensky convened a meeting of Ukraine's National Security and Defence Council (NSDC) to declare a state of emergency. Outwardly, Zelensky continued to dispel the rumours of war, reassuring the public via the secretary of the NSDC – Oleksiy Danilov – that the state of emergency was merely a preventative measure to keep the economy functioning. Behind closed doors however, the atmosphere within the NSDC was extremely tense. Intelligence reports from Washington and Ukraine's own agencies poured in, warning that the invasion was imminent. Simultaneously, massive cyberattacks were already beginning to target Ukraine's online infrastructure. Nevertheless, even at this late stage, Zelensky remained unsure of whether Putin would launch a full-scale invasion, a limited incursion, or even attack at all. It was only late that evening, as VSRF units began to move into the separatist areas of eastern Ukraine, when Zelensky finally realised war was upon him. Meanwhile, amongst the forests and fields of southern Belarus and south-western Russia, OSK East's armies began to leave their staging areas for the border. Following the effort to maintain secrecy, most of the tactical-level commanders had received the news they were invading Ukraine less than 24 hours before. Accordingly, many Russian units were in a state of considerable confusion, having not had time to calibrate their radios, stock up on supplies, nor find out exactly what their objectives were.[28] Even if Moscow had been dimly aware of this disorganisation, its own planning assumed the war would be over long before any serious problems could manifest.

3
THE BATTLE BEGINS

As planned, the Russian invasion had begun with a sophisticated and intensive series of cyberattacks designed to paralyse the Ukrainian government and military. During the late afternoon of 23 February, hackers from the GRU's cyberwarfare unit deployed a wiper malware against Ukrainian government computers, corrupting and deleting files as it spread across machines. It was dubbed 'HermeticWiper', based on the name of the Cypriot IT company whose identity it used as a trojan horse. Fortunately, American National Security Agency (NSA) and Microsoft response teams, in dialogue with Ukrainian officials, were quick to first identify, then contain the wiper. However, whilst this first attack was still underway, at around 1800hrs a separate cyberattack began against the American ViaSat company's SAT-KA satellite broadband system, which provided broadband services across Ukraine and formed the backbone of the ZSU's strategic communications network. This wiper malware, dubbed 'AcidRain', knocked out the SAT-KA system, whilst follow-up attacks prevented the system being restored by flooding ViaSat servers with spoofed requests at a rate of over 100,000 in a five-minute span.[1] The NSA could do little to help, taken off guard by an attack on an internet provider rather than the political and military targets it had prepared to defend. As a result, the ZSU's strategic communications network essentially ceased to exist, leaving the brigades of OC North and AC Centre largely to their own devices in the first days of the war.[2]

Dance of the Iskanders

Against the backdrop of this confusion, between 0300–0400hrs on 24 February, the Russian strike campaign in support of the advance on Kyiv began with salvos of Iskander-Ms and Iskander-Ks launched from Belarus.[3] Their primary targets were the array of AC Centre's air defence sites, airfields, and command posts defending the capital, with a particular focus on targets along the planned axes of the ground advance and on the approaches to Antonov IAP. Secondary targets engaged with subsequent salvos included the home bases of OC North's brigades. First, Ukrainian radars were lured out using E-95M decoy unmanned aerial vehicles (UAVs), which spoofed the radar profiles of incoming Russian attack aircraft.[4] Once they had illuminated, the radars were then jammed by the Il-22PPs orbiting north of the border, leaving them blind to the Iskanders already rapidly approaching their positions. Simultaneously, VKS fighter-bombers threaded through the pre-scouted gaps in air defence coverage to strike with Kh-31 and Kh-58 anti-radiation missiles. Overall, the campaign showed considerable sophistication, with Ukrainian air defence units facing multi-layered attacks from both non-kinetic and kinetic systems. Indeed, this was one area of the invasion where Russia's centralised planning process proved at least initially effective. Focusing on largely static targets, and with ample time already spent reconnoitring and planning the strikes, later problems with the lethargic responsiveness of the RUK cycle were yet to emerge.

The results of the opening bombardment were particularly lethal for AC Centre's heavy SAMs and radars. Although these systems took the most time to reposition, most had still not begun dispersing even as the peace drew into its final hours. The reason for this remains a matter of controversy,[5] especially as the commander of the PSZSU – Lieutenant General Mykola Oleshchuk – would later state he gave orders at 0302hrs to bring Ukraine's air defences to full-alert (implying a dispersal).[6] It is possible that the collapse of SAT-KA prevented these orders reaching the brigades in the field. Regardless of exact responsibility, the net result was AC Centre being caught unprepared. Sited at Danylivka, south-west of Kyiv, the 96th Anti-Aircraft Missile Brigade had one of its S-300PS battalions destroyed by multiple Iskander-M strikes around 0500hrs.[7] The 138th Radio Technical Brigade, stationed at Vasylkiv Air Base (AB), was also hit hard. A cruise missile demolished a barracks building still filled with its sleeping troops, though, miraculously, 50 of those inside managed to survive. Nonetheless, despite these setbacks, the personnel of the 96th and 138th quickly rallied and started restoring their damaged radars and launchers. By the morning of the 25 February, operating in tandem, these brigades were engaging their first targets. They were joined in the Kyiv area by an S-300PS battalion of the 160th Anti-Aircraft Missile Brigade and the S-300V1 equipped 210th

A still from a video showing the deployment of an Iskander-K cruise missile from its transporter erector launcher in Belarus. The footage was taken when the war was already well underway in mid-March 2022. (Russian Ministry of Defence)

Anti-Aircraft Missile Regiment, both of which had also suffered missile strikes in the opening hours of the war but restored combat capability.

Better off in the opening barrage against AC Centre were the significantly more mobile Buk M1 medium SAMs of the 156th Anti-Aircraft Missile Regiment. One battalion under the command of Lieutenant Colonel Andriy Kruglov was deployed forward on the Belarussian-Ukrainian border when the war began. It found itself suppressed by intensive jamming, then threatened by the first Russian ground units approaching from the north. All-the-same, thanks to some skilful manoeuvring, it was able to reposition southwards to the town of Borodyanka without losses, despite being actively hunted by the Russians (according to intelligence intercepts).[8] Another battalion of the regiment under Lieutenant Colonel Volodymyr Vesnin went similarly unscathed after quickly dispersing from its barracks, taking up firing positions amongst Kyiv's suburbs.

Here, the practical failure of the VSRF to deliver on the RUK concept begins to rear its head. Though Russian fires planning had proved effective against initial static targets, as Ukrainian SAMs began to reposition it struggled to keep up. After a SAM battery was spotted by GRU assets, for instance, the information would first be reported up to Russia's National Defence Management Centre (*Natsionalnomu Tsentru Upravleniya Oboronoy*, NTsUO) located in Moscow. Once there, it would be fed into the NTsUO's 'Akatsyia-M' automated command and control (C2) system and passed down to OSK East's HQ, who would then assign an asset to destroy the battery in their next 24-hour strike plan. The whole process frequently took over 48 hours to complete, by which time the Ukrainian batteries had already moved again.[9] As a result, many Russian missiles were wasted on empty fields. In total, in the first 48 hours of the war, an estimated 75 percent of all the PSZSU's static SAM sites were engaged. By contrast, just 10 percent of its mobile SAM sites were targeted. It was these same mobile systems, particularly the comparatively nimble Buk M1s, which would prove most effective against Russian aircraft in the subsequent weeks.

Overall, the opening Russian strike campaign against AC Centre had succeeded in its initial goal of suppressing Ukraine's air defences. The EW activity alone was so intense that many PSZSU SAMs and radars suffered serious damage to their electronics, sometimes requiring new components and multiple system resets to bring them back online. Crucially though, the opening strike campaign had failed to capitalise on this suppression of AC Centre's air defences to then destroy them in detail. As shrapnel holes were patched, fried systems reset, and nerves collected, Ukrainian SAM crews recovered in the breathing room provided by the lethargic RUK cycle. The optimistic assumption of Russian planners that shock-and-awe alone would be enough to knock out AC Centre, reflected in the comparatively limited number of missiles actually allocated for the opening strikes, had proven fatally mistaken.[10]

The optimism of Russian planning also hobbled the effectiveness of the strikes directed against OC North, along with the fact that

The consequences of failure in the cat and mouse game of air defence warfare are as violent as they are sudden. Stills from drone footage of an Iskander-M strike on a Ukrainian Buk-M1 in the Kyiv Oblast circa late March 2022. As the fighting progressed, the Russian RUK loop began to improve in efficiency. (Russian Ministry of Defence)

most of its units had already dispersed from their bases. At around 0500hrs, a missile blew up a warehouse on the 72nd Mechanised Brigade's base at Bila Tservka. Fortunately, the 2nd Mechanised Battalion had departed toward its assembly area west of Kyiv three hours earlier and the warehouse stood empty. Colonel Vdovychenko, still asleep in his room, was jolted awake by the explosion, hastening him from there to his forward command post inside the capital.[11] In Honcharivkse, the base of the 1st Tank Brigade was hit by cruise missiles at 0620hrs, but it was only occupied by elements of the brigade's training battalion. The blasts were impressive, as the battalion's commander – Lieutenant Colonel Artem Linkov – recalled later: 'honestly, I thought it was a nuclear explosion', but losses minimal.[12] At Antonov, four cruise missiles struck the base of the 4th Rapid Reaction Brigade without notable result, with two even failing to explode.[13] Despite the ineffectiveness of these initial attacks, few if any follow ups were launched. This can be attributed both to the misplaced optimism of Russian planners and the widespread culture of dishonest reporting between leaders and their subordinates in the VSRF, meaning a target fired on was usually considered as good as destroyed.[14] Also significant was the decision of Russian planners not to target Ukraine's rail infrastructure in the knowledge that it would be needed for the VSRF's own logistics. As a result, OC North was able to receive crucial reinforcements via rail over the following days and weeks, largely unmolested.[15]

4
THE RACE TO KYIV

Shortly before 0400hrs on 24 February, the 35th CAA, commanded by Lieutenant General Aleksandr Semyonovich Sanchik, began its advance to Kyiv on the north-western axis, invading Ukraine through the Chernobyl Exclusion Zone. Facing the onslaught from ambush positions on the P56 highway, the paratroopers of the 80th Air Assault Brigade's 2nd BTG waited and watched. At 0412hrs, they saw a bright flash as the anti-tank mines forward of their line exploded. Aircraft streaked overhead and artillery began to fall, one paratrooper recalled: 'I remember watching lights emerge from the whole forest. At first I thought they were car headlights. But then I realised they were Grads. They were firing at us'.[1]

Ordered to withdraw, the 2nd BTG retreated to defensive positions in Chernobyl, finding it in chaos as the few civilians and border guards living inside the city prepared to evacuate. Meanwhile, nine kilometres further down the P56, the personnel of the 205th Engineering Support Centre went to work preparing the demolition of the bridge supporting the highway over the Uzh River at Cherevach. A tense hour passed whilst the charges were set, then the BTG pulled back over the bridge, which was blown up immediately after its last Humvee was across. The BTG's column withdrew southwards under prowling Russian Su-25 attack aircraft, with the paratroopers having to dive from their vehicles into the woods for cover at least once.

Fortunately for the 2nd BTG, Sanchik's main thrust on 24 February was initially directed not toward Chernobyl but instead further north toward Pripyat and the Chernobyl nuclear power plant (NPP). Crossing the border at Belaya Soroka, the 5th Guards Tank Brigade (5th GTB) lead the advance in a column of some 353 vehicles, stretching over 17 kilometres long. Immediately behind it was the 76th GAAD in a column of about 495 vehicles spread over nearly 25 kilometres of road. A second grouping, including the 155th NIB, struck across the border toward Vilcha along the T1035 road. Facing this concentration was the National Guard's 1st Battalion of State Facilities Protection, defending the Chernobyl NPP. It numbered only 169 strong and lacked anti-tank weapons. All the worse, its commander, Colonel Yuri Pindak, was being told to surrender by the NPP's deputy head of security, Colonel Valentin Viter, who had been turned by Russian intelligence.[2] By 1200hrs the NPP was surrounded. Approximately two hours later, operators of the Bryansk Rosgvardia's "Arsenal" detachment stormed the plant with support from tanks and BMPs of the 5th

Table 1: Known units assigned to the 35th CAA, February–early April 2022

Unit	Known number of BTGs	Comment
5th Guards Tank Brigade	2	From 36th CAA
19th Operational Brigade		Rosgvardia
28th Bridging Brigade	N/A	
30th Artillery Brigade	N/A	From 36th CAA
31st Guards Air Assault Brigade	1.5	From VDV. One BTG shared with 45th GSB
36th Motor Rifle Brigade	1	From 29th CAA
37th Guards Motor Rifle Brigade	2	From 36th CAA
38th Motor Rifle Brigade	1	
40th Naval Infantry Brigade	1	
45th Guards Spetsnaz Brigade	1.5	From VDV. Elements of Redut Private Military Company (PMC) "Wolves" battalion attached
64th Motor Rifle Brigade	1	
69th Covering Brigade	1	
76th Guards Air Assault Division	4	From VDV
98th Guards Airborne Division	4	From VDV
106th Guards Airborne Division	4	From VDV
127th Motor Rifle Division		From 5th CAA. Limited confirmatory evidence
141st Special Motorised Regiment	1	Chechen Rosgvardia
155th Naval Infantry Brigade		
388th Rocket Artillery Brigade	N/A	

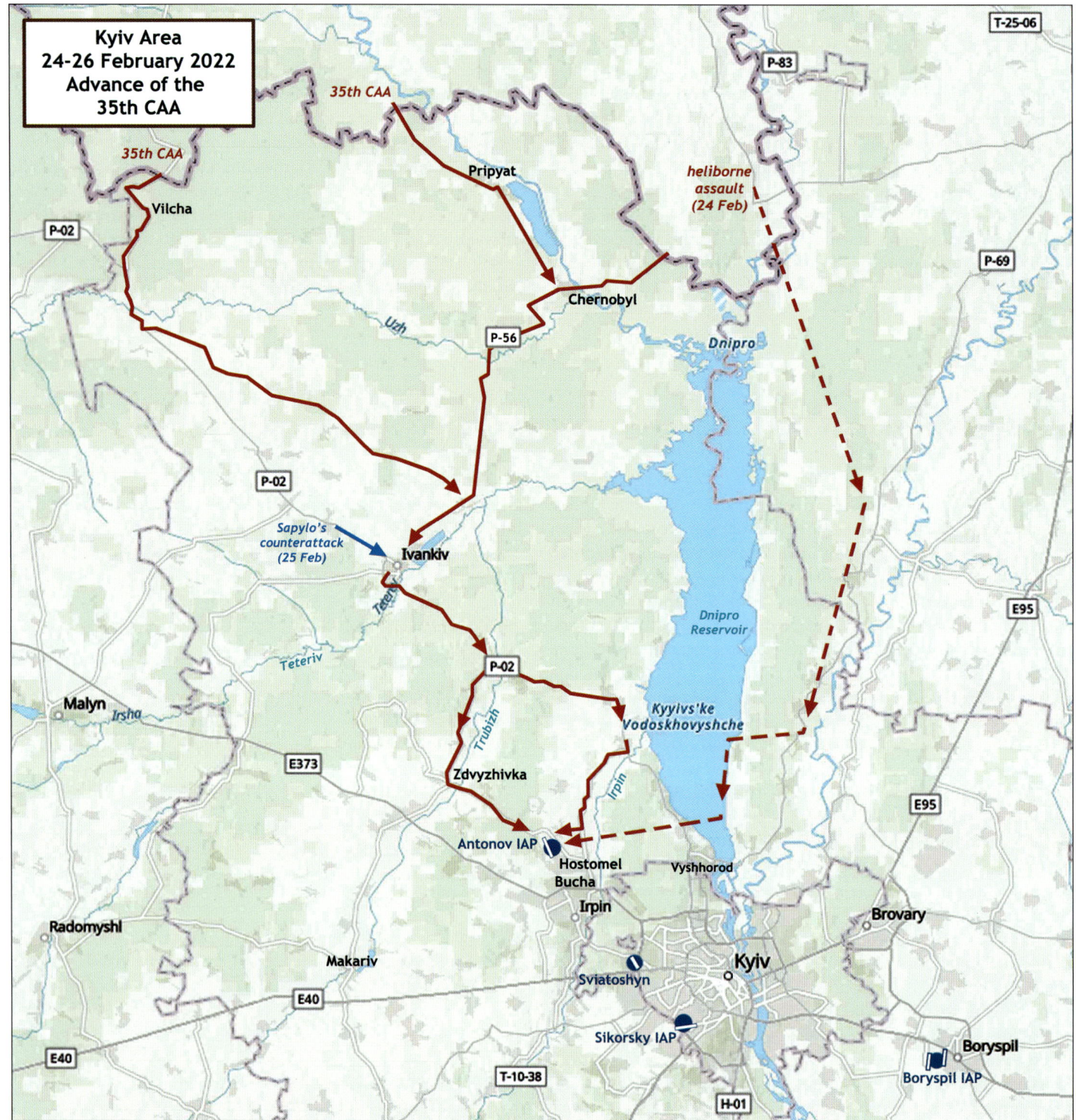

A map illustrating the approximate main routes of advance taken by the 35th CAA from 24–26 February 2022. The exact locations of the pontoons constructed by the Russians in the far north remain unknown, so routes of advance are shown as proceeding over destroyed bridges. (Map by Tom Cooper)

GTB. The outgunned Ukrainian guardsmen surrendered without a shot being fired.

Despite this early success, the advance of the 35th CAA was hardly proceeding to schedule. The sappers of the 250th Engineering Centre, after starting the demolition process of the Cherevach bridge, handed over responsibility to the 80th Air Assault Brigade to complete its demolition and rushed upriver to blow the bridges at Maksymovychi and Poliske, the latter supporting the crucial P02 highway. Though under fire from the approaching Russian armoured columns, the sappers completed their tasks, reportedly collapsing the Maksymovychi bridge even as the first Russian vehicles were racing across it. The loss of these bridges slowed the 35th CAA's advance significantly, forcing its spearheads to wait for pontoon bridges to be erected before they could continue southwards. Making matters worse, the army's routes of advance had been planned with obsolete Soviet maps. These still showed roads which had long since fallen into disrepair, leading some columns into swamps. The communications of the army were also severely disrupted by the VKS's EW activity aimed at the Ukrainian air defence network,[3] deepening the confusion. As a result of these frictions, columns of the 5th GTB were still trundling through the exclusion zone at 1600hrs when, according to their synchronisation matrixes, the brigade should have reached Kyiv's suburbs two hours prior.[4]

T-72Bs of the 5th GTB filmed on CCTV passing through the exclusion zone on 24 February 2022 (State Agency of Ukraine on Exclusion Zone Management)

A column of Russian T-72B3s and BMP-2s on their way south. Note the Soviet flag. (Russian Ministry of Defence)

Heavy vehicles are laboriously guided across a pontoon bridge over the Uzh River, built beside the fallen span of the P56 highway. (Russian Ministry of Defence)

The Battle for Antonov IAP

Regardless of the delays already befalling the 35th CAA's advance, at 1000hrs, the operation to seize Antonov IAP swung into motion.[5] The first wave of the 31st GAAB/45th GSB's BTG lifted off from its staging area on a road near Bagrin, southern Belarus, in a formation of some 15–16 Mi-8AMTSh assault helicopters.[6] The Mi-8s were escorted by 20+ Ka-52, Mi-24, and Mi-35 helicopter gunships, along with several pairs of Su-35S and Su-30SM interceptors providing a combat air patrol. Passing through the gap carved in AC Centre's air defences by the preliminary strikes, this formation was initially unmolested as it winged its way southward along the eastern bank of the Dnipro reservoir. The first Ukrainian resistance was presented by several MiG-29s from the 40th Tactical Aviation Brigade, approaching at low level in a bid to hide from Russian radar scans amongst the ground clutter. Equipped with semi-active radar homing R-27R missiles, which rely on the shooting aircraft's own radar to guide the weapon to target, the Ukrainian pilots were at a serious disadvantage against the active radar homing R-77-1 missiles of their Russian opponents, which can track targets autonomously using the missile's own radar transmitter.[7] In successive engagements, four MiG-29s were shot down, although one still managed to get close enough to loosen off a volley of S-8 80mm unguided rockets at the helicopters, apparently without effect.

The formation's first confirmed losses came as it turned west to cross over the Dnipro reservoir toward Antonov. Engaged by a pair of Ukrainian Igla MANPAD teams, a Mi-24P and a Mi-35M were both downed into the water. Crammed inside their assault helicopters, the paratroopers could only watch in dismay. Corporal Ponomarov, a soldier in the 31st GAAB, recalled later: 'people turned grey'.[8] Pressing on, the formation arrived over Antonov IAP at approximately 1100hrs, with the gunships fanning out to strike the Ukrainian positions; already betrayed to them by informants among the airfield's employees.

For Lieutenant Colonel Vitaly Rudenko, commanding the 4th Rapid Reaction Brigade's CTG, the appearance of the swarm of Russian helicopters came as an unpleasant surprise. His unit had been preparing to repel a small reconnaissance force in a few helicopters, not a concerted effort to seize the airfield. Regardless,

A smoke plume rises and a parachute descends after a Ukrainian MiG-29 was shot down into the Dnipro south of Kyiv on 24 February 2022. (Ukrainian Social Media)

alongside several teams from the GUR's 10th Special Purpose Unit (SSO),[9] the guardsmen opened fire with Iglas, small arms, and three ZU-23-2 anti-aircraft guns.[10] The leading Ka-52 was hit by an Igla as it swept over the airfield, crashing less than 150 metres from the hanger housing the famous An-225 transport aircraft, killing both pilots. Three more Ka-52s would be forced down by a mixture of gunfire and Iglas over the course of the battle, together with an Mi-8AMTSh, though all their crews survived and escaped capture.

Initially caught off guard by the fierce Ukrainian resistance, some Russian gunships switched tactics to snipe with their anti-tank guided missiles (ATGMs) from behind the woods surrounding the airfield, destroying two vehicles of an arriving Omega SOF team and one of the few BTR-3s the guardsmen had pulled from the base's storage.[11] Others continued to strafe with autocannons and rockets, providing suppressive fire as the Mi-8s disgorged their paratroopers

A Mi-8AMTSh (Bort 61 Yellow, registration RF-91175) seen underway over the Minsk area on 23 February 2024. Notably, the helicopter had not only the Russian tricolour on the armour plates under the cockpit, but also the white 'V' quick identification insignia, and exhaust diffusers – both already in preparation for the invasion. (Photo by Homoatrox)

A still from a video recorded by Major Ivan Boldyrev, pilot of Ka-52 Bort 17, showing the moment he launches a pair of unguided rockets toward Ukrainian positions on the outskirts of the airfield. Boldyrev's Ka-52 would later be damaged and forced down near the runway. He and his co-pilot Lieutenant Colonel Roman Kobets escaped unharmed. (Russian Ministry of Defence)

onto the runway. The CTG's positions were a distance from the airfield's apron among a group of two-story buildings, and so they could not immediately see the landings, as Rudenko remembers: 'I started to receive information over the radio that the paratroopers were landing. We didn't know where, and on which side, so I jumped in an armoured vehicle to go to the runway to see. (As I drove) my vehicle was under machine gun fire'.[12]

These shots opened a two-hour long firefight between the guardsmen and the paratroopers, in which several Russians were seen falling under the Ukrainian fire. Nonetheless, by 1300hrs, the CTG was completely out of MANPADs, and down to their last rifle magazines. More Ukrainian SOF had arrived as reinforcements, including several Georgian and Western volunteers,[13] but they lacked the ability to communicate with the guardsmen because of incompatible radios and had no further MANPADs to answer the Russian helicopters with. Running out of options, and with the first VDV elements nearing their positions, the Ukrainian forces decided to withdraw. Twenty guardsmen were isolated at a radar station on the north side of the airfield and captured, but the rest of the CTG and SOF escaped without casualties. With the facility secured, the second wave of the Russian BTG arrived in another formation of Mi-8s at 1320hrs, having completed their own journey from VD Bolshoy Bokov airfield (near Mazyr in Belarus). Fanning out, the paratroopers set about emplacing Kord heavy machine guns and Kornet ATGMs in preparation to defend the airfield.[14] They would not have long to wait.

Right above: A still from helmet camera footage recorded by a VDV paratrooper showing his team collecting themselves after landing. Several Russian Mi-8s are visible circling low to the horizon. (Russian Ministry of Defence)

Right: A still from the same paratrooper's camera, showing his team jogging across the exposed tarmac as parked aircraft burn in the distance after being struck by fire from the Russian helicopters. (Russian Ministry of Defence)

Ukrainian Counterattack

In the bunker beneath the presidential compound on Bankova Street, central Kyiv, Zelensky and his staff watched the events unfolding at Antonov on their social media feeds.[15] Presidential advisor Mykhailo Podolyak recalled later: '[Zelensky] gave the harshest possible orders. "Show no mercy. Use all available weapons to wipe out every Russian thing that's there."'[16]

In their own bunker beneath the Ministry of Defence building, Syrskyi and Zaluzhny were already busy assembling forces to retake the airfield. Their plan for defending Kyiv hinged on allowing the invaders to advance up to an outer defensive ring centred on the capital's suburbs, leaving Russian logistics bottlenecked along the P02 and P56 highways and vulnerable to ambushes. Once the Russian forces were starved of their logistics, a Ukrainian counterattack would encircle and destroy them. The capture of Antonov fundamentally threatened this plan. VDV mechanised forces could now land well inside the outer ring, leaving only 10 kilometres between the Russians and the heart of the capital. All the worse, the airfield, if still operational, would also provide the Russians a major logistics hub with which they could keep their forces supplied by air even if the P02 and P56 were cut.

In the absence of the ViaSat network, it took the *GenStab-U* hours to coordinate the counterattack. Fortunately, however, the expected Russian airlift never arrived. Its exact nature remains a mystery. An original report claimed 18 Il-76s had departed from Pskov AB bound for Kyiv,[17] but later interviews describe as many as 41 Il-76s.[18] The reported origin at Pskov also makes little sense given the 76th GAAD garrisoned there was already with the 35th CAA driving south. Instead, it seems the airlift originated from Ivanovo Severny AB, transporting elements of the 98th GAD. Whatever the case, by mid-afternoon, Antonov's runway was already being shelled by the 4th Rapid Reaction Brigade's two D-30 howitzers located in Horenka, making an airlanding untenable. Their mission aborted, the transports instead disembarked the 98th GAD in Belarus over that evening. The division would subsequently form Sanchik's operational reserve.

At 1700hrs, the 2S3 self-propelled howitzers of 2nd Battery, 2nd Artillery Battalion, 72nd Mechanised Brigade, took up position in Stoyanka to support the counterattack, having just completed their long journey from Bila Tserkva along roads crowded with refugees. Meanwhile, arriving from Chernobyl, the 80th Air Assault Brigade's 2nd BTG formed up west of the airfield to act as an assault force. The battalion organised its Humvees and BTR-80s into a battle line, planning to storm across the runway and assault the airfield's buildings directly under the cover of the 2nd Battery's fire. At 1730hrs, the attack began, the Humvees and BTR-80s surging through the perimeter fence as the 2S3s blanketed the facility. After 200–300 metres progress, Russian return fire began to rattle against the Ukrainian vehicles, inflicting the battalion's first casualties.

Whilst the battle developed, 50 Ukrainian paratroopers disembarked from three Mi-8s on the south-western side of the airfield, having flown in from the 199th Training Centre in Zhytomyr. As this group began vaulting the airfield's perimeter wall, their lead man was hit directly by a VOG-25 grenade. This was followed by sniper shots which pinned the Ukrainians down, then fire from the Kord machine guns emplaced amongst the buildings, as 199th Training Centre paratrooper *Zeus* described:

> When the enemy started to use heavy machine guns that could penetrate the concrete wall, our situation worsened and became really dangerous. Fragments of the wall and rounds were injuring the men. My deputy commander was wounded by a concrete fragment. The enemy fired randomly, the wall shattered, and the fragment hit and broke his leg.[19]

Meanwhile, the 2nd BTG's attack was also faltering in the face of the staunch Russian resistance, and it withdrew after being warned of approaching Ka-52s. Its retreat into Kyiv was not an easy one, losing several vehicles in a chaotic close-range ambush in Bucha, likely one of the first of many friendly fire incidents caused by over-enthusiastic TDF volunteers over the following days. Meanwhile, the 199th's group, with casualties out of reach on the Russian side of the wall, fought on until 0400hrs, when they finally ran out of ammunition and had to withdraw. Crucially, however, a team of four from this group under *Zeus* remained behind to direct artillery fire, concealing themselves in the airfield's outbuildings. This decision would pay dividends later.

Though the Ukrainian counterattack had failed to dislodge the Russians from Antonov, the airfield was useless to them with its runway cratered. With this immediate threat contained, overall the Russian advance was developing almost exactly as Syrskyi and Zaluzhny had planned, with the 35th CAA's columns spread along the P56 highway between Ivankiv and Chernobyl in what was rapidly becoming a giant traffic jam, still some 60 kilometres away from their assigned objectives for the day. Pairs of PSZSU Su-24M bombers, Su-25s, and roving teams of Ukrainian SOF contributed further to the chaos. Nonetheless, Kyiv remained extremely vulnerable. OC North's strategic communication network was still paralysed and the Ukrainian units defending the approaches to the capital were spread extremely thin. In an emergency online summit with dithering

A MAZ truck of the 80th Air Assault Brigade's 2nd BTG, destroyed in Bucha. TDF accounts describe the column being hit by Russian helicopters, but accounts from paratroopers describe an ambush with RPGs and small arms. Whatever the case, TDF fighters would subsequently salvage several vehicles and other equipment from the column's remains, later proving vital in the defence of Irpin on 27 February 2022. (Ukrainian social media)

Servicemen of the 4th Rapid Reaction Brigade pose with their bullet riddled flag after being evacuated from Antonov IAP, 24 February 2022. (4th Rapid Reaction Brigade)

European heads of state that night, Zelensky reminded them: 'this may be the last time you see me alive'.[20]

Paranoia

Early on the morning of 25 February, elements of the Rosgvardia's 19th Operational Brigade (drawn from the Rosgvardia units of the Siberian Federal District), somehow managed to slip ahead of the main body of the 35th CAA to become the foremost Russian units driving southward along the P02.[21] Lightly armed and equipped, it remains unclear what chain of mistakes led to these rear-area units spearheading the advance. Rosgvardia officer Lieutenant Colonel Dmitry Astakhov recalled later: 'I don't know what happened. We rode at the tail of the column, but for some reason, we got in the front, and there was no one else there'.[22]

In the confusion, two company-sized Rosgvardia detachments from the Kemerovo and Krasnoyarsk regions drove toward Kyiv on their own after receiving vague orders to establish a strongpoint inside the capital. Around 0811hrs, they passed through Hostomel and onto the E373 road bridge over the Irpin River, just 500 metres from the city limits. This brought them under the waiting guns of 4th Company, 2nd Mechanised Battalion, 72nd Mechanised Brigade, which had taken up positions opposite the bridge in Horenka the day before. Completely exposed on the bridge's span to the resulting machine gun, tank, and ATGM fire, the Kemerovo detachment's column was shot apart in matter of moments, their Ural and KamAZ trucks providing little protection against the fusillade. Seventy-seven Russians were killed and another three captured. Seeing this disaster, the Krasnoyarsk detachment retreated back into Hostomel, where – in an apparent act of revenge – they proceeded to shoot at passing civilian cars for the next six hours, killing five people and injuring six more. This was the first of many atrocities committed by Russian troops in Kyiv's suburbs.

The Kemerovo detachment's column seen burning on the E373 road bridge, 25 February 2022. (Ukrainian social media)

A still from CCTV footage capturing the Krasnoyarsk detachment collecting in Hostomel. Moments later they would begin machine-gunning passing cars. (Office of the Prosecutor General of Ukraine)

AN UNHAPPY ODYSSEY: THE KEMEROVO SOBR/OMON DETACHMENT

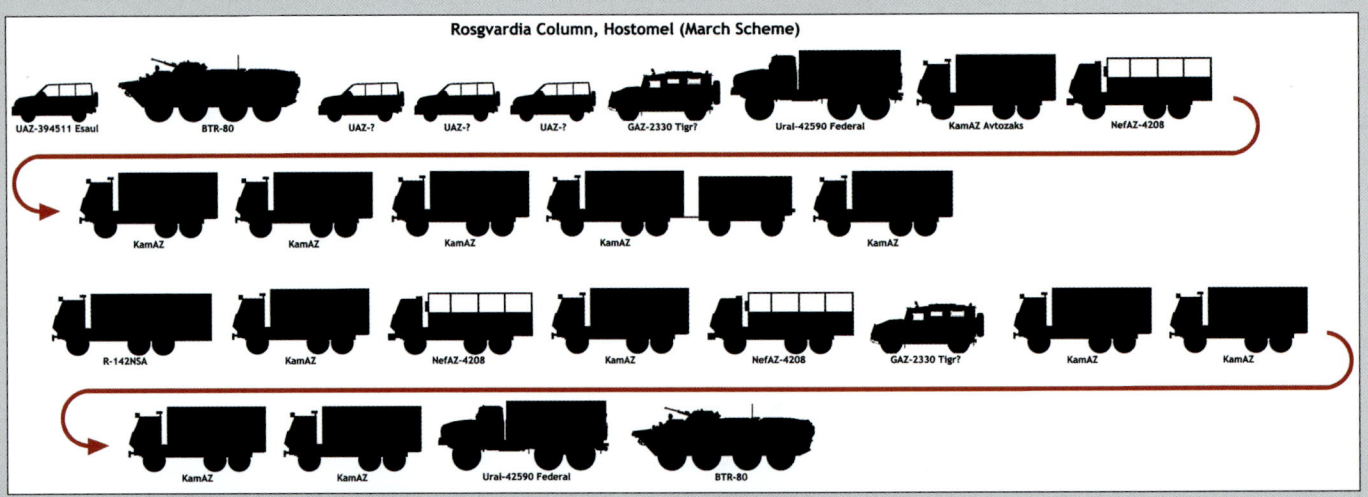

A diagram showing the marching scheme of the Kemerovo SOBR/OMON detachment's column, as reproduced from an original Russian military document published by the SBU. Many of the precise vehicle variants were left unspecified in the document beyond their maker's brand (e.g. NeFAZ, UAZ, GAZ) and have thus been deduced using photographs of the wrecked Kemerovo column and its sister from the Krasnoyarsk region (specifically the NefAZ-4208 buses, Ural-42590 Federal armoured trucks, and UAZ-394511 Esaul utility vehicle). Unfortunately, no GAZ vehicles of any make were pictured as wreckage nor in service with the Krasnoyarsk detachment, despite being listed on the original march scheme. Accordingly, the author speculates that these unknown GAZ's were GAZ-2330 Tiger MRAPs, as commonly seen in service with other Rosgvardia units during the invasion. Likewise, a series of UAZ vehicles were listed in the original document with no obvious analogues, and are thus left as 'unknown' in the diagram.[23] (Diagram by Tom Cooper)

Judging by subsequent interviews with survivors, the officers of the Kemerovo SOBR/OMON detachment appear to have been ignorant of the fact they were participating in an invasion almost until the very moment they met their fate on the E373 road bridge. Most commanders of the Rosgvardia formations attached to the 35th CAA were briefed of Putin's plans only a week before the war during a meeting in Smolensk. Among those present was Colonel Daniil Martynov – commander of the Chechen Rosgvardia's 141st Special Motorised Regiment and close confidant of Ramazan Kadyrov, President of the Chechen Republic. Describing the meeting afterwards to Kadyrov in an intercepted phone call, Martynov reported how the assembled Rosgvardia commanders received the news of the invasion with a mixture of consternation and dismay – their 'eyes bulging'. Many raised concerns that their men would refuse to fight. For this reason, several commanders apparently decided not to brief their units about the invasion at all, even after they had crossed the Ukrainian border, including the commander of the Kemerovo detachment. Indeed, Lieutenant Colonel Astakhov later recalled that the first moment he knew for sure he was in Ukraine was when he took a smoke break in the detachment's laager on the night of 24 February and came across a sign marked 'Exclusion Zone'.

In a twist of fate, the two Rosgvardia detachments were filmed by CCTV as they passed through Hostomel. This footage quickly spread across Ukrainian social media, where the column was mistakenly reported to be Russian infiltrators using captured vehicles in posts by Ukrainian officials. In Kyiv, with the city's armouries already emptied into the hands of civilian volunteers, this information sparked mayhem. Across the Obolon district, a peculiar firefight raged between a Ukrainian army anti-aircraft battery and elements of the National Guard's 27th Brigade, leading to the crew of a truck mounted ZU-23-2 being shot dead. Though originally reported as the destruction of a Russian SRG, this was almost certainly a friendly fire incident. Similar sporadic firefights would rage across the city long into the night, some genuine instances of SRGs being destroyed,[24] most more tragic instances of friendly fire.[25] The violence would only be curbed after a curfew was declared on 26 February.[26]

A still from a video filmed of the Obolon firefight on 25 February 2022. A gunman, likely a TDF volunteer, raises his AK-74 to dispatch a wounded man lying beside the truck mounted ZU-23-2. In the background a Ukrainian Strela-10 SAM system reverses after running over a civilian vehicle in the confusion. (Ukrainian social media)

Battle of Ivankiv

Though the Kemerovo and Krasnoyarsk Rosgvardia detachments had been able to make it to Hostomel apparently unopposed, the same could not be said for the rest of the 35th CAA: which remained strung out along the roads north of the capital.[27] Already arriving on its flank from the west were forward elements of the 14th Mechanised Brigade, which had spent the previous day marching from the Rivne training area. Faced with a frontage some 300 kilometres long, the brigade's commanding officer, Colonel Oleksandr Ohrimenko, broke his battalions down into small battlegroups to raid the Russian convoys:

> We used small mobile combat groups that could work from ambushes, inflict damage on the enemy, who outnumbered us by a ratio of one to twenty, or even to thirty, and advanced in large columns, battalion-tactical groups, entire regiments, and divisions. It was a 'pounce tactic' – two or three tanks, together with anti-tank means, including Javelins and NLAW [ATGM systems], would destroy several units of enemy equipment and withdraw in another direction, and so on. This allowed us to disperse the enemy's forces, to create panic among his personnel, since the enemy did not understand where the next attack would come from.[28]

Around mid-morning, one such battlegroup, centred on a T-64BV platoon commanded by Lieutenant Vitaliy Sapylo, struck across the intersection of the P02 and P56 northwest of Ivankiv, destroying several Russian vehicles in the process. This success proved short lived as, after withdrawing west to the village of Termakhivka for nightfall, Sapylo's battlegroup was set upon by Russian Su-25s. The lieutenant's tank was hit by an air-to-ground missile, instantly killing his crew and mortally wounding him. Another T-64BV and two BMPs were also destroyed. Nonetheless, the small battlegroup had managed to briefly cut the main supply route of the entire 35th CAA, contributing significantly to the chaos enveloping the Russian advance. Indeed, it was not until dusk that the first Russian ground elements finally reached the beleaguered paratroopers at Antonov IAP, led by a platoon of T-80BV tanks from the 40th Naval Infantry Brigade (40th NIB).[29]

Shaping Operations

As the 35th CAA approached, the Ukrainians scrambled to shore up their outer defensive ring by demolishing bridges along the Irpin River.[30] The E373 bridge crossed by the Rosgvardia earlier in the day was badly damaged, whilst the P30 and E40 bridges further south were completely destroyed, the latter in such haste that several civilians were injured and killed when the span collapsed beneath their vehicles. Outside of the ZSU's operations, a local businessman named Oleksandr Dmitriyev hatched his own plan to thwart the Russian advance after realising that the Irpin could be flooded by breaching the dam where it meets the Dnipro reservoir near the village of Kozarovychi, rendering it impassable even to pontoon bridges. Leveraging his government contacts, Dmitriyev was able to present the idea to Syrskyi, who received the proposal with characteristically blunt enthusiasm. With the assistance of loaned engineers and explosives, Dmitriyev's team blew a small hole in the dam around 1530hrs on 25 February, releasing the first of what would eventually amount to 117.5 million cubic metres of water into the Irpin floodplain.[31] Unfortunately, a small dam downriver at Chervone initially prevented the river flooding south of this point.[32] Though the front had been somewhat shortened, a wide opening remained for the 35th CAA to stage a crossing, which Sanchik would later exploit in full.

The Vasylkiv Events

According to multiple Ukrainian and Western accounts, a concerted Russian air assault was made against Vasylkiv AB overnight between 25–26 February in an attempt to seize a new airhead, this time south of Kyiv.[33] Official accounts describe two Il-76s, two Mi-24s, and an Su-25 subsequently shot down, along with many Russian paratroopers killed on the ground by the security company of the

A T-64BV from Lieutenant Sapylo's battlegroup seen advancing during the battle at the P02/P56 intersection on 25 February 2022. Russian vehicles are visible, ablaze. (14th Mechanised Brigade)

40th Tactical Aviation Brigade and TDF elements defending the airfield. Though dramatic, this narrative does not hold up to scrutiny. Crucially, no visual evidence of these alleged Russian losses nor any corroboratory Russian testimonies exist to the author's knowledge. Given the failure of the Antonov operation, and the difficulties incurred in reaching the IAP on the ground, it also makes little sense that Sanchik would have attempted to seize an airfield even further behind enemy lines. Ukrainian eyewitnesses themselves describe sporadic firefights with possible Russian SRGs at the AB and in Vasylkiv town itself over consecutive nights, not a major landing operation. The situation at the airfield stabilised with the arrival of a company from the 8th Mountain Assault Battalion, 10th Mountain Brigade in the early morning of 26 February,[34] but fighting around the town would continue, with an arriving convoy of artillery from the 128th Mountain Brigade losing eight killed and five wounded in an ambush that same day.

A group of Ukrainian soldiers find time for a meal in the immediate aftermath of the Vasylkiv skirmishes, 27 February 2022. (Marian Kushnir)

5
THE TIPPING POINT

26 February passed as an operational pause for both sides whilst they reorganised after the chaos of the previous two days fighting. The communications issues which had dogged the 35th CAA were slightly alleviated on this day with the lifting of the VKS EW campaign against Ukraine's air defences, Russian command having finally decided that its effectiveness did not outweigh the havoc it was wreaking upon their own C2 networks. At the same time, Sanchik was able to establish his forward HQ in the village of Zdvyzhivka. This settlement would become a centre of gravity for the Russian advance on western Kyiv, eventually housing a logistics hub, field hospital, and the HQ of the 98th GAD, among other units. Despite these improvements in command and control, Sanchik's overall position remained unfavourable. Ahead, the bridges over the Irpin were disappearing one by one whilst, to his rear, the army's logistics remained severely congested along the P56 and P02. Nonetheless, running out of time and under direct pressure from Putin for

A Russian checkpoint in Zdvyzhivka, note the emplaced BMD-2 on the far side of the road. The troops here are from the 331st Regiment, 98th GAD, which provided the initial garrison force for Sanchik's HQ. (Russian Ministry of Defence)

This satellite photo taken on 28 February 2022 reveals something of the logistics nightmare the 35th CAA was facing. Stacked three across, a column of Russian trucks sit in a traffic jam on the P02 south of Ivankiv. (Satellite Image © 2024 Maxar Technologies Provided By European Space Imaging)

results, Sanchik began planning a major offensive to reach Kyiv, commencing the next day.¹

Meanwhile, on the Ukrainian side, the situation remained desperate if beginning to improve. Syrskyi at least did not have Zelensky breathing down his neck: the President instead concerning himself with leading the nation and pleading for Western support rather than intervening in operational matters. The frontline along the Irpin River was still thinly held, with the 2nd Mechanised Battalion, 72nd Mechanised Brigade, spread between the villages of Huta-Mezhyhirska, Moschun and Horenka, whilst elements of the 80th Air Assault Brigade's 2nd BTG occupied Romanivka. However, reinforcements were already arriving in the form of hundreds of reservists, re-enlisting ATO (anti-terrorist operation) veterans, and fresh recruits.² For example, the 2nd Mechanised Battalion's 5th Company, holding north of Moschun, had begun the war with just 22 soldiers. Now, it numbered some 70 strong. Meanwhile, thousands more TDF volunteers readied to defend their own towns and villages. One such unit, vital in the next day's fighting, was the self-described 'Irpin CTG,'³ a band of ATO veterans and civilians numbering about 200 strong. On their own initiative, they established a checkpoint at the Giraffe shopping centre on the northern outskirts of Irpin, overlooking the bridge over the Bucha River and the southern outskirts of Bucha beyond. They also salvaged several BTR-80s from the 80th Air Assault Brigade convoy wrecked nearby, which they used to strengthen their positions.⁴

Alongside the tactical reinforcements generated from inside Kyiv and its immediate surroundings, Syrskyi was also receiving significant operational reinforcements from Ukraine's south and west. First among them, the 14th Mechanised Brigade was still arriving on Kyiv's west from Rivne, closely followed by the 95th Air Assault Brigade on its way from Zhytomyr. Also arriving around the city were elements of the 26th Artillery Brigade (equipped with 2S19 Msta-S and 2S5 Giantsint-S self-propelled 152mm howitzers) from Berdychiv, elements of the 43rd Artillery Brigade (equipped with 2S7 self-propelled howitzers) from Divychki, and elements of the 44th Artillery Brigade (equipped with 2A65 Msta-B and 2A36 Giantsint-B towed 152mm howitzers) from Zhytomyr. With these artillery brigades, Syrskyi now had the means of not only blunting Russian attacks, but of destroying the Russian units themselves. The next day of fighting would illustrate this point in graphic detail.⁵

A Day of Disasters: Central Axis

Sanchik's offensive was divided into three axes on western, central, and eastern approaches to the capital. The central axis was to strike south from Antonov IAP and cross the Irpin into Kyiv.⁶ Within this axis, a CTG of the 155th NIB would advance over the E373 bridge from Hostomel toward Horenka, whilst a BTG of the 104th Regiment, 76th GAAD, would drive straight through Bucha and Irpin toward the P30 bridge.⁷ Bringing up the rear was the 31st GAAB, which had now brought up its own vehicles and a second BTG to join the joint BTG already at Antonov IAP. First, however, the brigade had to refuel after its long journey from Belarus.

Following an order given at 0400hrs on 27 February, the 31st GAAB's vehicles collected on the apron outside the An-225's hanger for the procedure, along with the better part of a Rosgvardia brigade. The decision to concentrate so much equipment in an area less than 500 square metres remains a mystery. *Zeus* and his team had already made their presence known by directing Ukrainian artillery around the IAP over the previous days, even downing an Mi-28UM helicopter gunship with an Igla on 25 February.⁸ Nonetheless, the Russians ignored this threat completely and the refuelling proceeded without any haste. The concentration was soon spotted by both *Zeus* and a Ukrainian UAV. Shortly after 0900hrs, a massive artillery barrage was called down upon the refuelling point from the guns of the 43rd Artillery Brigade and the 2nd Artillery Battalion, 72nd Mechanised Brigade. The bombardment lasted for two hours, destroying over

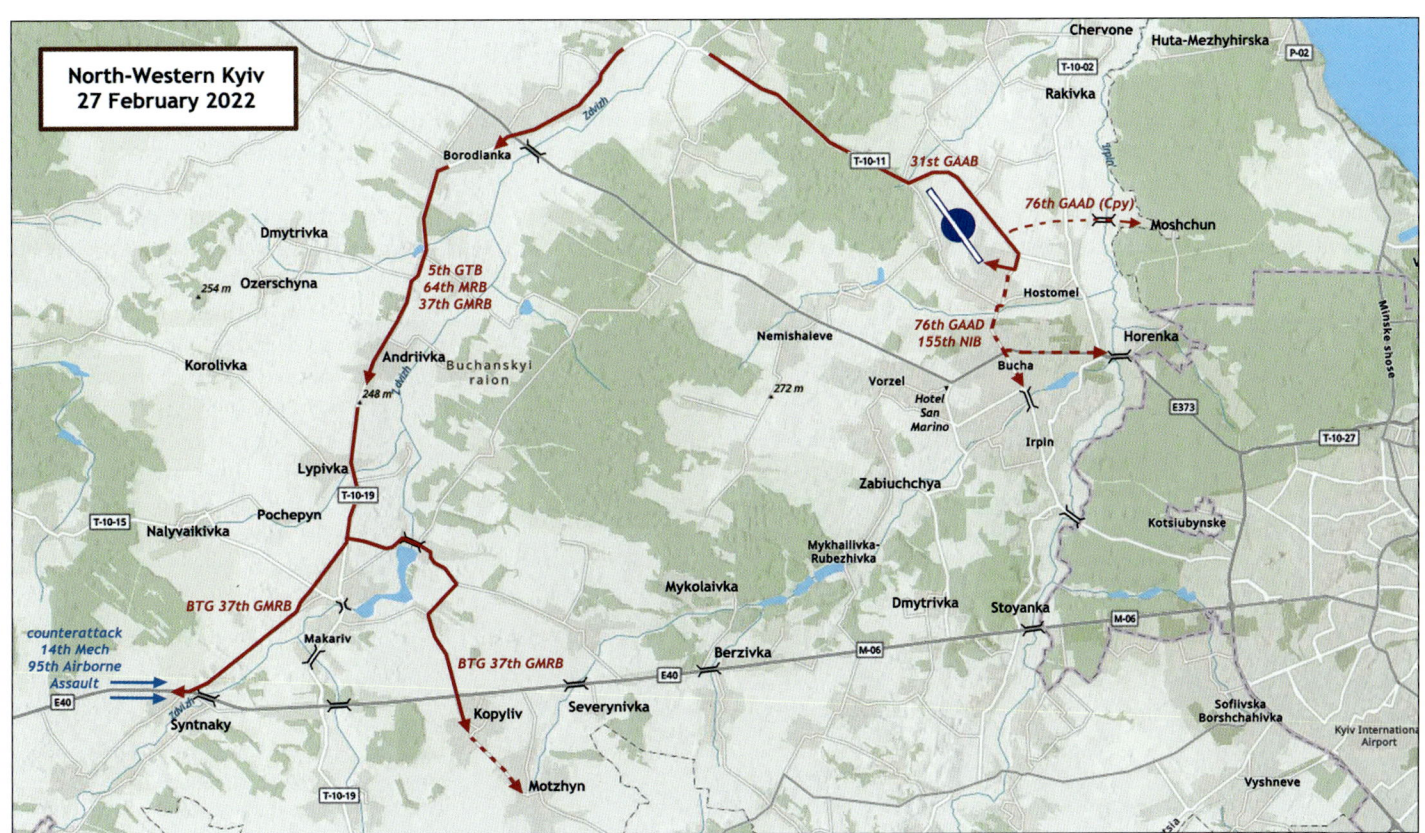

A map illustrating the Russian offensive against Kyiv on 27 February 2022. Dotted arrows denote failed attempts to advance. (Map by Tom Cooper)

The aftermath of the 27 February artillery strike at Antonov International. Photos were taken in April 2022 after many of the more intact vehicles had already been dragged away. (Kyiv City Government, Oleksii Samanov)

100 armoured fighting vehicles (AFVs) and trucks in the vicinity of the hangers and killing at least 60 Russians. Corporal Nikolayevich later recalled of these casualties: '[they] could only be scraped off the asphalt'.[9] So ended the participation of the 31st GAAB in the day's offensive.

Meanwhile, the 155th NIB's CTG and 104th Regiment's BTG were facing their own disaster inside Bucha. The Russian convoy had entered the town at 0640hrs, with the 155th's CTG splitting off toward the E373 bridge as the 104th's BTG continued southward. The marines found their bridge partially destroyed and were met with tank and machine gun fire from 4th Company, 2nd Mechanised Battalion, 72nd Mechanised Brigade, still holding firm in Horenka. With no hope of crossing here, they turned around and joined the tail of the 104th's column proceeding down Vokzal'na Street. The sound of a developing firefight could already be heard up ahead.

The 104th's BTG had not expected to meet Ukrainian resistance in Bucha. Most of its paratroopers were riding on the decks of their BMDs. Some were even singing.[10] Positioned around the Novus supermarket on Vokzal'na, a group of 20 local TDF volunteers cut short this parade spirit with Molotov cocktails and RPGs, destroying a BMD-2 and a BMP-2.[11] The Russian response was fierce, and the TDF group only narrowly escaped in civilian cars under a hail of autocannon fire. Their retreat was bravely covered by a second TDF group, consisting largely of pensioners. After 30 minutes of fighting, all 12 volunteers of this latter group had been shot and evacuated to hospital. The ambush neutralised, the Russians continued on toward the Giraffe checkpoint, now in combat formation.

Advancing cautiously, the Russian column was halted again after another ambush at Bucha railway station. This pause allowed the TDF group escaping from the Novus supermarket to join the Irpin CTG at Giraffe. Also present at the checkpoint were a dozen stragglers from the 80th Air Assault Brigade, some national guardsmen, and a SOF team from the 8th SSO Regiment. Apparently unaware of the Ukrainian position, around 0900hrs the leading elements of the Russian column crossed over the Bucha River, straight into the waiting ambush. Immediately, a Ukrainian paratrooper hit one BMD with an RPG-22, then a second with an RPG-7B. The Russian vehicles responded with autocannon bursts, setting the Giraffe shopping centre and surrounding houses ablaze. Meanwhile, towards the rear of the Russian column – still inside Bucha – pensioneer TDF volunteer Valentyn Didkovskiy was preparing his own ambush:

I saw a big column approaching from the Bucha railway crossing. I prepared my grenade launcher [an RPG-18] and four grenades. I ran to the gate, but it wasn't a good position. The column was just 30 meters away. I walked behind the house, there was a trailer parked by the fence. I climbed on it quietly. The first BTR drove by, then an BMP, another BTR, a tank. Suddenly, I spotted a fuel truck and thought: "maybe this will stop some of them." I fired my grenade launcher. When I hit the fuel truck, a huge fire started.[12]

With this inferno behind them, and the fighting at Giraffe up ahead, the Russian column became boxed in along Vokzal'na Street. Directed by TDF spotters, artillery fire from the 128th Mountain Brigade and 43rd Artillery Brigade began to devastate the concentration of men and equipment. A pair of PSZSU Su-24Ms competed the destruction of the column, though one was shot down after completing its bombing run, the aircraft's crew – Major Ruslan Bylus and Captain

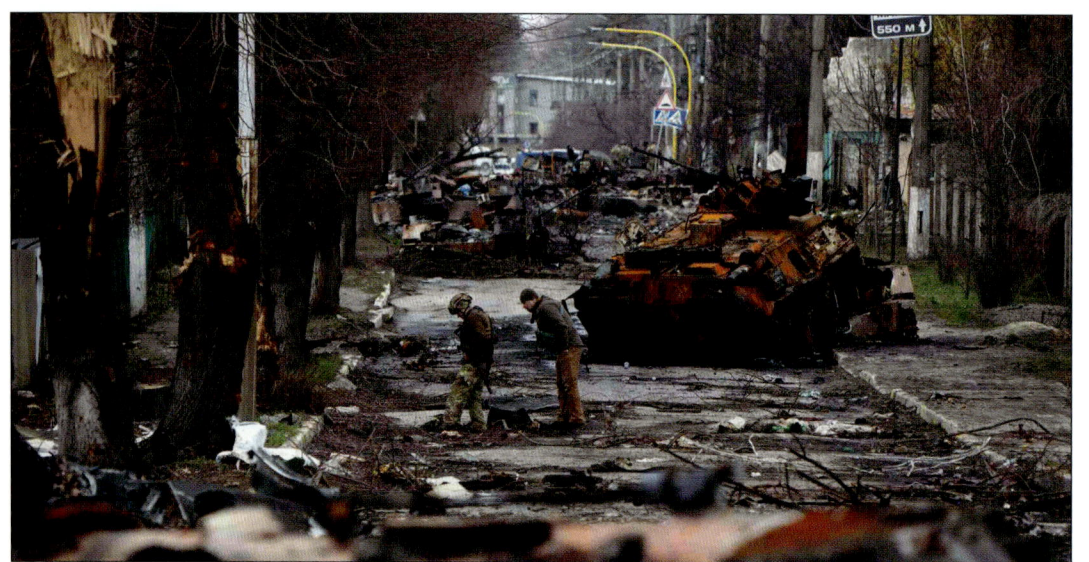

The aftermath of the 27 February artillery strike on Vokzal'na Street. Photo taken on 4 April 2022. (Ukrainian Presidential Release)

Roman Dovgalyuk – dying in the crash.[13] Their morale broken, Russian paratroopers and marines began surrendering as the survivors of the column fled back toward the IAP. In the aftermath, the Irpin company advanced to clear the battlefield. They captured several BMDs, a Strela-10M SAM system, and an MT-LBu based Barnaul-T air defence command post, which was promptly put in service with the 72nd Mechanised Brigade.[14] In total, the Russians had lost an estimated 95–200 personnel, along with around 40 AFVs and trucks. The central axis of Sanchik's advance on Kyiv had thus proven an utter disaster, with two BTGs destroyed between Antonov IAP and Vokzal'na Street for no real gain.

A column of 64th Motor Rifle Brigade vehicles enroute in Kyiv Oblast in early March 2022. (Russian Ministry of Defence)

The First Battle of Moschun: Eastern Axis

On the eastern axis of the offensive, a CTG from the 104th Regiment was sent to probe a crossing over the Irpin through Moschun.[15] At mid-morning, this group's 14 AFVs crossed the river over a small concrete bridge and began driving into the village itself, defended at the time by only a few TDF volunteers and the scout platoon of 5th Company, 2nd Mechanised Battalion, 72nd Mechanised Brigade. Outgunned by the Russian patrol, these forces fought a delaying action until another platoon from 5th Company, riding three BMP-2s, arrived on the Russians' flank from the north. This platoon was accompanied by the 5th Company's commanding officer, Captain Roman Kovalenko, a fortuitous choice, as the platoon's own commander was shot in the face and killed almost immediately. Surprised by the appearance of Ukrainian armour on their flank and disorientated by the fire and smoke overtaking the village, the Russians began to turn back towards the river. Their route of retreat was completely exposed over the river's wide floodplain, allowing the Ukrainian BMPs to knock out one BTR-MDM command vehicle and damage a BMD-2 as the Russian patrol withdrew. In the aftermath, the 5th Company secured new positions in Moschun, and the small concrete bridge was blown up. Though the overland approach to the village was now gone, the Irpin's waters here remained shallow, the Chervone dam still holding back the flood upriver. As a result, the 5th Company would face another Russian assault just a few days later, this time amphibious, much larger, and much more determined.

Drive on the E40: Western Axis

Sanchik's western thrust was by far the most successful of the day's offensive.[16] Here, BTGs of the 64th Motor Rifle Brigade (64th MRB), 37th Guards Motor Rifle Brigade (37th GMRB), and 5th GTB drove down the T1019 road running west of Kyiv in an attempt to encircle the city. Captured documents indicate their ultimate objectives were as ambitious as Kalynivka and Vasylkiv, well to Kyiv's south.[17]

The first major settlement in the way was Borodyanka, defended by only lightly armed TDF volunteers. They met the vanguard Russian column entering the town with Molotov cocktails. The Russian response to this resistance was brutal, civilians standing in the open were machine-gunned whilst residential properties along the roads were shelled with tanks. Violence would continue across the town for days. During the night of 28 February, columns of the 64th MRB and 5th GTB were attacked again on Borodyanka's central street, losing several AFVs and trucks.[18] In revenge, VKS Su-25s bombed an apartment block the following day, killing 41 people.[19] It was only on 12 March that the Russians completely secured the town, but raids, looting, and executions went on. Though most of the Russian grouping had continued south along the T1019 after the first resistance on 27 February, the failure to quickly secure their lines of communication here would later create major logistical problems.

South of Borodyanka in the village of Andriivka, the 64th MRB established its HQ and orientated to protect the push's western flank, whilst the 37th GMRB and 5th GTB drove on toward the next town of Makariv.[20] A single team from the 3rd SSO Regiment mounted on Humvees delayed the Russian advance using Javelins and NLAWs, but eventually their luck ran out and they were run down by BMPs

A Russian Tornado-G 122mm MRLS burning in central Borodyanka, presumably after being hit by a Molotov. (Ukrainian social media)

Immediate aftermath of the nocturnal attack on a Russian column inside Borodyanka. Photo taken on 1 March 2022. (Security Service of Ukraine)

The Borodyanka apartment block destroyed by a Russian airstrike on 1 March 2022. (Kyiv City Government, Oleksii Samanov)

and tanks. Only by hiding amongst the tall grasses and playing dead were the operators able to escape. By 1500hrs on 27 February, the 37th GMRB and 5th GTB had reached the outskirts of Makariv. As with Borodyanka, the town was relatively thinly defended, in this case by a National Guard company 120 strong and around 100 TDF volunteers, the latter with only eight RPGs between them.[21] Wary following Borodyanka however, the Russian columns opted to bypass Makariv after they met initial resistance, effectively encircling its defenders. Continuing south, the 37th GMRB reached the E40 highway, severing Kyiv's direct connection with western Ukraine. One BTG drove west along the E40 toward Nebelystya, whilst the second was dispatched through Kopyliv toward Motzhyn, continuing the push south-east as dusk fell.[22] Sanchik's western envelopment of the capital was halfway complete. However, the tactical situation was rapidly slipping out of his control. The 37th GMRB was low on fuel, with vehicles stalling in the road, and the brigade's communications were being jammed. Then, at this critical moment, Ukrainian forces began appearing from the west on the E40, opposite the 37th GMRB's first BTG. These were leading elements of the 95th Air Assault Brigade and 14th Mechanised Brigade, arriving to launch a major counterattack. Fierce fighting began immediately between Nebelystya and Syntnaky. In the latter village, a civilian medical post struggled to cope with the number of Russian wounded. Meanwhile, the second BTG's push on Motzhyn also fell apart after it met determined Ukrainian resistance there.

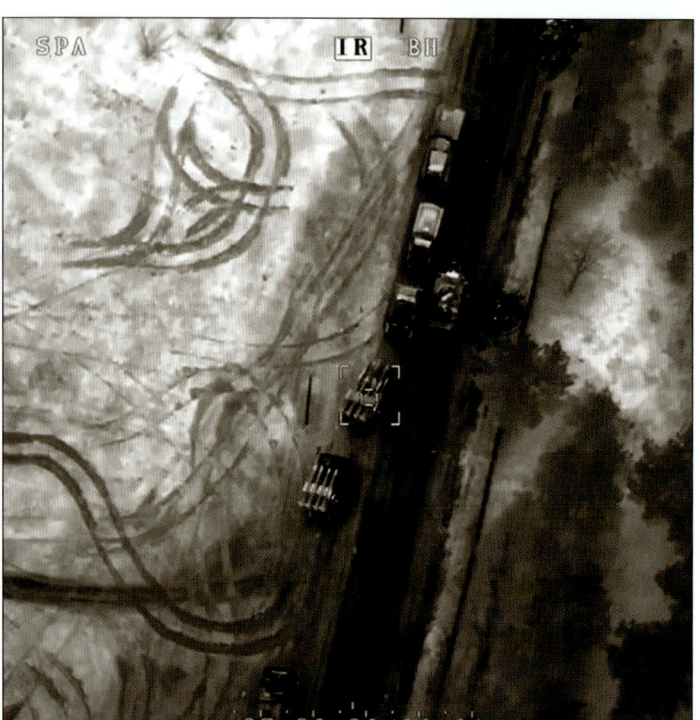

Adding insult to injury. At 1900hrs on 27 February 2022, PSZSU Bayraktar TB2 attack drones bombed a column of the 37th GMRB still northwest of Makariv, destroying a Buk battery in the process. (ZSU)

6
REINFORCING FAILURE

Though the 27 February offensive had proven an overall failure, Sanchik continued to push on the offensive's western axis where he had enjoyed relative success, itself attributable more to the initial absence of regular ZSU units here rather than any superiority on the part of 37th GMRB, 5th GTB, and 64th MRB vis-à-vis the Russian units on the other axes. At 0600hrs on 28 February, the entire 5th GTB advanced around Makariv to push eastward along the E40 toward Kyiv. Entering the village of Berezikva, the brigade was hit by a Ukrainian artillery strike, losing several vehicles, and dispersed into the surrounding woods. Continuing on, during 1 March, the brigade reached the Irpin River after fighting through several TDF ambushes. However, the E40 bridge here had long since been demolished and the Russians could do little more than wait, Kyiv just 500 metres away.[1]

On the same day, the 14th Mech and 95th Air Assault's counterattack broke through the 37th GMRB's BTG holding Sytnaky and reached the Ukrainian force still defending Makariv. In the process, this BTG was effectively shattered. Over 137 Russian bodies would later be recovered in the vicinity of Sytnaky and Zavalivka.[2] The counterattack also cut off the 5th GTB and the second BTG of the 37th GMRB from their already stretched logistics, which severely limited the ability of the Russians to continue the push south-east of the E40. The Russian commanders themselves were reaching saturation point. Continuous airstrikes by VKS aircraft overhead had not saved the situation and a Su-34 had been shot down in return, killing the crew. In intercepted communications, one 37th GMRB commander was heard sobbing over the brigade radio net.[3] Another lamented: 'The boys are suffering, suffering.'[4]

The Battles of Bucha, Irpin, and Hostomel

Thanks to the arrival of StarLink satellite communication terminals in theatre from 28 February, OC North (and AC Centre) began restoring its strategic communications network.[5, 6] Benefiting from this development, Syrskyi was able to coordinate a plethora of different units for an operation to clear Kyiv's northern suburbs of Russian forces. The reasoning behind this operation remains unclear, but the northern defensive line had recently been bolstered by the 214th OPFOR Battalion and the newly formed Kyiv Azov Regiment. With this new strength, Syrskyi likely saw an opportunity to increase the depth of his defence forward of the Irpin. Accordingly, on 2 March, Ukrainian SOF from the 3rd SSO Regiment and 10th SSO 'Shaman' Battalion occupied positions in central Hostomel beside a glass factory and dug in. They were reinforced by the 214th OPFOR Battalion and local TDF. Meanwhile, a company from the 80th Air Assault Brigade's 2nd BTG crossed the destroyed P30 bridge on foot. They joined the Irpin CTG, National Guard, and Azov Regiment elements sweeping north through Irpin and Bucha. On 3 March, a group from these assorted units occupied the San Marino hotel complex west of Bucha in Vorzel, which held commanding views of the E373. The same day would see the defenders of the glass factory and the San Marino put to the test.

An armoured column from the 5th GTB seen heading heading eastward on the E40 – toward Kyiv – in this video-still taken by a Ukrainian UAV on 1 March 2022. (Vlad Podol)

THE BTG CONCEPT IN PRACTICE: THE 37TH GUARDS MOTOR RIFLE BRIGADE'S 2ND BTG

This diagram reconstructs the combat elements of the 2nd BTG of the 37th Guards Motor Rifle Brigade as of late February 2022, using a synthesis of sources, including captured Russian military documentation,[7] a personnel roster leaked by the GUR (detailing the BTG's sub-units, and the number of personnel and vehicles assigned to each),[8] footage of the brigade taken prior to and during the battle,[9] and open-source vehicle loss reporting.[10] Unfortunately, the lack of a complete table of organisation and equipment for the BTG means the exact vehicle complements of some of its sub-units are unknown or partly speculative, leaving the diagram an approximation at best. On paper, the unit comprised 74 officers, 125 NCOs, and 509 enlisted personnel, giving a total strength of 708 soldiers, although – according to the battalion's own roster – actual manning was closer to 650 total. This discrepancy can be explained by a lack of available conscripts, an issue shared with many other contemporary BTGs of the VRSF. In terms of combat strength, this meant the unit only had around 247 infantry dismounts, illustrating how vulnerable the overall formation was should its combat elements be attrited.

The BTG's complement of personnel was transported within a total of some 180 vehicles. Many of the precise variants used can be stated with a high degree of confidence thanks to a partial brigade vehicle roster captured by the Ukrainians, further supplemented by contemporary footage and loss reporting. In particular, the formation's use of BMP-1Kshs, BMP-2s, T-72B3s, BM-21 Grads, 2S3(M) Acacias, BRM-1K reconnaissance vehicles, Strela-10s, ZSU-23-4 Shilkas, MT-LB ambulances, and 2S12 120mm mortars with Ural 2F510 trucks is widely corroborated. Although not detailed on the leaked personnel roster, at least two 9P162 Kornet-T ATGM carriers were filmed travelling with the BTG's column through Kopyliv out of a total of six seen on the brigade's transport train to Belarus, indicating they were concentrated specifically within the 2nd BTG for the operation. The two BTR-80 K1Sh1 jammers were captured in the same footage, whilst SNAR-10 battlefield surveillance radars were named on the brigade's vehicle roster – suggesting the BTG's radar reconnaissance section possessed this type for their single assigned vehicle. A similar supposition was made regarding the BTR-82s assigned to the 2nd Reconnaissance Platoon. Unfortunately, the remainder of the EW and signals platoons' vehicles are based purely off doctrinal tables of organisation and equipment. As a final note, the support elements attached to the BTG have been omitted from the diagram for the sake of space but can be detailed here as follows: an NBC section (one vehicle and three personnel), a flamethrower section (one vehicle and seven personnel), an engineering platoon (12 vehicles and 24 personnel), an evacuation and workshop platoon (five vehicles and 20 personnel), two supply platoons (16 vehicles and 34 personnel), and a water tanker section (five vehicles and nine personnel).

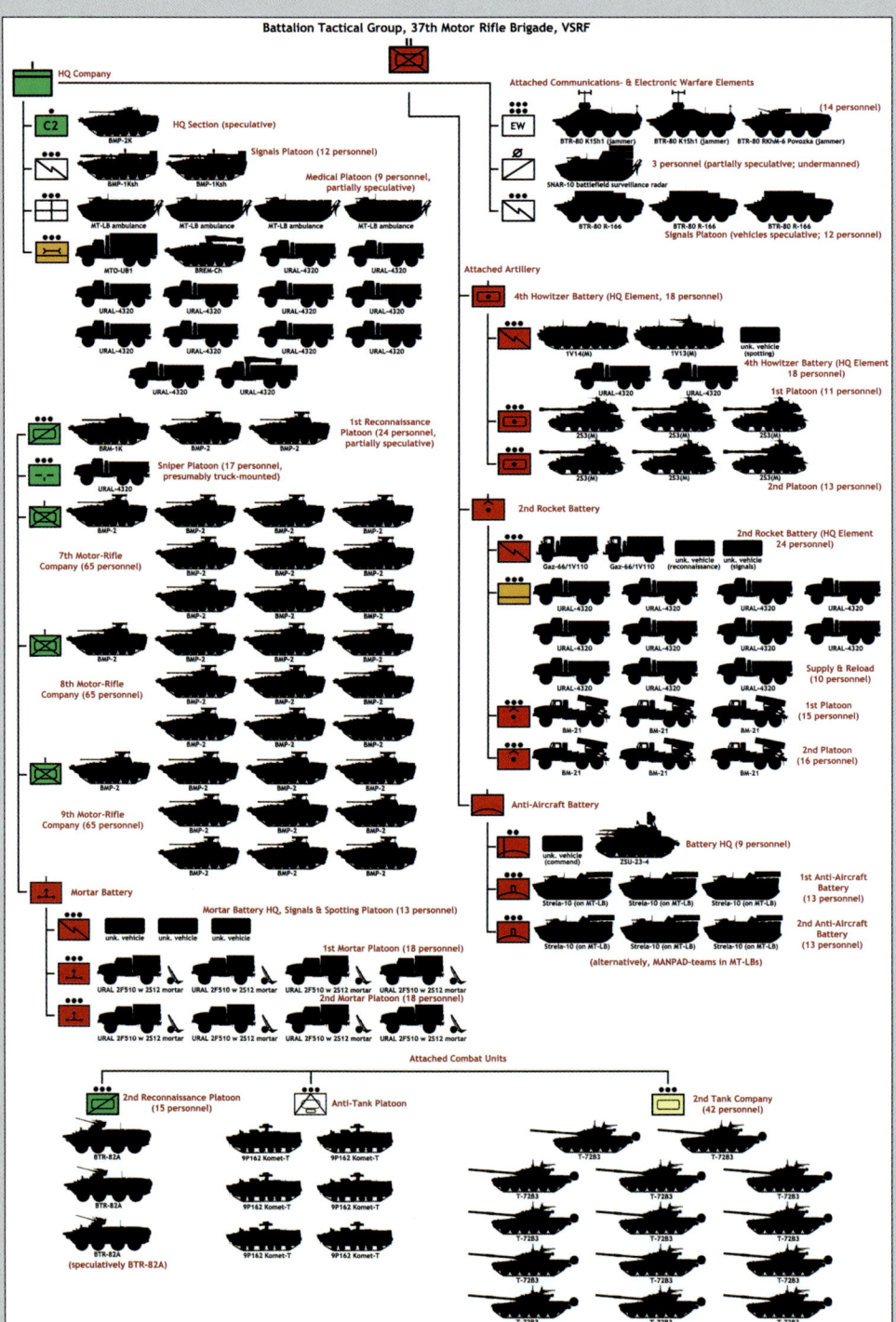

Diagram showing organisation and equipment of 37th Guards Motor Rifle Brigade's 2nd BTG. (diagram by Tom Cooper)

Under continued pressure from Putin, Sanchik had been preparing another offensive of his own. Critically, he needed to reestablish connection with his units isolated on the E40 to continue the western envelopment of Kyiv. With Ukrainian resistance persisting in Borodyanka and Makariv, further attempts down the T1019 were futile. Instead, on 3 March, Russian units advanced along the minor north-south roads connecting the E373 to the E40. Fortunately, almost no Ukrainian units were in the area, besides a single company of signallers defending the village of Mykolaivka, which was soon encircled.[11] The eastern flank of the attack however, advancing along the E373 to turn south at Vorzel and proceed down the western side of Bucha and Irpin, shortly encountered the San Marino strongpoint.

At 1400hrs, the hotel's defenders saw a large column of Rosgvardia and VDV vehicles approaching them via the E373. A rocket barrage was called down from the 72nd Mechanised Brigade's BM-21s, which prompted the Russians to turn off the road into Vorzel. Their advance continued, covered by the settlement. Still unaware of the Ukrainian position, the leading element drove right past the hotel and was ambushed at close range with small arms, RPGs, and NLAWs, losing several AFVs and trucks. Now alerted, the Russians began to level the San Marino with tank and autocannon fire, inflicting heavy casualties on the Ukrainians inside. Azov fighter *Whale*, a pro-Ukrainian Belarussian volunteer, later described the dire choice facing the hotel's defenders: 'We had two options: to defend ourselves and fight bravely to the end, or to run into an open field under the threat of guns and tanks and save the personnel, which was very risky. Our commanders decided to accept the battle'.[12]

Despite the hotel being effectively encircled, TDF volunteers in a civilian vehicle were able to evacuate some of the more heavily wounded, surviving machine gun fire on their way back to Irpin. The remaining Ukrainians fought on as VDV elements began to assault into the hotel. The fighting was extremely brutal, at times even hand to hand. Calling down artillery on themselves, the 10–15 Ukrainian survivors retreated into inner rooms and stopped firing in the hope the Russians would think they had been killed. The ruse worked, allowing them to escape back to friendly lines later that night.

As the San Marino battle raged, the 76th GAAD's 234th Regiment used a railway line shielded by embankments to enter Bucha from the west. Unlike their sister regiment's fatal ride a few days before, the 234th advanced with ruthless caution. Civilians going about their routines on the street were mown down with autocannon fire and any TDF volunteers caught alive were summarily executed. Dozens would die according to this pattern over the following days. Outflanked by the 234th's advance, the Irpin company was briefly caught in an encirclement. It took the loss of several of their number and a commandeered Kozak mine-resistant ambush protected (MRAP) vehicle for the company to escape southward. By the day's end, the Russians had occupied Bucha and much of Irpin. This tactical success allowed Russian forces to advance from Vorzel, via Zabiuchchya, to the E40, relieving pressure on the 5th GTB. By 5 March, BTGs from the 106th GAD were using this route to advance on Irpin from the south-east (the division having been committed from Sanchik's operational reserve).[13] Despite this, the Russians were unable to convert their tactical victory into any operational breakthrough: the fundamental problem of the Irpin River remained.

If the Russians' 3 March advance on Bucha had gone well, their advance launched against Hostomel on this day ended in disaster. Here, the 2nd BTG of the 31st GAAB was dispatched from Antonov to clear Hostomel, likely as a supporting effort for the larger operations occurring to the west. Around 1830hrs, the 5th Air Assault Company of this BTG ran straight into the waiting positions of the Ukrainians holding the glass factory. The leading BMDs were hit with RPGs and caught fire, their crews and dismounts shot dead before they could even make it off their vehicles' decks. Disorientated, the few survivors stumbled towards the Ukrainian positions. Ukrainian SOF commander *Shaman* described later:

> They ran from the damaged vehicles in the direction of our positions. I don't know [why]… we can't ask them now anyway. One of my soldiers picked up a trophy RPK [a light machine gun] and, gripping the trigger, killed an enemy, and it was clear [he] had [a] good quality bullet proof vest because a lot of sparks were flying. From the whole magazine that was going into his chest it seemed like you were looking at welding.[14]

In total, 11 VDV vehicles were lost in the vicinity of the glass factory and some 50 paratroopers killed. Among them was the 2nd BTG's commander – Major Alexy Osokin – and his deputy – Major Insur Kinyakaev.[15] In the following days, supported by constant artillery fire, the 31st GAAB was nonetheless able to recapture most of Hostomel. However, as with the advances made in Bucha and Irpin, the Irpin River blocked any hope of a breakthrough into Kyiv.

A still from a video showing a Ukrainian Kozak-2 MRAP engaging Russian targets outside the glass factory with its KPVT heavy machine gun. (Ukrainian Social Media)

Left and above: The aftermath of the glass factory ambush. (GUR)

Final Advances South of the E40

With their immediate logistics situation rectified, the 37th GMRB continued pushing south of the E40.[16] Following preliminary air and MRLS strikes, scouting elements of the brigade advanced upon the village of Yasnohorodka on 5 March. Defending the settlement was a single TDF platoon armed predominantly with hunting rifles. The local priest, Father Rostyslav Dudarenko, was helping man the platoon's checkpoint, though unarmed himself. As the leading Russian element of two BMPs and a BTR appeared, the priest went out alone to confront them. *Nimble*, the commander of the TDF platoon, recalled later: 'When the Russian BMP went at them, Father raised the cross to the sky. He thought it would stop the heathens, but it didn't. They shot him through the chest with a machine gun'.[17]

These shots opened a fierce firefight which saw four more TDF volunteers killed in return for seven Russians and a BMP-2 destroyed. Fortunately, ZSU elements arrived just in time to drive the rest away. This defeat proved enough to halt the 37th GMRB's advance, and the brigade withdrew into the woods around Severynivka. Indeed, Yasnohorodka would mark the high tide point of the 35th CAA's southward advance and with it, the end of Sanchik's hope to envelope Kyiv from the west.

Morale among the 37th GMRB collapsed and, on 11 March, the brigade's commander, Colonel Yuri Medvedev, was reportedly run over with a tank by his own men, mortally wounding him.[18] Meanwhile, Ukrainian artillery constantly worked over the brigade's positions as local civilians helped spot targets for them. For instance, around 12 March, a 70-year-old Motzhyn woman discovered a Russian Borisoglebsk-2 EW complex outside of Severynivka and reported its position. This complex had been jamming Ukrainian UAVs overflying the area, frustrating the work of Ukrainian artillery, but now with its position betrayed it was soon suppressed by artillery fire, then subsequently destroyed in detail by Bayraktar TB2 attack UAVs. In revenge, Russian troops later found and shot the elderly woman.[19] Indeed, throughout March, civilians were tortured and killed in similar reprisals across Kopyliv, Severynivka, and Motzhyn by soldiers of the 37th GMRB. Over the same period, the 5th GTB also killed dozens of civilians along the E40.[20] One particularly vicious major of this brigade led a gang suspected of raping local women and girls. *Nimble*'s TDF platoon eventually ambushed this group and the major in question was almost cut in half by machine gun fire.[21]

The only noteworthy success achieved by the 5th GTB over March was defeating the company of Ukrainian signallers encircled at Mykolaivka. Here, the signallers had been holding out alone under constant air and artillery bombardment for weeks, having already destroyed one T-72B during an initial Russian assault. At 0600hrs on 20 March, the 5th GTB attacked again in strength, supported by Spetsnaz and VDV elements. Completely outgunned, the signallers still managed to knock out another T-72B with an RPG-18, killing its crew, and destroy one of the Spetsnaz's Iveco light mobility vehicles (LMVs) before they were forced to surrender. Ten Ukrainians were killed. Another 67 were taken prisoner.

The Battle of Makariv

As the 5th GTB and 37th GMRB bogged down along the E40, bitter fighting continued for Makariv to their west.[22] Here elements of the

95th Air Assault Brigade,[23] reinforced with the local TDF and National Guard, held the central part of Makariv against the repeated assaults of the 64th MRB, which had occupied the town's northern outskirts. Upon arriving in the town centre on 2 March, the Ukrainian paratroopers had immediately lost three killed and five wounded when a BMP-1TS operated by the brigade was destroyed by a Russian tank watching down the T1019. These were the first of many ZSU casualties sustained in Makariv. Russian aircraft and artillery, including BM-30 Smerch self-propelled 300mm multiple rocket launchers, devastated the town, inflicting heavy casualties on the civilian population and armed defenders alike. In one instance, at around 2000hrs on 7 March, VKS aircraft bombed a local bread factory filled with soldiers from the 95th Air Assault Brigade, causing dozens of casualties. The Makariv hospital and its crucial medical supplies were also eventually destroyed, forcing the local medical volunteers to improvise tourniquets from bicycle tires. Nevertheless, the Ukrainian garrison held on, downing at least one Su-25 and an Mi-8AMTSh on 4 March alone with MANPADs.[24]

With their southward advance stalling in the urban fighting, the 64th MRB began flanking Makariv from the west on 2 March, with Russian elements advancing upon the villages of Pochepyn and Nalyvaikivka northwest of the town. A civilian using her car to drop off Ukrainian soldiers in their positions in Nalyvaikivka later described the scene:

> My car was full of weapons, Javelins, NLAWs. As we reached Shevchenko Street, I saw Mykola Omelchenko running towards my car, screaming: "Turn around, their tanks have broken through!" I didn't know what to do. The lads jumped out of the car and prepared to fight. I drove away, Russian tanks firing from the rear.[25]

This Ukrainian unit defending Nalyvaikivka was the 9th Company, 3rd Mechanised Battalion, 14th Mechanised Brigade.[26] They were among the first of several company-sized 14th Mechanised Brigade battlegroups meeting the 64th MRB in individual counterattacks north of Makariv. Whilst this battlegroup tactic had been effective in ambushes against the disorganised Russian columns around Ivankiv, fighting piecemeal in this fashion against a deployed motor rifle brigade supported by artillery and airpower was to invite disaster. During the early morning of 8 March, a company from the 14th Mechanised Brigade advanced upon the villages of

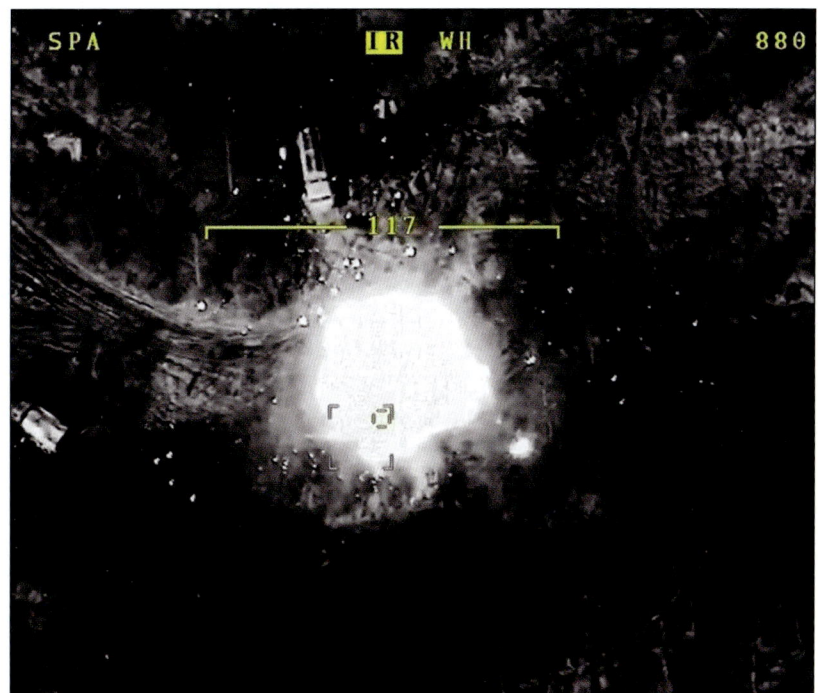

A still from a video showing the moment a MAM-L guided munition released from a TB2 attack UAV destroys an R-330Zh 'Zhytel' electronic warfare station outside Severynivka. A Buk battery co-located with the EW complex was also destroyed. (ZSU)

The 5th GTB T-72B destroyed in Mykolaivka. (Russian Ministry of Defence)

The Ukrainian signal company is marched into captivity in the aftermath of the battle. (Russian Ministry of Defence)

Ozerschyna and Dmytrivka, located halfway between Makariv and Borodyanka. Lost in the darkness, the company's seven AFVs and one captured Russian tank halted in the middle of Dmytrivka to re-orientate themselves. Unfortunately, they had already wandered into the waiting ambush of a 64th MRB BTG holding the village. In moments, the company was destroyed, with only 30 of its 100 soldiers managing to escape. A local eyewitness saw at least two Ukrainian soldiers attempt to surrender, only to be executed by the Russians. *Poltava*, a tank commander in the 14th Mechanised Brigade, said later of the battle: 'That was people going to slaughter, like meat, without any intelligence or preparation. I personally know four or five tank crew members who died there'.[27]

On the same day, the 9th Company faced its own disaster as it counterattacked toward Makariv from Nalyvaikivka. Advancing across open fields, the company was exposed to the 64th MRB positions dug into the northern outskirts of the town and took heavy casualties. Senior Sergeant Serhiy Vasich led his T-64BV platoon in support of the attack until his own tank was hit by an ATGM, sparking an ammunition fire which killed the other two crewmembers: Senior Soldier Vitaliy Parkhomchuk and Soldier Oleh Svynchuk. Escaping the burning tank, Vasich had made it inside a BMP-1 evacuating survivors when that too was hit, killing him instantly. Unfortunately, the ordeal of the 9th Company continued even as its wounded remnants returned to Nalyvaikivka. Around 2130hrs, two VKS aircraft hit the company aid post in the village with 500kg bombs, badly wounding the company commander and killing the company medic, Sergeant Kateryna Stupnytska.[28] Tank crewman Vasyl Shvets recalled of the day's fighting: 'It was very hard, almost the entire 9th Company was killed there, plus a tank platoon. I was the only one who was able to leave in my burnt but still operating tank'.[29]

Despite these defeats, the 14th Mechanised Brigade's company groups doggedly continued to counterattack. On 11 March, 5th Company, 2nd Mechanised Battalion, advanced from Korolivka toward Lypivka, the village directly north of Makariv on the T1019. The attack was led by a T-64BV under the command of Senior Soldier Yevgeny Fedosov. Fedosov's tank first destroyed a Russian checkpoint, then advanced deep into the village, expecting the BMP-mounted infantry behind him would follow. Unfortunately, the BMPs came under intensive artillery fire at that moment, forcing them to halt as Fedosov continued on alone. One BMP-1P was hit directly by a shell which blew off its turret and wrecked its forward hull. Miraculously, the vehicle did not explode, allowing some of the dismounts inside to escape. Meanwhile, unsupported by infantry, Fedosov's T-64BV was soon also destroyed, killing him and his crew. As at Dmytrivka, Russian soldiers reportedly executed Ukrainian survivors attempting to surrender in the battle's aftermath. The severely wounded driver of the wrecked BMP-1P – Senior Soldier Yurii Kindratyshyn – was left pinned in the remains of his vehicle. His body was still there when Lypivka was finally liberated on 1 April.[30]

Ultimately, the piecemeal attacks of the 14th Mechanised Brigade north of Makariv had seen at least three company groups mauled for little immediate gain. The 64th MRB continued to hold its positions from Borodyanka to Makariv and, by extent, maintained the southwestern flank of the 35th CAA. However, the attacks had at least halted the Russian attempts to flank Makariv and dissipated their combat power, which might otherwise have been directed against the town itself. Enduring repeated airstrikes and barrages, Makariv's defenders held on. By 24 March, Russian assaults in the town had devolved into probing attacks conducted by small teams using RPGs and machine guns, with some Ukrainian officials already claiming the town liberated.[31] Though the town in fact seemingly remained contested until the 35th CAA's withdrawal at the end of March,[32] the Russian failure to secure Makariv had denied Sanchik the T1019/E40 route to Kyiv, contributing to the culmination of the 37th GMRB and 5th GTB's own attacks.

Above: A still from a video taken by a Russian UAV, showing the 5th Company's BMPs being hit with Krasnopol 152mm laser-guided shells as they enter Lypivka on 11 March 2022. The blurring is due to the censor. In total, three Ukrainian BMPs were destroyed during the battle. (Russian Ministry of Defence)

Left: A T-80BVM from the 64th MRB burns outside of Lypivka, circa 10 March 2022. (Ukrainian internet)

7
THE BATTLE OF MOSCHUN

As early as the end of 3 March, Sanchik foresaw that the 35th CAA would struggle to reach Kyiv on its current axes of advance. The bridges over the Irpin River were gone, denying him the possibility of a breakthrough into the capital even if his units grinding through Hostomel, Bucha, and Irpin could drive as far as the river. Meanwhile, the attempt at a western envelopment of the capital had fallen far short of its objectives and the arrival of the 14th Mechanised Brigade and 95th Air Assault Brigade limited the potential for further advances in this direction. As the Russian attacks continued on these central and western axes, Sanchik began planning a new offensive which would instead attempt to force a way to Kyiv via his eastern flank, retracing the steps of the previous Russian crossing of the Irpin at Moschun on 27 February. The terrain ahead was extremely unfavourable. Dense pine forests covered the Ukrainian side of the river here, along with a network of bunkers last fought over in 1943 when the Soviets had driven the Wehrmacht from Kyiv. Still worse, only the Chervone dam stood between the Russian bridgehead and the floodwaters building upriver, though this detail escaped both sides' attention until much later. Nevertheless, if Sanchik did have misgivings, unrelenting pressure from Putin proved enough to overcome them. Spetsnaz teams scouting for crossing points confirmed that the river remained shallow opposite Moschun and so the lieutenant general collected his units for what would become the final concerted offensive of the 35th CAA towards Kyiv.[1]

The Crossing and Subsequent Struggle

On 5 March, an intense artillery barrage began against 5th Company, 2nd Mechanised Battalion, 72nd Mechanised Brigade, which had now occupied positions along the western-most houses of Moschun.[2] Massed on the Russian side of the river were the 2S1 self-propelled guns and MRLS batteries of the 155th NIB's artillery group sited in Hostomel, alongside the D-30s and 2S9 Nona 120mm self-propelled mortars of the 1065th Artillery Regiment, 98th GAD, located around the village of Ozera. Sanchik had drawn the latter division from his operational reserve for the operation, with the BTGs of its 331st Regiment forming his main striking force. First, though, a bridgehead had to be won across the river.

As night fell, an assault group centred on 1st Company, 47th Airborne Assault Battalion, 155th NIB, (elements of the 40th NIB were also attached) waded their way across the river north of the village under the cover of the darkness, EW activity, and a smoke screen. Accounts diverge significantly as to what happened next,[3] but it seems the Russian marines were able to fight their way into the north-western corner of the village. An initial counterattack was conducted by Ukrainian SOF before dawn broke, but faltered after one operator was shot. A second attempt by the 5th Company also failed after one of their BMP-2s was driven off with RPGs. Having repulsed these attacks, the marines began working their way southward through the village, attempting to cut off 5th Company

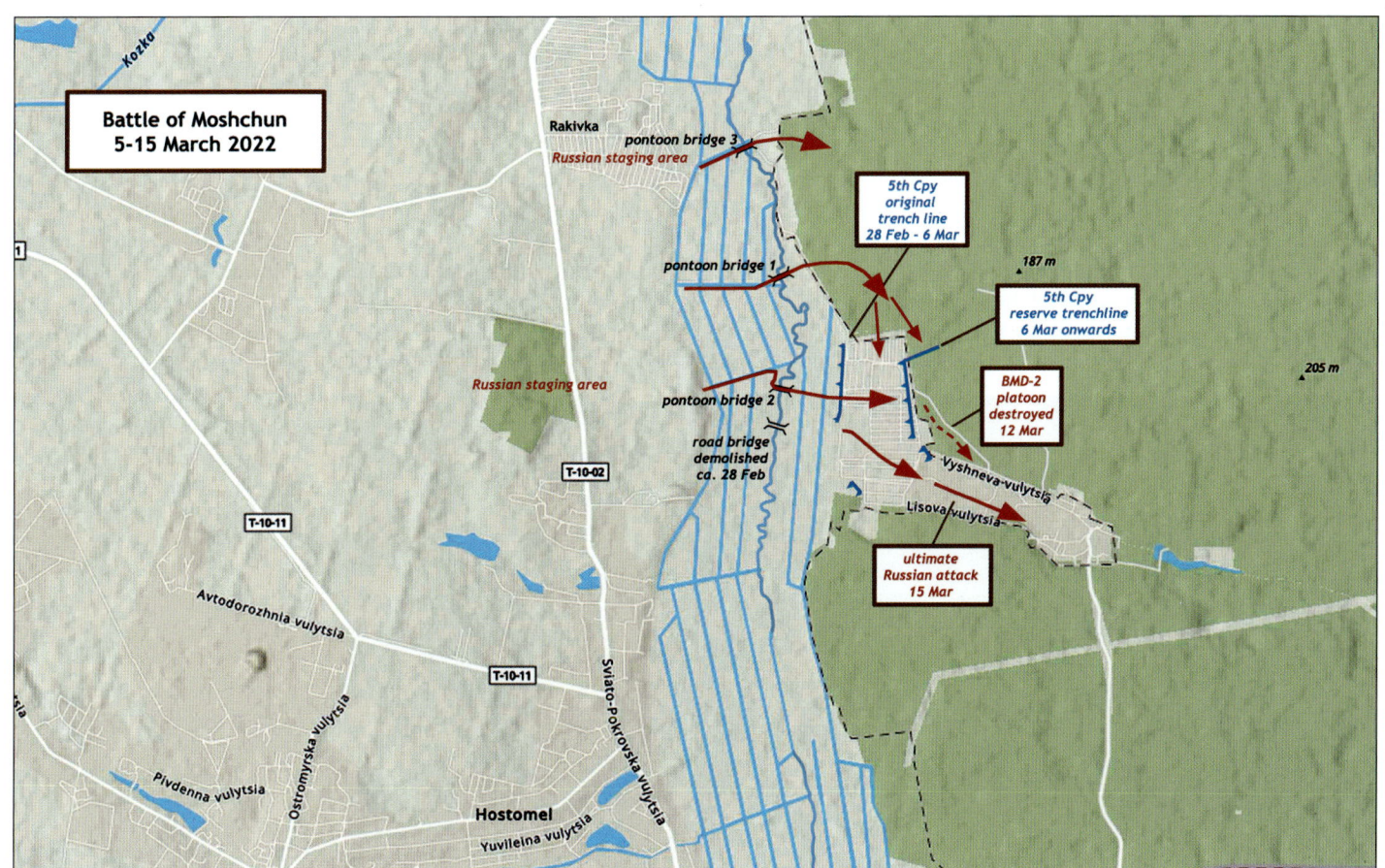

Map illustrating the main Russian crossing points, lines of advance, and Ukrainian defensive positions in the Moschun area, from 5 March to 15 March 2022. The order of pontoon bridges should be treated as approximation. (Map by Tom Cooper)

Vehicles of the 331st Regiment halted whilst enroute to Moschun, 3–4 March. (Russian Ministry of Defence)

before it could retreat. Captain Kovalenko called forward another BMP-2, but this was hit by two RPGs, badly injuring the driver and concussing the rest of the crew. A mortar barrage landing on his HQ caused several more casualties, prompting Kovalenko to withdraw his company to a reserve trench line dug into the forest edge on the eastern side of the village. The Russians had won their bridgehead, but behind them a calamity was unfolding as the 331st Regiment attempted to cross the river.

With their objective reportedly the city of Vyshhorod, located immediately north of Kyiv (roughly 13 kilometres away), the 331st Regiment needed to cross with its vehicles, unlike the dismounted marines seizing the bridgehead. Though BMDs are nominally amphibious, in reality a great effort is needed to maintain such vehicle's 'seaworthiness',[4] and those of the 331st Regiment were probably not capable of fording the river as a result. Accordingly, engineers of the 28th Pontoon Bridge Brigade constructed a pontoon bridge north-west of Moschun, and the regiment assembled to cross in a group of some 200–300 vehicles. By chance, a Ukrainian Furia UAV underway on a different mission spotted the concentration and an immediate call for fire went out. The howitzers of the 72nd Mechanised Brigade and 43rd Artillery Brigade soon scattered the Russians, destroying the pontoon bridge.

Without their expected reinforcements, the Russian marines had to hold on inside the bridgehead alone, suffering heavy casualties from the constant Ukrainian artillery fire. The loss of the pontoon bridge forced their wounded to swim back across the river, a feat one marine managed despite missing his arm.[5] BMP-3s would then ferry the casualties back, but several were lost to Javelins in the process. Over the day's fighting, at least 21 marines were killed, including company commander Captain Andrey Ivanov.[6] Most of those still alive in Moschun were wounded to varying degrees. Nonetheless, the bridgehead survived, and over 7 March two further pontoon bridges were constructed. The first was emplaced directly opposite Moschun, beside where the destroyed road bridge had spanned, whilst the second was positioned much further north along the river near the village of Rakivka.[7] Continuously screened by EW and artillery, these bridges initially went unseen, allowing the two BTGs of the 331st Regiment to cross the river, along with the 155th NIB's 59th Amphibious Assault Battalion (mounted on BMPs). The Russian mechanised forces were finally in position, but the way to Vyshhorod would not be easy.

Artillery duel: the 2S3s of the 72nd Mechanised Brigade strike Russian supply trucks inside the village of Kozarovychi, 7 March 2022. These vehicles were supporting D-30 howitzers and 120mm mortars firing on Moschun. (72nd Mechanised Brigade)

Already holding the flanks of Moschun were elements of the National Guard's 1st Operational Brigade and the 112th TDF Brigade. Meanwhile, a plethora of other Ukrainian units were arriving to bolster the 5th Company's positions in the treeline, including a platoon of GUR International Legion soldiers, elements of the Kyiv Azov Regiment, and various SOF teams. The situation they were entering into was dire. Russian Orlan UAVs orbited constantly over Moschun, spotting artillery and airstrikes onto the defender's positions, whilst others ranged far beyond, directing counter-battery fire against the Ukrainian artillery in depth. Russian EW jammed Ukrainian UAVs in turn, whilst the kaleidoscopic variety of units in the battle zone made synchronising radio communication difficult. Nights in the village were freezing, and there was little food, forcing the Ukrainians to scrounge for supplies amongst the abandoned houses. Kovalenko later described the conditions his company faced:

> You get so exhausted that by night you are just passing out, you don't care about the shelling anymore, whatever is flying, you just need to sleep for an hour or two. You don't care if it's freezing, snowing, raining, if there's mud around you. You just lie down. Many couldn't cope mentally. It's hard not to break down. Sometimes I would break down myself.[8]

For the Russians, the supply situation was even worse, with one account stating *all* their food had to be scavenged from inside Moschun. Researcher Max Schönhausen speculates that the resulting starvation and exhaustion might explain the inhuman behaviour of Russian soldiers observed during the battle.[9] Indeed, several International Legion soldiers describe witnessing Russian soldiers abandon their wounded between 7–11 March.[10] One later recalled the moment a Russian was shot by his team's sniper: 'The Russians never fired a single shot back; they didn't do anything. That Russian soldier just laid there in the road, they didn't try to help him, they didn't try to do buddy aid. He basically just plopped down like a sack of potatoes and just bled out'.[11]

These attritional conditions were grinding down the Russians forces in the bridgehead and hope for the breakthrough to Vyshhorod was fading. Time was indeed running out: the waters along the Irpin had started to rise. Sometime after the Russian landings, the Ukrainians had finally discovered the stubborn dam at Chervone holding back the flood. Initial attempts to breach it – first with tank fire, then with a 2S7 of the 43rd Artillery Brigade – had both failed. The only option remaining was to destroy the main dam upriver at Kozavrovychi. On 8 March, Syrskyi gave the order and engineers from the 72nd Mechanised Brigade blew up one of this dam's sluice gates, unleashing a torrent which soon overpowered the smaller Chervone dam as hoped. Initially, the water level rise at Moschun was only gradual, though just days remained before the flood would swamp the remaining pontoon bridges.

Either ignorant of this danger or willing to persevere regardless, on 11 March, the Russians renewed their offensive against Moschun. Around 0430hrs, a massive artillery barrage commenced along the entire Ukrainian line. Between 0700–0800hrs, Russian units surged toward the Ukrainian positions in the forest edge. The 100mm guns and 30mm autocannons of the 155th NIB's BMP-3s proved particularly oppressive, but several suffered from mechanical issues affecting their turret traverses and were knocked out. Nonetheless, by midday Russian soldiers had reached the edge of the treeline. The fighting was now extremely close range, with one Russian element approaching within 20 metres of the 5th Company's trench, demanding the Ukrainians surrender, before they were driven away with grenades. During a lull in the shelling, the 72nd Mechanised Brigade's deputy commander, Lieutenant Colonel Vladyslav Naliazhnyi (callsign *Granite*), arrived leading two tanks and a SOF team, a clear sign of how desperate the situation had become for the Ukrainians. Joining Kovalenko in his trench, Naliazhyni personally directed the fire of the brigade's 2S3s onto the advancing Russians. One 5th Company soldier recounted the direct impact Naliazhyni had on the situation:

> There were about 15 people in this trench. The company commander and the deputy brigade commander were also there. I believe that it was the deputy brigade commander's merit that the soldiers did not run away from this trench. He instilled confidence. He didn't just sit, he fought. Out of 15 people, maybe five shot. The remaining ten lay terrified in the trench. Someone helped load the weapon. The deputy brigade

An artillery round explodes beside the second pontoon bridge, mid-March 2022. (ZSU)

commander fired from everything- from a grenade launcher, a machine gun, an RPO-A Shmel [thermobaric RPG]. *Granite* was wounded, but he continued to shoot. The attack was repulsed with rifles and hand grenades. If they had not shown determination, then our trench would have been destroyed.[12]

Though this intervention by Naliazhyni helped turn the tide in the 5th Company's sector, it was likely the destruction of the pontoon bridge directly opposite Moschun with 120mm mortar fire on this day which broke the back of the wider Russian assault. The third and final pontoon bridge meanwhile lay beyond the effective range of Ukrainian artillery, surviving as the final lifeline of the Russian bridgehead. With breathing room won, the remnants of 5th Company and the International Legion platoon were rotated out of the battle area. Their replacements included 2nd Company, 1st Mechanised Battalion, 72nd Mechanised Brigade, having arrived from the eastern flank of Kyiv, and the 10th SSO 'Shaman' Battalion.[13]

The End in Moschun
On 12 March, the Russians resumed their offensive and began to breakthrough the Ukrainian line.[14] By now, the 217th Regiment of the 98th GAD had also been committed. In one instance, a BMD-2 platoon from the 331st Regiment managed to drive around the Ukrainian positions using a forest road and strike toward the rear of Moschun. Unfortunately for them, an Azov UAV had observed the movement and a 72nd Mechanised Brigade T-64BV was directed to intercept them. In moments, two of the BMDs were ablaze and the third abandoned. Another breakthrough on 13 March was similarly repulsed by the 10th SSO's operators. Russian losses were severe during this fighting. From 11–14 March, 39 paratroopers of the 331st Regiment are confirmed to have been killed, including the regiment's commander, Colonel Sergei Sukharev. At least eight paratroopers of the 217th Regiment also died. The 155th NIB meanwhile had been so badly mauled that it was withdrawn from Moschun over the night of 13–14 March and sent to the Russian rear. In their stead, Sanchik committed the 106th GAD to the battle. Ukrainian losses were also heavy, and by March 15 the Ukrainian defence around Moschun was at breaking point, the village almost entirely in Russian hands. Colonel Vdovychenko remembered later:

> We thought that we are done. Contact with those people who were in Moschun was lost. Communication with the units that were north of Moschun was lost. We thought we were finished. The Commander-In-Chief of the Armed Forces [Zaluzhnyi] arrived along with the Commander of the Ground Forces [Syrskyi]. I told them we would not hold Moschun, we must retreat. But the Commander-In-Chief answered: "If we give them Moschun, this is the road to Kyiv".[15]

In fact, it was the Russians who would break first. The rising waters of the Irpin had transformed the floodplain between the bridgehead and the Russian staging areas on the west bank into a swamp. Russian vehicles attempting to cross were soon bogged in the mud and easily picked off by Ukrainian artillery. By 18 March, the crucial final pontoon bridge was swept away by the floodwaters, its original position marked by a platoon of BTR-Ds destroyed beside it. With their means of reinforcement and resupply now beyond a watery moonscape of artillery craters and wrecked vehicles, the Russian bridgehead was doomed. From 19 March, Ukrainian forces began to push the Russians into the river, flanking Moschun on both sides. Over 20–21 March, the remaining Russian force withdrew back over the Irpin. Piles of helmets, webbing, and other equipment subsequently found on the riverbank indicate many soldiers had to swim back to Russian lines. The Battle of Moschun was over.

Ukrainian losses had been heavy, officially 118 killed, but Russian losses were likely even worse. In an intercepted phone call, one 331st Regiment paratrooper complained that the whole of the regiment's

A 331st Regiment BMD-2 bogged on the floodplain and left abandoned. (ZSU)

600 strong 2nd Battalion was gone. Regardless of the exact numbers, Sanchik had exhausted his operational reserves and still not achieved the breakthrough Putin demanded. Meanwhile, the flooding along the Irpin precluded any further bridgeheads toward the capital being opened. In short, the 35th CAA's attempt to seize Kyiv had failed. On 23 March, OSK East commander Colonel General Chaiko arrived by helicopter at Sanchik's HQ in Zdvyzhivka. Though this trip was nominally to award medals, it seems likely it was also an attempt to see the operational situation for himself.[16] It would only take another week to prove that the 35th CAA's position was indeed untenable.

Chaiko speaks during a staged meeting with Russian servicemen in Zdvyzhivka on 23 March 2022. (Russian Ministry of Defence)

8
THE END IN THE WEST

As the Russian spearheads stalled, events occurring in the 35th CAA's rear area were also spiralling out of control. From the invasion's outset, bands of Ukrainian SOF and TDF irregulars had been picking off Russian supply convoys in depth, contributing to the logistical problems overshadowing the entire operation. By mid-March however, regular Ukrainian units were themselves well inside the Russian rear, though not before a bitter struggle to break into the 35th CAA's flank. Syrskyi, sensing the Russian attack was beginning to culminate, had begun the second stage of the *GenStab-U*'s plan for defending Kyiv: the counterattack aiming to encircle and destroy the 35th CAA.

The War in the Russian Rear Area

On 6 March, the 109th Mountain Assault Battalion, 10th Mountain Brigade, was ordered to the town of Malyn on the north-western flank of the Russian advance, the battalion having previously been defending the border in the Volyn region.[1] Here, it joined its sister 108th Mountain Assault Battalion, which had been holding Malyn since the war's outbreak, along with most of the brigade's artillery and support units. At 0000hrs on 7 March, the Ukrainian company commanders received their orders to strike into the Russian flank. The 109th Battalion would advance from Zaruddya toward the villages of Kukhari and Sloboda-Kukhar'ska, whilst the 108th would advance from Stari Vorobi on the villages of Morozivka and Varivs'k. Inexplicably, the attack began just four hours later, leaving no time for adequate reconnaissance. Had this been conducted, the Ukrainians would have realised they were driving straight into the prepared defensive line of the 69th Covering Brigade (69th CB), the unit assigned to screen the 35th CAA's flank opposite Malyn. The results were predictable. Immediately upon moving off, the 109th Battalion was hit with artillery and airstrikes. Pressing on, it then ran into ambushes and minefields on the approach to Kukhari which caused heavy casualties. Bloodied, the battalion returned to Zaruddya to spend the next days reorganising, its 2nd Company having suffered 75 percent losses in the ordeal. Little is known about how the 108th Battalion's attack unfolded, but it was likely also unsuccessful.

On 12 March, the 10th Mountain Brigade received orders to repeat the operation. This time, however, an extensive reconnaissance was conducted, aided by the arrival of the first quadcopter UAVs in the brigade's equipment pool. The attack began the next day and proved immediately more successful, with the 108th Battalion taking Morozivka and the 109th taking Kukhari. Seeking to break the momentum of the Ukrainian advance, on 14 March, the 69th CB responded with a counterattack on Kukhari from the north, sending a T-80BV platoon and two platoons of BMPs down the T-10-05 road from Sloboda-Kukhar'ska. The Ukrainians had foreseen this coming however, with the 109th Battalion's chief intelligence officer personally laying a mine barrier across the road just minutes before the Russian counterattack began. The first Russian tank blew up on these mines, causing the vehicles behind it to bunch up. Watching from a quadcopter UAV above, the Ukrainians then brought down fires from the 120mm mortar battery and three howitzer batteries attached to the battalion, smashing the Russian column. Two T-80BVs were damaged and abandoned, whilst five more BMPs and a truck were destroyed. The Russian counterattack defeated, the 109th Battalion continued its advance westward in the face of constant artillery and airstrikes. By the day's end, one company had reached as far as the village of Teteriv'ske, just 13 kilometres from Ivankiv and the crucial supply arteries of the 35th CAA.

Operating from the 10th Mountain Brigade's salient, Ukrainian UAVs and SOF teams began to rove along the P02 highway identifying Russian logistics depots. On 16 March, an MTO logistics battalion dug-in outside the town of Poliske was found by a Leleka-100 UAV of the Aerorozvidka group, a volunteer unit specialising in drone warfare. Three 152mm howitzers were dragged into range along a trail cut through the woods and StarLink terminals were brought up to relay communication between the spotters and the guns. The following artillery strike burned 44 supply trucks, four AFVs, and the brigade command post of the 38th Motor Rifle Brigade (38th MRB). On 19 March, another MTO battalion dug-in on a farm in Zdvyzhivka was hit by artillery, destroying at least 13 more supply trucks. These losses, though seeming small in the grand scheme, were disastrous to the already overstrained logistics of the 35th

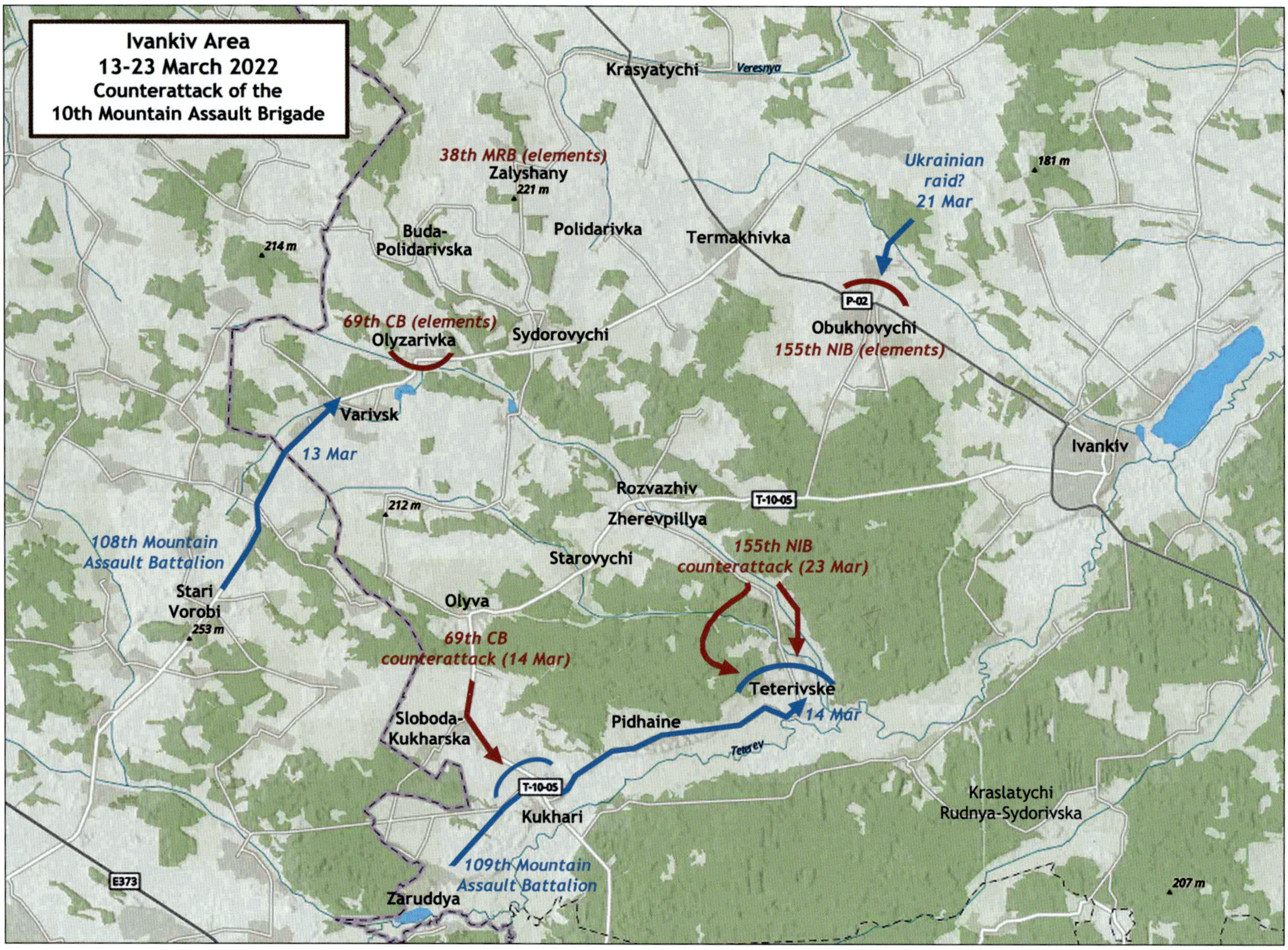

Map reconstructing the counterattack of the 10th Mountain Brigade's 109th and 108th Battalions north-west of Kyiv, 13–23 March 2022. (Map by Tom Cooper)

A BMP-1 from the 69th Covering Brigade abandoned in the aftermath of the Battle of Kukhari. (GUR)

CAA, for which every truck counted. Still worse, substantial Ukrainian units were beginning to raid onto the P02 itself.

At dawn on 21 March, unknown Ukrainian forces (possibly from the 108th Battalion) attacked the village of Obukhovychi, which lies directly on the P02 north-west of Ivankiv. The village was occupied at the time by the demoralised survivors of the 155th NIB, which had been rotated to defend the Ivankiv area after their ordeal in Moschun. The brigade's support battalion was hit hard, losing several men, but by midday the marines had managed to check the Ukrainian advance by rolling up a battery of 2S1s, which levelled suspected Ukrainian firing points over open sights. The Ukrainian raiders withdrew back into the woods, having destroyed a pair of R-934B 'Sinitsa' EW vehicles, a BMP-2, and several trucks. More importantly, however, they had managed to cut the P02 for the better part of a day and remained in a position to threaten it. The danger the 155th NIB felt itself under is well indicated by their decision to drag 150 civilians out

The logistics depot outside Poliske burns after being hit by Ukrainian artillery, 16 March. (Aerorozvidka)

of their cellars across Obukhovychi that evening and force them into the school gymnasium, which was next to the brigade's HQ. Though told this was for their own protection, there is little doubt the civilians were being used as human shields.[2]

Realising the threat the 10th Mountain Brigade's salient posed to his lines of communication, Sanchik ordered the remnants of the 155th NIB to attack Teteriv'ske in a bid to drive the Ukrainians away from Ivankiv. The Russian lines were already close to the outskirts of the village, just some 500 metres north amongst the forest belt, but far from safe. On the same day as the Obukhovychi raid, a company of BMP-3s had been moving up to the front when they had been hit by an intense 120mm mortar barrage, killing some 14 marines and destroying two BMPs, causing the rest to retreat. Despite this setback, the brigade was nonetheless able to collect together at least six BTR-82s, two T-80BVs, and six BMPs for the attack, along with a mixed complement of infantry from its 47th Airborne Assault Battalion and 59th Amphibious Assault Battalion. On 23 March, the attack began with the BMPs advancing on the village's west and the BTRs on the east. Advancing in pairs, the BTRs bore down on the Ukrainian infantry's positions amongst the ruined houses. The situation looked dire, the Russians nearly overrunning the local company commander's own position, until two tanks from the 109th Battalion's attached tank company arrived. One BTR, already disorientated after its optics had been damaged by small arms fire, was destroyed inside the village. Three more were hit and burning before they could make the safety of the treeline. Their attack broken, the remaining marines retreated.

With this battle, the 35th CAA's effort to dislodge the 10th Mountain Brigade was defeated. The situation facing the army was increasingly dire. Ukrainian elements were pressing toward Ivankiv and by 27 March were inflicting casualties on Russian soldiers in the town itself. Making matters worse, the Ukrainians had begun flooding the Zdvyzh and Teteriv rivers. This operation was restrained in comparison to the demolition of the Kozarovychi dam, using a network of engineers and observers to gradually raise the

A 120mm mortar of the 10th Mountain Brigade in action during the late March fighting around Teteriv'ske. (Maryan Kushnir)

rivers' water level until the surrounding ground was saturated, thus avoiding a dramatic flooding akin to the Irpin. Though subtle, for the Russians the flooding of the Zdvyzh and Teteriv was a far more ominous development than the flooding of the Irpin. Most of the northbound minor roads were now waterlogged, leaving only one remaining route for withdrawal: the P02 highway, carried over the Teteriv by a single bridge at Ivankiv.[3] The 35th CAA was no longer fighting for the capital, but for its own survival.

Suburban Struggle

Though the Russians had lost hope of seriously threatening Kyiv, local attacks continued against the Ukrainian line in Irpin.[4] Vicious street fighting had been raging here since 3 March, with an eclectic mix of Ukrainian volunteer and regular units holding off alternating assaults by the 31st GAAB, 76th GAAD, 98th GAD, and 106th GAD – the latter two divisions having been rotated into the suburbs after Moschun.[5] On 23 March, after screening artillery fire, VDV mechanised forces came forward again to probe the Ukrainian defences, held at the time by the 130th Battalion, 112th TDF Brigade, and a CTG drawn from the AFVs and personnel of the 184th Training Centre. The VDV advance was repulsed, but in the process the Ukrainian firing positions exposed themselves. The next morning, a massive artillery bombardment suppressed these identified positions and, around 1400hrs, VDV forces began advancing along the entire breadth of the Ukrainian defence. The first assault was repulsed, but a second attempt managed to flank the Ukrainian line with a BMD platoon. This platoon did not get far however, meeting a determined squad from the 184th Training Centre under the command of Junior Lieutenant Ihor Dykun. The lieutenant damaged one BMD with an RPG and then destroyed a second, narrowly escaping death himself after a Russian mistook the dark patterned Polish uniform he was wearing for Russian fatigues. This bravery contained the Russian attack.

The purpose behind this final Russian assault is uncertain, especially considering the bridges beyond Irpin were gone. Rather than another attempt at the capital, it seems it was actually an aggressive rearguard action to push the Ukrainians back before the 35th CAA began its retreat. Indeed, on 25 March, heavy Russian artillery fire began to fix the Ukrainians in place across Irpin, Bucha, and Hostomel, even forcing some units, like the 114th TDF Brigade's 133rd Battalion, to retreat. Behind this artillery screen, Russian units started to withdraw from the suburbs. The 35th CAA was leaving.

Negotiations

The exact circumstances of the Russian withdrawal from Kyiv remain a hotly contested subject.[6] Putin has since characterised the move as a 'gesture of goodwill' given in support of the peace talks taking place at the time in Istanbul on 29 March.[7] Indeed, this was the language used at the time by Russian Deputy Defence Minister Colonel General Alexander Fomin when he emerged from the talks to announce the withdrawal to the press:

> The Ministry of Defence of the Russian Federation, in order to increase mutual trust and create the necessary conditions for further negotiations and achieve the ultimate goal of agreeing on the signing of the aforementioned treaty, [has] decided to radically reduce the military activity in the Kiev and Chernihiv directions.[8]

In reality, the decision to withdraw from the northern axes was made not on the basis of goodwill, but because of the dire military situation the VSRF was facing. As described over the proceeding chapters, the 35th CAA had been repeatedly defeated in its efforts to take Kyiv from the west and now faced encirclement and destruction as the Ukrainians encroached upon the P02. Similarly dire situations faced the 41st CAA, 2nd GCAA, and 1st GTA on their own axes on the eastern side of the capital as the Ukrainian counteroffensives there gained momentum (as will be elucidated over the next chapters). Far from benevolence, the decision to abandon the war's original aim of Kyiv was taken out of necessity, avoiding an even greater disaster than the one already enveloping the VSRF. The expression of 'goodwill' was purely a face-saving measure.

The Flight of the 35th CAA

The withdrawal of the 35th CAA began considerably before Fomin's statement on 29 March. The first definite sign was the abandoning of Bucha and Irpin from 25 March, together with a statement by the *GenStab* on the same day claiming the capture of Kyiv was never the objective of the war.[9] Nonetheless, despite these signs, the *GenStab-U* seemingly remained unaware that the Russian escape was occurring right beneath their noses. Ukrainian officials publicly recognised that Russian units were withdrawing into Belarus as early as 0000hrs, 26 March,[10] but others were still reporting as late as 30 March that this movement was a rotation of units rather than 35th CAA's complete retreat from Kyiv.[11] The same mistaken evaluation was widely repeated in the West, with the US Defence Department and NATO both treating the Russian announcements of withdrawal with scepticism and warning of further offensives against Kyiv.[12] As a result of these apparent intelligence failures, the bulk of the 35th CAA was able to withdraw in good order up the P02 in the last days of March.

A Russian column northbound on the P02 seen halted temporarily in Termakhivka during the retreat. (Russian social media)

Several other factors contributed to the withdrawal's success. Firstly, the movement was reportedly directly overseen by Colonel General Chaiko from a command post near Chernobyl (Sanchik having relinquished operational control), preventing the retreat devolving into a rout.[13] Secondly, fighting withdrawals, unlike offensive manoeuvres, were rehearsed extensively by the VSRF prior to the war, with Russia's annual strategic exercises typically premised around a manoeuvre defence against invading NATO forces.[14] Though mauled and demoralised, Russian troops could fall back on this ingrained layer of training. Thirdly, intensified airstrikes and artillery fire helped pin Ukrainian units in place, preventing them from interfering in the retreat.[15] Indeed, the pace and completeness of the withdrawal was shocking to Ukrainian soldiers. One battery commander from the 72nd Mechanised Brigade's 2nd Artillery Battalion recalled:

> My battery was on duty. I still remember this moment. It was either 31st March or 1st April. I got into the position and am waiting for the command. And I write to the [artillery battalion] commander [on WhatsApp] "give me a goal." And he writes "wait, I am looking." Half an hour passed. I told him again "give me a goal." He said, "there is nothing, there is no one." So, the Russians left.[16]

The Battle of Dmytrivka

Nonetheless, the withdrawal was not so successful everywhere.[17] Still holding on the E40, the 5th GTB was isolated well to the south of the rest of the 35th CAA. Retreat toward Ukrainian-held Makariv and the T1019 was out of the question, so the brigade decided to use the north-south roads between the E40 and E373 to escape. On 30 March, one of the brigade's BTGs left the E40 and began to drive north into the village of Dmytrivka (Bucha region) toward the E373. Meanwhile, a company of the 104th Regiment, 76th GAAD,[18] drove south to meet it with the intent of opening an escape corridor. Unfortunately for the Russians, the Ukrainians of 4th Company, 133rd Battalion, 114th TDF Brigade, had recently occupied Dmytrivka, blocking their retreat. Concealed among the houses, the TDF volunteers watched the first Russian vehicles pass, waiting for the right moment. Seeing the turret of the nearest T-72B was turned away, the commander of the 4th Company's 1st Platoon called forward his RPG-7 gunner – *Snake* – to initiate the ambush. *Snake*'s first shot hit the T-72B's explosive reactive armour (ERA) and did not penetrate, but the crew panicked and bailed out regardless. His next RPG then knocked out a BMP-2. In total, the 20-year-old fired no fewer than 24 RPG rounds during the battle. As the 4th Company began to run low on ammunition, the Russian BTG was able to disengage and continue north, only to find itself ambushed again as two Ukrainian T-64BVs began firing into its flank from a side street, first destroying a T-72B, then two more BMPs. Meanwhile, Ukrainian GUR SOF and the 184th Training Centre's CTG were also joining the battle.

Running the gauntlet of the pair of T-64s, the Russian column continued onto the road north of the village, desperate to escape. The Ukrainian tanks followed on its flank, knocking out vehicle after vehicle in a series of fireballs. The 104th Regiment's company arrived in time to help some of the survivors northwards, but were far too late to save overall the situation. By the time the fighting had finished, some 50 Russians were dead, and 16 AFVs lost. In the aftermath, Georgian Legionnaires and Ukrainian soldiers executed two wounded Russian paratroopers lying in the road.[19] So ended the last major combat operation undertaken by the 35th CAA at Kyiv.

A still from video filmed by a Ukrainian UAV showing a Russian BMP-2, already disabled by an RPG fired by *Snake*, exploding after being dispatched by the T-72B immediately behind it – apparently in a hasty scuttling effort. (Ukrainian Internet)

A still from the same video showing the Russian column attempting to escape Dmytrivka to the north. (Ukrainian Internet)

The aftermath of the battle. (ZSU)

This BMD-2 was captured intact in central Moschun following the Russian withdrawal in late March 2022. The tactical insignia of a white three inside a white triangle denotes its assignment to the 331st Regiment, 98th Guards Airborne Division. The BMD family of vehicles were originally conceived in response to the problem of the nuclear battlefield, which – at least under Soviet thinking – demanded even airborne forces have robust mechanised protection. The BMD-2 was introduced in the mid-1980s following the experience of the VDV in Afghanistan, where the low-pressure 2A28 73mm gun of the earlier BMD-1 was found to lack sufficient range and explosive power. Instead, the new vehicle was equipped with a much more effective 2A42 30mm autocannon. (Artwork by David Bocquelet)

This BMD-4M of the 31st Guards Air Assault Brigade was knocked out west of Bucha and abandoned in mid-March 2022. Designed as a replacement for the BMD-2, the BMD-4 boasts a 2A70 low-pressure 100mm gun capable of firing laser-guided 9M117M1-3 Arkan ATGMs, further supplemented by a co-axial 2A72 30mm autocannon and PKT 7.62mm machine gun. Unfortunately, this extensive firepower comes at the expense of the vehicle's survivability: its aluminium hull filled with unprotected 100mm and 30mm ammunition. Corresponding concerns regarding the BMD-4's fragility were raised publicly by the *GenStab* during its procurement, but these were overruled by Putin, who feared tarnishing the reputation of the Russian arms industry in the eyes of potential foreign buyers. (Artwork by David Bocquelet)

This BTR-MDM armoured personnel carrier of the 31st Guards Air Assault Brigade was abandoned during the infamous glass factory ambush in central Hostomel on 3 March 2022, which saw the brigade's 5th Air Assault Company badly mauled. This vehicle is shown without the usual remote-controlled PKT machine gun on the hull roof to highlight the NSV 12.7mm machine gun the vehicle's own infantry section emplaced in a bid to bolster its firepower. Similar ad-hoc additions of crew-served weapon systems were also seen on Russian BMD-2s and BTR-Ds during the initial invasion period, a prelude to the explosion of in-field adaptations during the subsequent years of the war. Capable of carrying 13 dismounts and two crewmembers, the BTR-MDM is spacious in comparison to the BMD-2 and BMD-4. (Artwork by David Bocquelet)

This Federal-42590 armoured truck of the Rosgvardia's 19th Operational Brigade was knocked out on the E373 road bridge over the Irpin River during the fighting on 25 February 2022. Based on the ubiquitous Ural-4320 truck chassis, the Federal-42590 was developed on the request of Russia's Ministry of Internal Affairs in the early 2010s following the experience of the Second Chechen War, where soft-skinned Russian trucks had proven highly vulnerable to road-side rebel ambushes. The vehicle's forward cab and engine compartment are armour-plated, whilst an armoured compartment for dismounts is fixed to the truck bed – the latter reportedly capable of resisting steel core 7.62mm rounds and explosive devices weighing up to 10kg. The vehicle's total carrying capacity is around 15 troops, with loopholes allowing passengers to use their personal weapons from inside both the rear compartment and cab. (Artwork by David Bocquelet)

This T-90A of the 27th Guards Motor Rifle Brigade was bogged down and subsequently abandoned in muddy fields north of Sumy around 27 February 2022. Its belonging to the brigade is denoted by the tactical insignia of an orange 27 in an orange triangle painted on the turret. Red identification tape has also been affixed to the wind sensor of the tank's 1A45T Irtysh fire control system. A late 1980s development of the T-72, the T-90 initially saw only limited orders in the context of the collapse of the USSR. However, an export order by India had a large production run of the T-90S variant produced, prompting the Russian government to renew their interest in the design, with the new T-90A variant being procured for the VRSF from 2005 onwards. Equipped with the Essa thermal sight and the improved 2A46M-5 125mm smoothbore gun, the T-90A is one of the more modern VRSF tank models. This particular vehicle seemingly went on to serve with the Ukrainian 117th TDF Brigade. (Artwork by David Bocquelet)

This T-80BV No. 516 was knocked out by Ukrainian anti-tank mines on the approaches to the village of Kukhari on 14 March 2022. The small white crosshair tactical symbol painted on its side skirt denotes its belonging to the 69th Covering Brigade. Powered by the GTD-100TF gas turbine engine, the T-80BV enjoys a better power-to-weight ratio than comparable T-64 and T-72 variants, although its higher fuel consumption makes any difference in operational mobility relatively negligible. Its Kontakt-1 ERA and composite armour is also comparable to the T-64BV, as is its 1A33 Ob fire control system. The lack of a thermal sight for its 2A46-1 125mm smoothbore gun nor a remote-controlled mount for the commander's NSV Utyos machine gun reveals its age as a 1985 modernisation of the original T-80. (Artwork by David Bocquelet)

WAR IN UKRAINE VOLUME 8: THE BATTLE OF KYIV, FEBRUARY–APRIL 2022

This BMP-2K No. 315 of the 90th Guards Tank Division's 80th Tank Regiment was destroyed in the Nizhyn region in late March 2022. Note the distinctive orange and black stripes painted on the hull, representing the ribbon of St George – a contemporary Russian nationalist symbol frequently associated with the SVO. Several vehicles of the division have been pictured with it painted both laterally and vertically on their hulls, and it may be an identifying mark for the unit – if inconsistently applied. The BMP-2 was the most prolific IFV of the VRSF prior to the war and was also common among ZSU formations. The vehicle is armed with a 2A42 30mm autocannon and co-axial PKT machine gun – and can carry seven dismounts alongside its three crew. Its inadequate survivability, poor ergonomics, and obsolescing optics limits its performance compared to more modern IFV designs. (Artwork by David Bocquelet)

This 2S19 Msta-S self-propelled 152mm howitzer was knocked out near Trostianets in late February 2022. It fought with the 4th Guards Tank Division's 275th Self-Propelled Artillery Regiment, as indicated by the tactical symbols of a small paired white oak leaves and a black four in an orange rimmed white hexagon (the latter heavily obscured by scorching) painted on the turret: both common insignias of the division. Also visible on this vehicle's side skirts are the white cross and 'H-2200' markings denoting its status as oversized cargo for Russian railway transport. The Msta-S was one of the most modern self-propelled howitzers fielded by the VRSF at the war's outbreak, also seeing service in small numbers with the ZSU's 26th Artillery Brigade. (Artwork by David Bocquelet)

This 2S34 Khosta self-propelled 120mm gun-mortar was knocked out inside the village of Novyi Bykiv in late March 2022. The large 'O' identification markings common to the 41st CAA and 2nd GCAA are prominently displayed on the vehicle's hull and turret. Though based on the chassis of the prolific 2S1 Gvozdika self-propelled howitzer, the Khosta replaced the 2A18 122mm gun of the former vehicle with the unique 2A80-1 120mm gun-mortar. Combined with an improved fire control system, this arrangement allows the rapid fire of 120mm rounds at much greater ranges than could be expected with a usual mortar, including 3VOF112 Kitolov-2 laser-guided rounds (reserved primarily for anti-tank missions). Introduced in 2014, the Khosta saw only a limited production run and was fielded exclusively by the 21st Motor Rifle Brigade at the invasion's outbreak. This particular vehicle was later displayed in Prague as part of the 'Ukraine – Shield of Europe' exhibition in summer 2022. (Artwork by David Bocquelet)

This M1151A1 up-armoured Humvee was pictured in service with the 80th Air Assault Brigade in April 2022. Such vehicles were among the first Ukrainian elements meeting the Russian invasion north of Kyiv in the early hours of 24 February 2022. The vehicle retains the three-tone NATO camouflage scheme it was originally delivered in under the Ukrainian Security Assistance Initiative following the 2014 invasion. A winged trident tactical insignia on the front doors denotes its belonging to the Ukrainian Air Assault Forces, whilst yellow reflective tape has been fixed to the roof sides to assist in identification. As was common among Humvees delivered to Ukraine prior to the 2022 invasion, this vehicle is fitted with a DShK 12.7mm machine gun. (Artwork by David Bocquelet)

This BMP-1 No. 215 of the 15th Motorised Infantry Battalion, 58th Motorised Brigade, was destroyed just north of Ivanivka, likely during the Russian assault on the village on 5 March 2022. First introduced to service in 1966, the BMP-1 is still widely used by the VRSF and the ZSU at the time of writing in 2024. The vehicle is armed with a low-pressure 2A28 73mm gun and a co-axial PKT machine gun – and can carry eight dismounts in addition to its three crew. Whilst an innovative design for the 1960s, the BMP-1's one-man turret, lacklustre armament, and lack of protection against modern anti-tank threats leaves much to be desired on the contemporary battlefield. This vehicle was painted dark green overall, with sand, dark brown, and black applied in the typical Ukrainian 'digital' camouflage scheme. (Artwork by David Bocquelet)

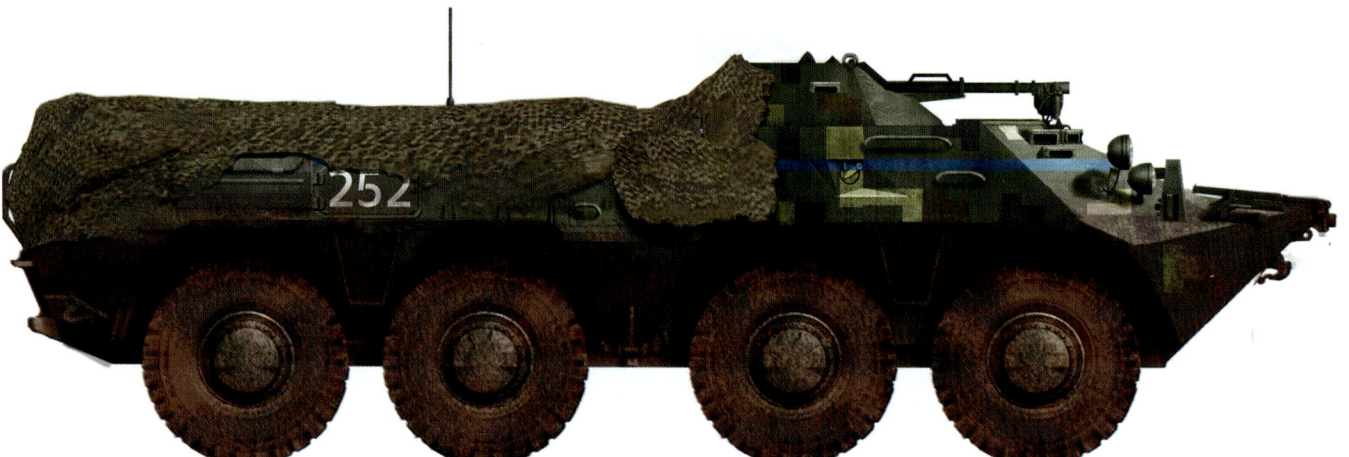

This BTR-80 No. 252 was knocked out beside the Giraffe checkpoint in Irpin during the fighting on 27 February 2022. Originally in service with the 80th Air Assault Brigade's 2nd BTG, it was abandoned during the unit's chaotic retreat through Bucha following the failed counterattack against Antonov IAP late on 24 February 2022. The vehicle was subsequently discovered and re-crewed by TDF volunteers from the Irpin CTG and positioned beside their checkpoint, with a camouflage net draped over it to provide some concealment. Entering service in the mid-1980s, the BTR-80 is armed with a KPVT 14.5mm machine gun – in addition to a co-axial PKT machine gun – and can carry seven dismounts alongside its three crew. The type has seen extensive service both with the ZSU and VRSF. (Artwork by David Bocquelet)

WAR IN UKRAINE VOLUME 8: THE BATTLE OF KYIV, FEBRUARY–APRIL 2022

This BTR-3E was found knocked out north-west of Antonov IAP in the village of Ozera, having likely been destroyed by a Russian helicopter during the initial assault on 24 February 2022. The vehicle belonged to the 4th Rapid Reaction Brigade and was one of several IFVs and tanks still left in the unit's garrison in various states of disrepair when the invasion began. Accepted into ZSU service in 2015, the BTR-3 is a development upon the design of the BTR-80, though the type itself is an all-new Ukrainian production. Its armament consists of a remotely operated BM-3M 'Storm' turret, featuring a ZTM-1 30mm autocannon, a co-axial 7.62mm machine gun, and two Barrier ATGMs. The vehicle has a crew of three and can carry six dismounts. (Artwork by David Bocquelet)

This T-64BV was pictured in service with the Rosgvardia in October 2022, having allegedly been captured from the garrison of the 4th Rapid Reaction Brigade at Antonov IAP during the Russian occupation of the airfield. The tank was evacuated during the subsequent retreat and later restored to working order, then crewed by Rosgvardia personnel who had previous experience as tank crew. The vehicle was repainted with 'V' identification markings and had its usual NSV Utyos machine gun replaced with a Kord 12.7mm machine gun. The ad-hoc use of such heavy armour by Rosgvardia forces reflects their experience of the initial full-scale invasion and the Ukrainian 2022 counteroffensives, where lightly equipped Rosgvardia units frequently found themselves outgunned by regular ZSU formations. Eventually, following the Wagner Group rebellion in 2023, the Rosgvardia was officially re-equipped with tanks and other heavy weapons. (Artwork by David Bocquelet)

This 2S7 Pion self-propelled 203mm howitzer named 'Kraken' was filmed in April 2022 as part of a propaganda video produced by the 43rd Artillery Brigade, the sole ZSU brigade equipped with 2S7s. Introduced into service in the 1970s as a heavy artillery piece capable of firing nuclear rounds into the tactical depth, the 2S7 continues to shine in both Ukrainian and Russian service as the heaviest howitzer employed by either side. Its 2A44 gun can loft 110kg high-explosive fragmentation shells over ranges of 37.5 kilometres at a rate of 1.5 rounds a minute. According to the staff of the 43rd Brigade, their 2S7s regularly fired as many as 50 rounds per gun each day during the Battle of Kyiv, illustrating the intensity of the fighting. (Artwork by David Bocquelet)

This SOBR operator of the Rosgvardia is shown in a typical fashion for the early invasion period. He is armed with a heavily accessorised AK-104 assault carbine – a shortened version of the AK-103 assault rifle (itself a derivative of the ubiquitous AK-74M rechambered from 5.45x39mm to 7.62x39mm) – and a GM-94 pump action grenade launcher, the latter capable of firing a variety of 43mm grenades, including thermobaric rounds. For protection, he wears a Classcom TOR aramid helmet with a cover and an SSO Pantsir plate carrier. His uniform appears to be a variant of the black Vympel overalls widespread amongst SOBR units. The white tape on his left arm is a typical identification symbol for Russian forces, along with red tape and St George's ribbons. Ukrainian forces typically use yellow, green, or blue tape. (Artwork by Giorgio Albertini)

WAR IN UKRAINE VOLUME 8: THE BATTLE OF KYIV, FEBRUARY–APRIL 2022

This Ukrainian special forces operator is shown as seen west of Kyiv on the E40 highway in early March 2022. He is armed with a Malyuk assault rifle chambered in 5.45x39mm, accessorised in this case with an Aimpoint CompM4 red dot sight, PEQ laser illuminator device, weapon light, and foregrip. Also known as the Vulcan, the Malyuk is a bullpup conversion of the AK series of rifles, wherein the breech of the weapon is moved behind the firing grip. The platform is manufactured by the Ukrainian company InterProInvest and has seen widespread service throughout the ZSU, most commonly within special forces units. Besides his weapon, he wears a MultiCam patterned uniform (standard issue among Ukrainian SOF by February 2022), plate carrier, and a Kaska-1M helmet. Note the yellow identification tape. (Artwork by Giorgio Albertini)

This Ukrainian soldier is shown as pictured during the battle of Rudynts'ke on 10 March 2022, suggesting he was a member of the 8th Mountain Assault Battalion, 10th Mountain Brigade, or perhaps a volunteer from the Bratstvo Battalion attached to the former formation for the operation. His firearm is an AKS-74 5.45x39mm assault rifle with an under-barrel GP-25 40mm grenade launcher. He also carries an RPG-7 rocket launcher in his hands and has a Spanish C-90 90mm rocket launcher slung across his back, the latter provided as foreign aid to Ukraine following the full-scale invasion. For the assault on Rudynts'ke, the 8th Battalion was equipped with a wide variety of portable anti-tank systems, including many examples donated by Ukraine's allies: German Panzerfaust 3s and MATADORs, British/Swedish NLAWs, and Spanish C-90s. (Artwork by Giorgio Albertini)

WAR IN UKRAINE VOLUME 8: THE BATTLE OF KYIV, FEBRUARY–APRIL 2022

Written off during the assault on Antonov IAP, this Ka-52 Bort 18 Blue (registration RF-13405) of the 18th Army Aviation Brigade was hit by an Igla MANPAD and force-landed west of Hostomel. The crew – Lieutenant Colonel Airat Safargaleev and Major Dmitriy Zlobin – were able to escape capture, although their machine was abandoned intact and later dismantled and transported away by the Ukrainians. As with many VKS helicopters involved in the operation, this example had its usual insignia (depicted in the upper right inset) painted over and prominent white 'V'(s) applied. The VKS Ka-52 fleet saw intensive service in the opening months of the invasion and suffered proportionately heavy losses as a result. Several downed examples of the type subsequently inspected by the Ukrainians were found to have their sensor covers still fitted and radio encryption keys left uninstalled, indicating poor levels of training among VKS groundcrews. This reconstruction of 18 Blue shows it equipped with the Vikhr ATGMs and PTB-450 external fuel tanks it carried for its final sortie. (Artwork by Luca Canossa)

Also a casualty of the assault on Antonov, this Mi-35M Bort 29 Blue (registration RF-13024) of the 16th Army Aviation Brigade was hit by an Igla whilst ingressing toward Hostomel and crashed into the Dnipro reservoir, killing the helicopter's entire crew – Major Nikolai Bugay, Major Roman Grovich, and Captain Aleksey Belkov. The wreckage of the machine was later raised from the reservoir in June 2022 and placed on display outside the Lyutizh Bridgehead Museum, located in the village of Novi Petrivtsi – north of Kyiv. A development of the famous Mi-24 helicopter gunship, the Mi-35M first entered service with the VRSF in the early 2010s. The retractable undercarriage of the original design was replaced with fixed landing gear and the wings shortened from three hardpoints to two, chiefly to save weight. Meanwhile, a variety of advanced avionics and sensors were installed, including the L370E24 Vitebsk self-protection suite and the GOES-342.10 electro-optical complex, the latter mated with a GSh-23L twin-barrelled 23mm autocannon. This reconstruction of 29 Blue shows it armed additionally with Ataka ATGMs and B-8V20A pods for 80mm S-8 unguided rockets. (Artwork by Tom Cooper)

This Mi-8AMTSh Bort 83 Blue (registration RF-91292) of the 35th Mixed Aviation Regiment was shot down north-west of Makariv on 4 March 2022 by an Igla MANPAD of the 95th Air Assault Brigade, operated by a paratrooper with the callsign *Seven*. The helicopter was shattered by the crash and subsequent fire, killing the crew – Captain Gennadiy Ismagulov, Senior Lieutenant Aleksey Trishin, and Captain Konstantin Kusov. Although the machine originally fell close to Russian lines, the bodies of the crew were not recovered from the wreckage of their aircraft until well after the VRSF withdrew from the Makariv area, leaving a stark scene later famously photographed by passing journalists. The helicopter is shown fitted with the two B-8V20A rocket pods it was carrying at the time of the incident. The small Russian tricolour flag and white 'V' were typical markings for VKS Mi-8AMTSh's operating over northern Ukraine at the time, although the near total destruction of 83 Blue leaves it impossible to tell whether the machine was wearing similar details at the time of its loss. (Artwork by Tom Cooper)

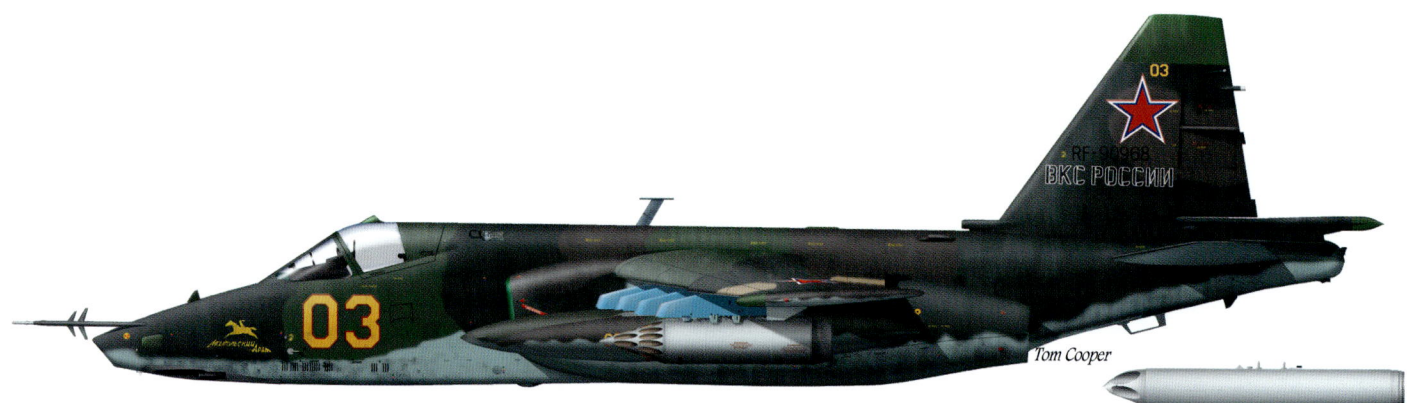

This Su-25 Bort 03 Yellow (registration RF-90968) crashed inside southern Belarus on 24 February 2022 whilst returning from a sortie in support of the Antonov operation. The pilot – Colonel Ruslan Igorevich Rudnev, commander of the 266th Assault Aviation Regiment – was killed in the incident. The exact circumstances of the machine's loss remain unclear, although it was likely damaged either by a Ukrainian MANPAD or a MiG-29 during the Antonov battle and subsequently became uncontrollable as Rudnev nursed it over the border. The aircraft is shown as last pictured in 2021 and with a typical wartime loadout of PTB-800 external fuel tanks and B-8M pods for S-8 unguided rockets (carried in addition to an internally installed Gsh-30-2 twin-barrelled 30mm autocannon). VKS Su-25s were also frequently seen armed with B-13L pods for 122mm S-13 unguided rockets, an example of which is depicted in the inset. (Artwork by Tom Cooper)

This Il-22PP EW aircraft (registration RF-96673) was one of only three examples in operation with the VKS in February 2022 and accordingly saw extensive service during the invasion's outset. Based on the venerable Il-18 turboprop airliner which first flew in 1957, the Il-22PP is one of several military variants of the type still in the VKS's inventory. The aircraft is equipped with the KNIRTI 1-145 electronic warfare suite, with antennas mounted inside the four large fairings located on each side of the fuselage and within the aft tail boom. Little is known about the system's precise capabilities, although it has demonstrated its practical effectiveness in jamming the radars of Ukrainian interceptors and SAM systems alike. For self-defence, the aircraft carries 16 32-round 26mm chaff/flare launchers in a ventral pod, along with two 14-round 50mm chaff/flare launchers in the fuselage. (Artwork by Tom Cooper)

This Su-34 Bort 05 Red (registration RF-81259) of the 2nd Mixed Aviation Regiment was shot down south of Bucha on 28 February 2022. The crew – Captain Artur R. Gubaiduin and Major Maxim M. Borona – ejected safely and were apparently able to escape capture. At the time of the incident the aircraft was carrying 500kg OFZAB-500 high-explosive incendiary bombs, although this illustration shows an alternate configuration of RBK-500 cluster bombs also frequently seen carried by Su-34s of that period. Besides ground attack munitions, the aircraft is armed with a pair of R-73/R-74 air-to-air missiles on the outboard underwing pylons and an internal GSh-30-1 30mm autocannon. VKS Su-34s typically employed unguided bombs in risky low-level strikes during the invasion's first months, despite possessing a ventrally installed 1255 B1/02 Platan laser and TV sight capable of targeting precision-guided munitions from stand-off distances. Only from mid-April did VKS Su-34s begin regularly employing Kh-29 guided missiles from medium altitudes, likely in response to previous losses. (Artwork by Tom Cooper)

WAR IN UKRAINE VOLUME 8: THE BATTLE OF KYIV, FEBRUARY–APRIL 2022

This MiG-29MU1 Bort 03 Blue of the the 40th Tactical Aviation Brigade was shot down north of Vasylkiv AB whilst covering the take-off of other Ukrainian MiG-29s on 24 February 2022, likely by a Russian R-77-1 missile. The pilot – Lieutenant Vyacheslav Radionov – was killed in the resulting crash. Whilst most Ukrainian MiG-29s were painted in a 'digital' camouflage scheme on their upper surfaces and sides by 2022, 03 Blue was among a handful of machines still sporting the striking scheme of the Ukrainian Falcons aerobatic team, which had been officially disbanded in 2002 following the Sknyliv air show disaster. It remains unclear whether Bort 03 Blue was still wearing the colourful livery at the time of its shootdown, but the appearance of other Falcons liveried MiG-29s in combat service in 2014 and following the full-scale invasion suggest it possible. The aircraft is shown with a typical armament of two R-27R and four R-73 missiles – carried in addition to its internal GSh-30-1 autocannon. (Artwork by Luca Canossa)

This Mi-8MTV Bort 133 of the 11th Army Aviation Brigade was one of three Ukrainian helicopters shot down in the Brovary area on 8 March 2022 whilst trying to slow the Russian advance toward Kyiv. The crew – Colonel Oleg Irodievich Gegechkori and Captain Ihor Moroz – were both killed in the crash. The distinctive pair of white bands around the tail boom are typical identification markings for Ukrainian helicopters, although Russian helicopters have also been seen using white stripes on their tail booms for the same purpose during the war. The machine is shown armed with a pair of B-8V rocket pods and a pair of UPK-23-250 gun pods, each containing a GSh-23 twin-barrelled autocannon. (Artwork by Luca Canossa)

This Bayraktar TB2 attack UAV Bort 403 Red was one of the early production examples of the type delivered to Ukraine before the invasion, as can be visually distinguished by its two-bladed propeller (in contrast to the three-bladed propeller of later production machines). Administratively collected under the command of the 383rd Regiment of Remotely Controlled Aircraft, in practice TB2s were operated in dispersed groups during the war, with a ground control station as a focal point for each groups' activities. One such station was established in the small city of Bilohorodka south-west of Kyiv in late February 2022, directing the efforts of TB2s in the vicinity of the capital. The machine above is shown armed with a typical payload of two 22kg MAM-L laser-guided mini-bombs, capable of mounting either tandem HEAT, high-explosive fragmentation, or thermobaric warheads. Ukrainian TB2s enjoyed great success against unprotected Russian columns and vehicle laagers in the opening weeks of the invasion, but were eventually relegated to more passive missions as Russian air defences became properly established. (Artwork by Goran Sudar)

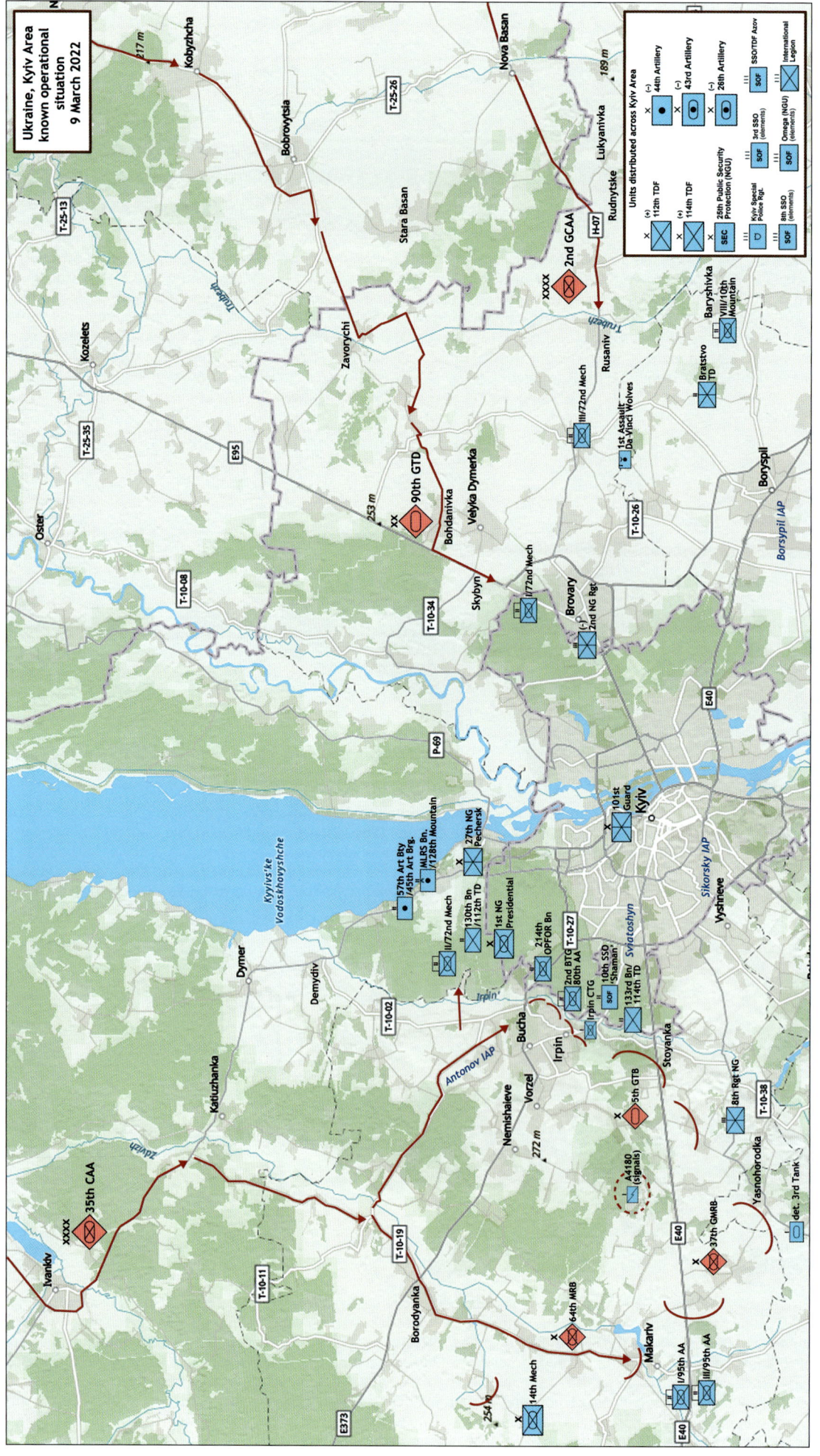

(Map by Tom Cooper)

9
EASTERN AXES

Whilst the 35th CAA struggled on the western side of Kyiv; a similar story was unfolding on the other side of the capital as the 41st CAA, 2nd GCAA, and 1st GTA were mauled in their attempts to envelop Kyiv from the east. Here, the battle area was much larger, spanning some 60,000 square kilometres from Kyiv's eastern side across the Chernihiv and Sumy oblasts, with terrain seemingly more favourable to the Russians: largely flat farmland crisscrossed with highways connecting the area's few towns and cities, rather than the dense woodland of north-western Kyiv. The Russian plan reflected this geography, aiming to bypass the few population centres and drive straight for the capital down the highways, Moscow's intelligence having assured them that these bypassed cities would then surrender, even greet them as liberators. Ultimately, this flawed assessment of Ukraine's will to fight proved as fatal here as it had in the west.

41st CAA

Beginning around 0400hrs on 24 February 2022, a series of drone strikes hit the Ukrainian border posts guarding the perimeter of the Chernihiv Oblast, catching some border guards in their sleep.[1] An hour later, the 41st CAA – commanded by Lieutenant General Sergey Borisovich Ryzhkov – crossed the border and began advancing down the E95 and P13 highways toward the city of Chernihiv. Unlike the other population centres east of Kyiv, Chernihiv was to be captured rather than bypassed. It contained a major railway station connecting lines running from Belarus and Russia, which would provide a crucial supply hub for the VSRF's advance, dependent as it was on rail-borne logistics. Nonetheless, Chernihiv was still only a preliminary objective for Ryzhkov, Kyiv was his main goal. Watching the 41st CAA's advance, the officers of OC North were amazed by the sheer scale of the Russian columns, as Lieutenant Colonel 'Oleksandr' recalled: 'At first we would get excited to see even 100 units of equipment – but then we wouldn't even bother to count if there were less than 500. The biggest column we saw was 34 kilometres long.'[2]

Table 2: Known units assigned to the 41st CAA, February–early April 2022

Unit	Known number of BTGs	Comment
35th Motor Rifle Brigade	2	
55th Mountain Motor Rifle Brigade		Deployed seemingly with all three manoeuvre battalions
74th Guards Motor Rifle Brigade	2	
90th Guards Tank Division	2	BTGs drawn from the division's 80th Tank Regiment and 228th Motor Rifle Regiment
120th Artillery Brigade	N/A	

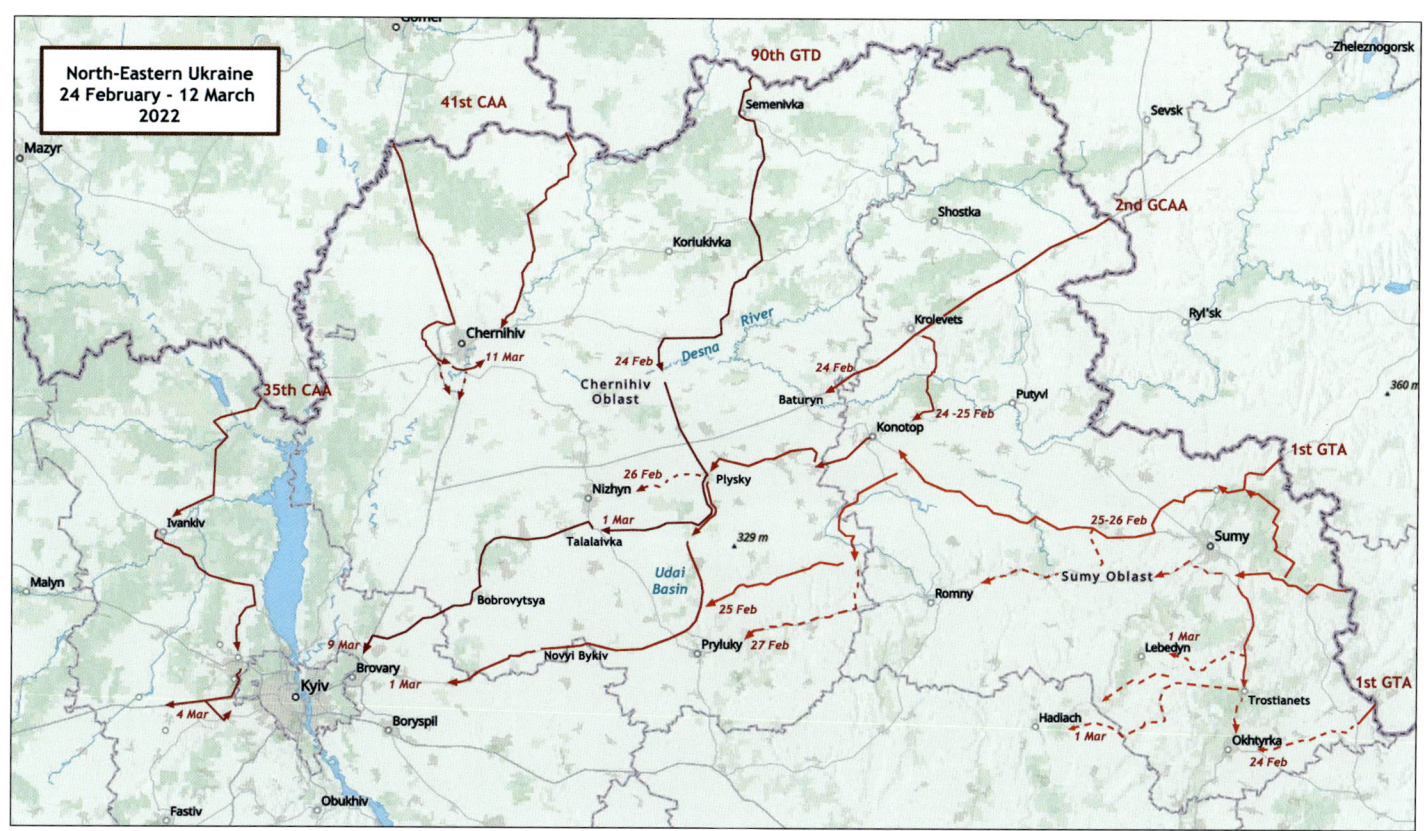

A map of the eastern axes of the VRSF advance on Kyiv, from 24 February until 12 March 2022. Path of the 90th GTD has been depicted in darker shade to prevent confusion with route taken by 2nd GCAA. (Map by Tom Cooper)

By midday, the Russian spearheads were driving through Ripky on the E95 and Horodnya on the P13 respectively, settlements OC North had originally planned to hold as an initial defence line. However, things were already going seriously wrong within the 41st CAA. For starters, many of its troops had not even been informed they were participating in an invasion. For example, the personnel of the 35th Motor Rifle Brigade (35th MRB) crossed the border in the belief they were simply 'demonstrating military equipment', having packed enough rations for only three days.[3] Inevitably, this resulted in a lack of all conceivable supplies across the army, widespread confusion as to where units were going or what their objectives were, and a loss of morale when Ukrainian resistance was encountered. These issues were further compounded by the obsolete equipment the 41st CAA possessed relative to the other combined armies committed around Kyiv. Often lacking satellite navigation systems or modern radios in their vehicles,[4] units frequently became lost or dropped out of contact. Still worse, Ryzhkov's HQ was itself facing major communications issues after its Era encrypted mobile communications system proved unable to work inside Ukraine, Ukrainian mobile operators denying it access to their networks. The theft of Ukrainian SIM cards eased the situation somewhat, though this compromised Era's encryption, likely later costing one of Ryzhkov's deputies his life after his position was triangulated.[5] In summary, the 41st CAA was already becoming combat ineffective before it had even begun to fight.

Facing the 41st CAA on Chernihiv's outskirts were the defences of the 1st Tank Brigade, under the command of Colonel Leonid Khoda. Khoda knew engaging the enemy directly would be suicidal, and so he worked to channel the Russians into the swampy terrain north of the city by demolishing bridges and forcing them off the roads. Once the Russians were slowed, he could then leverage his brigade's organic artillery and the Uragans of the 27th Rocket Artillery Brigade and the Tochkas of the 19th Missile Brigade to destroy them. A first clash that afternoon on the E95 just north of Rivnopillya played out exactly in this fashion, seeing forward elements of the 74th Guards Motor Rifle Brigade (74th GMRB) smashed by artillery, then mopped up by a company-sized counterattack from the 1st Tank Brigade. In the aftermath, an entire Russian reconnaissance platoon surrendered.[6]

The misery of the 41st CAA continued over 25 February as its columns were subjected to artillery and missile strikes, their locations constantly reported to OC North by local civilians. Outside Horodnya, a halted Russian engineering column was hit by multiple Tochkas, losing 19 vehicles. Nevertheless, Ryzhkov continued pushing. Advancing southwards on the E95 that morning, a BTG of the 74th GMRB bore down on a 1st Tank Brigade checkpoint at Khalyvan, manned by only two T-64BVs and a mechanised infantry platoon on three BMPs. An artillery strike halted the Russian's advance, allowing the Ukrainian armour to begin engaging. Sergeant Major Oleksandr directed the fire of his BMP-1 from outside the vehicle, a prudent decision, as he later found a tank round had passed straight through the turret. Having lost one T-64BV in exchange for at least two T-72Bs,[7] and with Russian elements flanking around their position, the Ukrainians opted to retreat to Chernihiv. The way back was not easy, Oleksandr's BMP was hit again: two RPGs wounding him and killing his commander – Senior Lieutenant Sergey Telushkov – but the crippled vehicle still managed to limp back to friendly lines. There, elements of the National Guard's 22nd Battalion held off the Russian pursuit, allowing Khoda to organise a counterattack which drove the 74th GMRB back.

Meanwhile, to the east, another Russian BTG (likely of the 35th MRB) advanced down the P13 highway and swung to attack Chernihiv across the Pivtsi airfield, defended at the time by a

A 1st Tank Brigade BMP-1P and dismounts watch on as a Russian vehicle burns on the approaches to Chernihiv. (1st Tank Brigade)

company of guardsmen from the 22nd Battalion and just five Ukrainian tanks.[8] Beginning at 1030hrs, the attack quickly faltered as the Russian vehicles sank into the mud on the northern outskirts of the airfield. Meanwhile, the Ukrainian tanks expertly used the vegetation on the south side of the airfield as cover for repeated shoot-and-scoot engagements, knocking out five Russian tanks. Defeated, the BTG retreated under the cover of a heavy artillery barrage, leaving the field littered with its bogged AFVs. Major General Nikoliuk recalled later:

> We tried to take them for ourselves. But [the Russians], realizing they could not evacuate them either, simply shot them, along with their crews. At first, it was surprising. Then I was no longer surprised. You're okay with it. That is, a good enemy is a dead enemy. They just destroyed them. On the contrary, even when we tried to evacuate their wounded, they covered them and our own with artillery.[9]

Realising that further frontal assaults were fruitless (at least for the moment), and with supplies running out, Ryzhkov next attempted to bypass Chernihiv. On 26 February, a BTG of the 35th MRB was ordered into blocking positions north of the city to facilitate this movement. Unfortunately, in the process, a company group under the command of the brigade's chief of staff – Major Leonid Shchotkin – became lost and wandered deep into Chernihiv itself. Around 0630hrs, near the *Epitsentr* supermarket, Shchotkin's company was ambushed by four Ukrainian tanks and 70 infantry, including a company from the 22nd Battalion and volunteers from the rapidly assembling 119th TDF Brigade. At least one of the 22nd Battalion's three BTR-70s was also present. Shchotkin's T-72B was knocked out almost immediately and caught fire, though he and his gunner managed to escape into a nearby shed. One 22nd Battalion BTR crewman recalled:

> We had a narrow task: work only on the infantry. Our tankers did a great job, they hit the first tank that was moving. I was on the machine gun [KPVT 14.5mm] and started shooting at the infantry. They immediately ran away. The tanks also turned around. They got scared. I don't know. But they just ran away as soon as they heard the shooting. Like there was nobody.[10]

Leaderless, the Russians had scattered, abandoning another T-72B, a BMP, and a BTR-80-based radio station in the process. Killed on the same day, the 35th MRB's deputy commander and chief of communications – Lieutenant Colonel Nikolai Pirozhkov – was likely a casualty of the same engagement.[11] Shchotkin, meanwhile, became a POW. Ironically, his mistaken ride was the furthest the 41st CAA would ever make it into the city.

Above: Shchotkin's T-72B burns, 26 February 2022. (1st Tank Brigade)

Right: Shchotkin is led away by guardsmen of the 22nd Battalion in the aftermath of the *Epitsentr* battle. (Ukrainian National Guard)

2nd GCAA and the Fighting Retreat of the 58th Motorised Brigade

The advance of the 2nd GCAA – commanded by Major General Vyacheslav Nikolaevich Gurov – was by far the most successful of the three combined armies approaching Kyiv from the east.[12] Preceded by artillery and MRLS strikes, around 0400hrs on 24 February 2022, the 2nd GCAA crossed the border and began driving west along the M02 highway. In its path was the 58th Motorised Brigade, commanded by Colonel Dmytro Kashchenko. However, this brigade was dispersed across the entire Sumy Oblast: the 13th Battalion at Shostka, the 15th Battalion at Sumy, and Brigade HQ at Konotop. In fact, only the 16th Battalion, holding Hlukhiv, was in position to check the initial Russian advance along the M02.

Table 3: Known units assigned to the 2nd GCAA, February–early April 2022

Unit	Known number of BTGs
15th Motor Rifle Brigade	2
21st Motor Rifle Brigade	2
30th Motor Rifle Brigade	1
385th Artillery Brigade	N/A

Around 0430hrs, the 16th Battalion's mechanised company advanced toward the intersection of the M02 and P65 highways just north of Hlukhiv. Leaving the rest of his company south of the intersection, the company commander – Captain Vitaliy Derevyanko – led a group of four BMPs eastward on the M02 to recon the situation. It was not long before he found himself being passed in the pre-dawn darkness by columns of Russian BTR-82As driving west. These were the first elements of two BTGs of the 15th Motor Rifle Brigade (15th MRB), spearheading Gurov's advance.[13]

Incredibly, neither side opened fire at first and Derevyanko had turned around and was returning to the intersection when the first engagement began at a range of less than 200 metres, as he recalled later: 'We started four [BMPs] on four [BTRs]. And we exchanged four for four. Two were burned, two were knocked out. And we had one burned down, three knocked out. We took as much ammunition as possible from our vehicles and evacuated'.[14]

Returning on foot, Derevyanko rejoined his company and then led it toward the intersection, over which Russian columns were already passing. The Ukrainians' BMP-1s and BRDM-2 armoured cars were at a serious disadvantage against the autocannons of the BTR-82As, as the commander of the 16th Battalion – Major Volodymyr Logush – described later:

> During the battle, it became clear that the BRDMs we had were ineffective. We all witnessed how when KPVT [machine gun] shoots point-blank range at BTR82A, sparks fly from it, and it drives on. But when the [BTR-82A] was hit by a Corsair [ATGM], it caught fire. But it continued to move and burned down in the area of Krolevets. Their 30mm guns easily pierced [our] BMP-1[s]. And [by comparison], the gun on this vehicle is not manoeuvrable, it just does not have time to react. Despite everything, we did what we could.[15]

As the battle raged, Russian columns continued over the intersection and down the M02. Kashchenko dispatched a battery of D-20 towed 152mm howitzers along the M02 from Krolevets to support the 16th Battalion, but this was run down and destroyed by marauding BTRs before it could even deploy. By now badly mauled and at risk of being destroyed itself, the 16th Battalion broke off the battle and retreated west to Baturyn, travelling via backroads to avoid the Russian spearheads. Meanwhile, with the Russians bearing down on Konotop, Kashchenko rushed the 15th Battalion back from Sumy to defend his HQ. Rapidly completing the 120-kilometre journey, the battalion was in position to block the first Russian attack on Konotop when it fell that evening, knocking out several Russian vehicles. Nevertheless, with Russian elements already bypassing Konotop on their way to Kyiv, Kashchenko knew he would have to withdraw further if his brigade was to survive. Accordingly, the 58th Motorised retreated overnight to Baturyn, where it blew up the M02 bridge over the Seim river, then retreated again to Vertiivka. With this, the 58th Motorised's odyssey was over, and the brigade was able to regroup. Meanwhile, the 2nd GCAA continued on toward Kyiv.

The chaotic aftermath of the battle of Hlukhiv. A knocked out Russian BTR-82A is seen rammed against a burning Ukrainian BMP-1. (Ukrainian social media)

The 90th GTD's Attempted Crossing of the Desna River

Advancing between the invasion axes of the 41st CAA and 2nd GCAA via Semenivka toward Sosnytsya on 24 February 2022, the 90th Guards Tank Division (90th GTD) appears to have been operating semi-independently from either CAA during the invasion, although most of its 80th Tank Regiment and 228th Motor Rifle Regiment were subordinated to the 41st CAA for the advance on Chernihiv.[16] Late on the invasion's first day, the division arrived on the Desna River in the Makoshyne area and began establishing pontoon bridges. Unfortunately for the Russians, the 16th Battalion, having completed its retreat from Hlukhiv, was already opposite this area of the Desna. Watching the bridging operation unfolding, the Ukrainians called down artillery fire on the pontoons, breaking up the Russian attempt. Though the 16th Battalion withdrew shortly after with the rest of the 58th Motorised Brigade to Vertiivka, Ukrainian fire continued to devastate further Russian crossing attempts over the following days, largely via Uragan and Tochka strikes directed by local civilians. The pace of firing was relentless. One Uragan battery crew, their reloader crane broken, manually loaded the 280kg rockets into the launchers using their trouser belts for a hoist. In total, at least nine 90th GTD vehicles were lost in the Makoshyne area, though Ukrainian accounts indicate still heavier casualties.

Table 4: Known composition of the 90th GTD, February–early April 2022

Subunit	Comments
30th Reconnaissance Battalion	
6th Tank Regiment	T-72A/AV/B, BMP-2, Msta-B howitzers
80th Tank Regiment	Largely assigned to 41st CAA; T-72A/B, BMP-2
239th Tank Regiment	T-72AV/B/B, BMP-2, Msta-S self-propelled howitzers
228th Motor Rifle Regiment	Largely assigned to 41st CAA; T-72AV/T-72B/ T-72B3, BTR-82A
440th Self-Propelled Artillery Regiment	BM-21 Grad, 2S3 self-propelled howitzers
288th Anti-Aircraft Missile Battalion	Tor SAM system

1st GTA

Whilst the 2nd GCAA advanced along the M02, the 1st GTA swept toward Kyiv on the H07 highway, which runs parallel to the M02 a hundred kilometres further south.[17] Commanded by Lieutenant General Sergey Kisel, the 1st GTA was considered the cream of the VSRF. Prior to the war, it was garrisoned around Moscow, defending the seat of Putin's power, and was always first in line for testing new equipment, such as the advanced T-90M tank.[18] The invasion objectives assigned to the army reflected this elite reputation. Advancing on an axis stretching from Bilopillya in the north to Velyka Pysarivka in the south, the 1st GTA was to drive 300 kilometres to positions on Kyiv's southeast and secure the bridges over the Dnipro at Kaniv and Cherkasy. Once there, the army would dig in and block any Ukrainian counterattacks aiming to break the encirclement of the capital. The entire movement was to be completed in under a day.

Table 5: Known units assigned to the 1st GTA, February–early April 2022

Unit	Known number of BTGs
2nd Guards Motor Rifle Division	6
4th Guards Tank Division	8
27th Guards Motor Rifle Brigade	3
47th Guards Tank Division	5
96th Reconnaissance Brigade	
288th Artillery Brigade	N/A

Needless to say, the 1st GTA's actual performance fell far short of these expectations. Receiving its orders only hours before the invasion commenced, the army began the war short of supplies, without established communications, and morally unprepared to fight. The southern flank of the army's advance, centred on the vaunted 4th Guards Tank Division (4th GTD), can only be described as a disaster. Arriving in the town of Okhtyrka early on 24 February 2022, an advance column of the division was ambushed and destroyed by the ZSU's 91st Operational Support Regiment and the 3rd Mechanised Battalion, 93rd Mechanised Brigade. Colonel Denys Dykiy, commanding Okhtyrka's defence, knew he had to keep delaying the 4th GTD as long as possible to allow the rest of the 93rd Mechanised Brigade to deploy: its 1st and 2nd Mechanised Battalions still enroute to the front. Blowing bridges outside the town and mining the approaches, the Ukrainians held

A group of 4th GTD T-80Us and T-80BVs seen abandoned in the village of Chupakhikva, east of Okhtyrka. The tanks were lost around 26 February. (93rd Mechanised Brigade)

on, enduring heavy artillery fire from Russian artillery batteries stationed in the neighbouring town of Trostianets, which became the 4th GTD's main base of operations. Russian airstrikes were also a constant feature of the battle. On 26 February at 1355hrs, a pair of Su-34s bombed the base of the 91st Operational Support Regiment, followed by a second pair which struck the base's medical station at 1406hrs in a classic 'double-tap' airstrike. 70 Ukrainian soldiers were killed and scores more injured. Yet, despite such heavy losses, Okhtyrka's defenders continued fighting.

Meanwhile, the 93rd Mechanised Brigade, having now fully arrived, was able to defeat a spearhead of the 4th GTD on the approach to Hadyach around 28 February with support from the 116th TDF Brigade, then begin rolling the Russians back towards the border in vicious battles across the Lebedyn and Okhtryka area. By 15 March, according to its own reports, the 4th GTD had suffered 156 casualties and lost over 120 vehicles, including 71 T-80s.[19] Making matters worse, the division was always short of supplies, with Russian troops forced to loot civilian homes for food.[20] On 23 March, the 93rd Mechanised Brigade began a counteroffensive to liberate Trostianets, subjecting it to heavy artillery fire. Already completely demoralised, the 4th GTD abandoned the settlement without a fight between 25–26 March, leaving behind piles of wrecked and abandoned Russian equipment. Essentially shattered, the division never got within even 250 kilometres of Kyiv.

Aftermath of the 26 February airstrike on the base of the 91st Operational Support Regiment. (Ukrainian social media)

A Ukrainian soldier inspects a Russian KamAZ truck abandoned after the initial fighting inside Okhtyrka, photo circa 28 February. (93rd Mechanised Brigade)

The scene of devastation in central Trostianets after the town's liberation in late March. A pair of Russian 2S19 self-propelled howitzers lie shattered beside a Soviet war memorial. The T-34/85 atop the memorial was reportedly part of the battalion which originally liberated Trostianets from German occupation in 1943. (93rd Mechanised Brigade)

Meanwhile, the northern flank of the 1st GTA's advance performed somewhat better than the south, though it too ended ultimately in failure. Here, the 2nd Guards Motor Rifle Division (2nd GMRD) bypassed Sumy city from the north and south over 24 February and rushed west along the H07 highway. This decision not to secure Sumy from the invasion's outset, based upon Moscow's flawed intelligence assessments that bypassed Ukrainian cities would surrender, would have fatal consequences for Kisel's overall operation. Though the 58th Motorised Brigade's 15th Battalion had withdrawn from Sumy to Konotop by mid-morning, the city remained defended by a considerable Ukrainian force, including the 5th BTG of the 81st Airmobile Brigade (the rest of the brigade remaining in the Kharkiv Oblast) and the local 117th TDF Brigade, which was rapidly constituting itself as armouries emptied and volunteers flocked to enlist. When night fell, confused fighting spread out across the city as the TDF volunteers and paratroopers ambushed passing Russian supply columns in the darkness, destroying at least one. Unfortunately, a 2S1 battery of the 5th BTG was itself ambushed by the TDF in a friendly fire incident, killing several paratroopers.[21] Though the 5th BTG withdrew from Sumy shortly afterwards, this initial resistance had bought enough time for the 117th TDF Brigade to organise its own defences. Over the following days, the brigade defeated a few probing attacks by the 27th Guards Motor Rifle Brigade (27th GMRB) into Sumy, then began to sally out of the city to ambush the passing Russian convoys heading west. Conducted at first with improvised explosive devices and small arms, these ambushes gradually increased in intensity as more weapons were captured and turned against their former owners, eventually including a handful of tanks and IFVs. Some were even conducted in conjunction with airstrikes by PSZSU TB2 attack UAVs, the TDF volunteers communicating directly with their operators via WhatsApp. The net result of these attacks was that Sumy became a kill zone for Russian supply convoys, the city an island of Ukrainian resistance in the very heart of the 1st GTA's rear area. The logistical nightmare this posed would contribute significantly to the failure of the 2nd GMRD's own advance along the H07.

Driving rapidly west, the leading BTGs of the division bypassed the city of Romny overnight between 24–25 February via backroads around Talalaivka and continued toward Pryluky. Here, the Russians encountered a major terrain obstacle. Lying across their path to Kyiv was the vertical stretch of woodland and swamps of the Udai River basin. Pryluky lies in the basin's south where the H07 crosses the Udai, whilst the city of Nizhyn lies to the basin's north, just beside the M02. Unless either Nizhyn or Pryluky could be seized, the only other navigable routes over the basin available to the Russians were the minor roads crossing its centre in the vicinity of the town of Ichnya. Unfortunately for the Russians, Ukrainian units were already in position to block the M02 and the H07. In Nizhyn, the sappers of the 250th Engineering Centre were preparing their defences after an exhausting journey from Kyiv's northwest (having completed the mining of the bridges in the Chernobyl zone). Armed only with RPGs and light weapons, they salvaged some Second World War-vintage 14.5mm anti-tank rifles and an 82mm mortar from the local museum to bolster their arsenal. Meanwhile, in the path of the 2nd GMRD at Pryluky, the 54th Separate Reconnaissance Battalion readied its own defences, emptying the city's arsenal of all available anti-tank weapons. Both units were small and without armour, but they were determined.

A T-90A of the 27th GMRB burns after being ambushed by the TDF outside of Sumy, 27 February 2022. (ZSU)

The Culmination of the 2nd GMRD's Attack

Late on 25 February, a BTG from the 2nd GMRD attempted to advance across the Udai basin north of Pryluky.[22] However, its logistics were already exhausted after the 200+ kilometre journey from Sumy and it only took some 120mm mortar fire from the 54th Reconnaissance Battalion for the BTG to halt in Kolinsky and dig in. Here it remained for the following days, apparently out of fuel. Resupply columns never arrived, having likely been destroyed in the vicinity of Sumy. The BTG was psychologically exhausted too, its officers even attempting to ask the 54th Battalion for a ceasefire so it could withdraw, an offer refused with more mortar fire. The rest of the 2nd GMRD was also suffering badly from logistics issues, and it was only on 27 February that more of its BTGs arrived in the area. Driving down the H07, two BTGs from the division's 1st Tank Regiment approached Pryluky from the east. Standing in the way of this onslaught was just a 44-strong detachment from the 54th Battalion and local TDF. However, this group had carefully positioned their ambush where the H07 bridges the Udai River, near the so-called Mi'lky mountain, a natural choke point.

As the leading Russian element crossed the bridge, the Ukrainians opened fire with Corsair ATGMs from the column's flanks, destroying several vehicles. A T-72B3M platoon attempted to charge the Ukrainian positions but was destroyed after two of its tanks were hit by Corsairs and the third bogged in the mud beside the highway, the crew abandoning it. With the Russian column now halted, the Ukrainians directed airstrikes from Su-25s and TB2 attack UAVs along its length. Further along the H07 at Sribne, another group of TDF attacked the rear of the column, setting several trucks ablaze.

Their morale broken; the remaining Russians fled, abandoning much of their equipment in the process. In total, the 54th Battalion captured at least nine T-72B3Ms, 17 trucks, and an Osa-AKM SAM battery in the aftermath. Another 11 Russian vehicles were destroyed. This attack was the last concerted effort of the 2nd GRMD to push west, the division paralysed by the spiralling logistics situation in its rear area. For the same reason, the wider 1st GTA would get no significant elements across the Udai basin.[23] Once earmarked to deliver Putin's counterstroke against NATO, the army had been stopped in its tracks by a handful of Ukrainian brigades and scattered support units.

The 1st Tank Regiment T-72B3M bogged down and abandoned beside the H07 after the platoon it was part of attempted to charge Ukrainian positions at the Mi'lky mountain, 27 February 2022. (OC North)

10
THE BREAKTHROUGHS OF THE 2ND GCAA AND 41ST CAA

Whilst the 1st GTA's attack against the Udai basin had failed, the *GenStab* had a second hope in the form of the 2nd GCAA. Unlike Kisel, Gurov had maintained much of his army's combat power over the journey from the border, having successfully swept aside the 58th Motorised Brigade. He also enjoyed a comparatively better logistics situation, though bad weather and terribly poor road-security for his supply columns still made going difficult. After an initial attempt to break through the basin in the vicinity of Nizhyn over 25–26 February was foiled by the 250th Engineering Centre, TDF forces, and Uragan strikes,[1] Gurov instead directed his forward units south to where the beleaguered BTG of the 2nd GMRD was still holding out north of Pryluky in Kolinsky. On 27 February, Ukrainian scouts of the 54th Battalion watched in horror as several massive Russian columns passed through Kolinsky on their way west. The 2nd GCAA was crossing the basin.[2]

Now clear of the obstacle, Gurov's forces rejoined the H07 and rushed on toward Kyiv. Their advance was ruthless. Arriving in the neighbouring villages of Stariy Bykiv and Novyi Bykiv, Russian soldiers immediately rounded up six men, tortured them, and executed them.[3] Continuing along the highway, the Russian spearheads had reached the village of Peremoha by evening on 28 February. Here, soldiers of the 15th MRB tortured and executed another five men who were part of the local TDF.[4] These were not isolated cases. Kidnappings, torture, and summary executions would become a common feature of life for Ukrainians in the occupied settlements along the H07.[5]

Though the 2nd GCAA had made good progress along the highway, it was beginning to receive artillery fire as it came within range of the Ukrainian batteries defending Kyiv. These guns were supporting the outer ring of Syrskyi's defences on the eastern side of the capital, held primarily by the 72nd Mechanised Brigade's 1st and 3rd Mechanised Battalions. The specific subunit facing the approaching Russian columns on the H07 was 3rd Company, 1st Mechanised Battalion, defending the village of Rusaniv.[6] The settlement was an excellent defensive position. The Trubizh river runs vertically along its western side, presenting a natural barrier against the Russian advance. Only one major bridge carried the H07 over the river, and this had already been demolished by the 3rd Company. Its fallen span was well covered by their dug-in positions among the houses. On 1 March, artillery began falling on Rusaniv as a leading CTG of the 21st Motor Rifle Brigade (21st MRB) approached down the H07 from Peremoha, just three kilometres away. Apparently unaware that the bridge was destroyed, the first Russian AFVs were within 100 metres of it when they were hit by Javelin ATGMs from across the river, exploding into fireballs. A quadcopter UAV operator within 3rd Company described the battle in his journal:

I have the drone lift off, and we fly from the houses. On the frontline, mines and shells periodically explode around us. We see an assault group of nine units with a couple of tanks and BMPs. We are in the air, and we aim our artillery and

A T-72B3 from the 21st MRB after being hit by a Javelin outside of Rusaniv on 1 March 2022. (ZSU)

correct their fire. Direct hits, and the enemy is on fire! The orcs' attack is choked off.[7]

Its nose bloodied, the 21st MRB reorganised for another assault the following day, this time approaching using a small wood for cover rather than along the highway. Regardless, as the attacking force concentrated in the wood, it was spotted by the 3rd Company's UAVs and dispersed again with artillery fire. This would prove the last Russian assault against Rusaniv for some time: the 21st MRB's staging areas in Peremoha were themselves beginning to receive artillery fire, knocking out several vehicles and degrading the brigade's ability to re-attack. With the rapid resupply of fresh quadcopters to replace losses, the 3rd Company's UAVs were eventually able to direct this harassing fire around the clock. In return, Russian howitzers and MRLSs continued to bombard Rusaniv, but this fire failed to dislodge the Ukrainians from their cellars and dug outs. Seeing an opportunity to regain the initiative, the 21st MRB instead attempted to bypass Rusaniv by crossing the Trubizh further south at Baryshivka on 3 March. However, met by Ukrainian SOF and local TDF volunteers, this attack also failed after the town's bridges were blown.[8] Two Russian BMPs were cut off on the wrong side of the river and captured. The 2nd GCAA's advance west was stalling.

For Gurov, the situation was indeed looking unfavourable. The roads through the centre of the Udai basin were small and of a poor quality, straining the logistics of his army's advance. Making matters worse, the 250th Engineering Centre at Nizhyn and the 54th Reconnaissance Battalion at Pryluky were beginning to raid into the basin itself to ambush his supply convoys and mine the roads. At first, these operations were of a small-scale, relying on improvisation and bravery to succeed. Lieutenant Colonel Serhii Burkovskyi, deputy commander of the 250th Engineering Centre, later recalled:

> At first, we didn't have live mines. At that time, there were no combat units in our staff, so there was no provision for the storage of engineering ammunition. We made mine barriers from training mines. In terms of size and the fuse, they do not differ from combat ones, only they have a white stripe, which we erased. But, they have sand inside. We also combined training mines with tree debris and used them as a way to mislead the enemy. The occupiers stopped in front of them, and we fired at them from ambushes.[9]

Nonetheless, as more weapons arrived from Kyiv and others were captured, Ukrainian raiding and ambushing across the Udai basin grew in intensity and effectiveness. By mid-March, the 250th Engineering Centre was using layered minefields of both remotely operated and 'dumb' mines to catch out Russian convoys. Meanwhile, the 54th Reconnaissance Battalion employed roving mortar teams and even a pair of captured T-72B3Ms for its own raids deep into the basin. Local villagers helped by spotting targets and providing food and shelter to the raiding parties. The 2nd GCAA's supply convoys, usually escorted by vehicles no heavier than BMPs or BTRs, stood little chance against such attacks.

Despite this poor logistical situation, Gurov was actually receiving more units to push through the basin: around 2 March, the 90th GTD began arriving in the Talalaivka area, south of Nizhyn.[10] How the division had managed to cross the Desna after the repeated Uragan and Tochka strikes on its crossings in the Makoshyne area

The remains of a Russian column ambushed by the 250th Engineering Centre. (ZSU Support Forces)

A T-72A of the 6th Tank Regiment, 90th GTD, abandoned south of Nizhyn after an ambush by the 250th Engineering Centre, circa 2 March 2022. (ZSU Support Forces)

remains a mystery, but it seems possible that it was finally able to force a crossing in this area, or else find an unseen one further east. Regardless, the division's arrival gave Gurov a new opportunity to strike at Kyiv from the north-east rather than the easterly direction his army was currently pursuing on the H07. Negotiating the minor roads running south-west from Talalaivka, the division advanced almost unopposed toward Kyiv over 3–4 March. As it happened, it would be the last hope of reaching the capital for all the Russian forces on Kyiv's east.

The 41st CAA Crosses the Desna

After the destruction of Shchotkin's company inside Chernihiv during the *Epitsentr* battle on 26 February, Ryzhkov had continued with his original plan to bypass the city and push the 41st CAA on to Kyiv.[11] Not wishing to let the *Epitsentr* defeat go unavenged however, on 27 February a joint strike using an Iskander-M and artillery was ordered against the Ukrainian positions outside the supermarket. Lieutenant Colonel Linkov, emerging in the aftermath of the Iskander landing, recalled the scene:

> I was wounded in the head. The gunner's leg was broken by the shockwave. I was already lying on the ground, and I saw the tank crews begin to get out, and that's when the artillery began its work. The 152 calibre was working, and the tank of the Hero of Ukraine was hit right in front of my eyes. Oleksiy Senyuk [was] the tank commander. I already lifted my head. I saw the tank was on fire. [Senyuk] shouts 'I am burning!'. Then, the ammunition set detonated, and he was thrown out of the tank. That was it.[12]

Chief Sergeant Senyuk would be posthumously awarded the Hero of Ukraine for his actions during the previous three days fighting. The 27 February strike was one of the first of many similar artillery, missile, and aviation attacks levelled against Chernihiv, typically directed by the numerous Russian informants and SRGs inside the city. Colonel Khoda later stated there were as many as 500 such agents operating simultaneously within Chernihiv at the war's outset. The intelligence this network provided was often mixed, leading to strikes equally deadly to civilians and military personnel alike, a situation further worsened by the VKS's almost exclusive use of unguided bombs. For example, on 3 March, Russian informants betrayed the position of a TDF headquarters located in School No.18 on Haharina Street. Shortly after 1215hrs, a Su-35 hit the school with six 250kg FAB-250 bombs, killing upwards of 50 TDF volunteers and civilians inside the building, along with several others nearby. Simultaneously, a Su-34 dropped at least four 500kg FAB-500 bombs on apartment buildings along Chornovola Street. There were no military targets here, just civilians queuing at a pharmacy and a breadline. 47 people were killed and scores more injured.[13]

Whilst traumatic for Chernihiv's population, these airstrikes were of limited military value against the dug-in and dispersed Ukrainian positions around the city, even if there were exceptions such as the School No.18 bombing. In turn, the sorties, flown during daylight and at low level, were exceptionally dangerous for VKS strike aircraft. On 5 March, around 1120hrs, Su-34 Bort 24 was shot down over Chernihiv under a fusillade of fire from small arms, truck mounted ZU-23-2s, and Igla MANPADs of the 1st Tank Brigade.[14] Later that same day, Su-34 Bort 26 was shot down south-east of the city. Of the Russian crews, only Major Alexander Krasnoyartsev piloting Bort 24 survived. Such losses were hard felt amongst the already small pool

Above: A Su-34, laden with eight FAB-500M-62 bombs, lifts off for a combat sortie, circa 8 March 2022 (Russian Ministry of Defence)

Left: A fireball rises from the crash site of Krasnoyartsev's Su-34. (Ukrainian social media)

of Russian combat pilots,[15] with some reportedly refusing to fly further raids behind Ukrainian lines altogether. In response, the VKS switched largely to night raids. Whilst these proved less costly in terms of aircraft, they were also significantly less accurate, leading to still more civilian casualties.

As Chernihiv was bombarded, the 41st CAA continued pushing around the flanks of the city. Still suffering from morale, communications, and logistics issues, this task was far from easy for Ryzhkov's units. Initially, several attempts were made to assault down the E95 highway running just west of Chernihiv. However, each attack was halted by determined Ukrainian infantry dug into the woods outside of Kyinka, which overlook the intersection of the E95 and P56 highways. This group was drawn from the local military commissariat and was armed with only four RPGs and small arms, but they could also count on the support of a few tanks from the 1st Tank Brigade. These tanks employed shoot-and-scoot tactics, giving the Russians the false impression they were facing a much larger force, frustrating their efforts. In the course of the fighting, Ryzhkov's deputy – Major General Andrey Sukhovetsky – was shot dead by a Ukrainian sniper on 28 February. Though the exact circumstances of his death remain unknown, it seems possible his location was betrayed by the compromised Era communications system.

Despite these setbacks, on the same day the 41st CAA was finally able to flank Chernihiv by driving through the village of Mykhailo-Kotsiubynske, located eight kilometres further west of Kyinka. Spearheading the advance here were several BTGs from the 55th Mountain Motor Rifle Brigade (55th MMRB) and 74th GMRB, driving in a column some 258 vehicles long. This concentration of equipment did not go unnoticed however, as a local security guard transmitted the column's coordinates to Ukrainian artillery, an act for which he was later executed by the Russians. The resulting artillery strike destroyed several logistics trucks but, undeterred, the column continued on toward the village of Shestovystya and the Desna River beyond. Arriving in Shestovystya around 1100hrs, the Russians immediately occupied the Lan farm on its western outskirts as a forward HQ for the coming river crossing. The account of the farm's owner, Oleksiy Luhina, conveys the urgency with which the Russians were pressing their advance:

> My brother Serhiy was in the garage on the farm at the time. They entered, pointed a gun barrel at his abdomen, and ordered him to show what was there. They found 40 cubic meters of diesel fuel, brought over their tankers, pumped it all out in an hour or two, and left.[16]

Though local civilians constantly informed on the Russians' actions, the pace of their advance had still taken OC North by surprise, and the grouping in Shestovystya was able to establish a pontoon bridge and cross a whole BTG over the Desna before it could be decisively engaged. The bridge did not survive long enough, however, for further BTGs to cross, as a direct hit from a Tochka soon ripped it to pieces, which were swept downstream. With this strike, the 41st CAA's envelopment of Chernihiv was halted, if only temporarily.

On 3 March, Ryzhkov established a new pontoon bridge in the Shestovystya area. Again, the Ukrainians struck the bridge with missiles and artillery fire, but this time it refused to sink. Unlike the previous bridge, this model was a special foam-impregnated version originally meant for the Strategic Missile Forces and was thus highly resilient to damage.[17] Braving the Ukrainian fire, the Russians rushed the BTGs of the 55th MMRB and 74th GMRB across the bridge and began advancing eastward in a bid to encircle Chernihiv, occupying the villages of Ladynka, Zolontynka and Yahidne. Facing this advance were the 58th Motorised Brigade's 15th and 16th Battalions, having been dispatched from Vertiivka to hold open Chernihiv's lines of communication and prevent the 41st CAA breaking through toward Kyiv.

As the fighting raged, Major General Nikoliuk himself arrived on the frontline, intent on seeing the situation with his own eyes. Leading a vehicle of the 15th Battalion in his SUV, Nikoliuk drove out toward Yahidne to conduct a personal reconnaissance of the Russian positions. In the process, the small convoy was ambushed, with Nikoliuk's driver being shot dead and another of his escorts wounded. Leading his men, the general returned fire using an AK-74 and disposable RPGs until autocannon fire from a Russian BTR-82A forced the Ukrainian group to retreat. The following day, Nikoliuk led a successful raid against Yahidne to recover the body of his driver, destroying a Tiger MRAP in the process. Whilst in retrospect it might seem irresponsible, even foolhardy, for such a senior commander to lead tactical actions, it must be remembered that the collapse of the SAT-KA communications system meant OC North's units were already largely fighting according to their own devices, a situation only eased as more StarLink terminals arrived throughout March. Nikoliuk's visible bravery also raised the morale of his subordinates and won their trust, in the general's own words: 'In the army, everyone is equal – both generals and soldiers. Before you send a soldier to his death, you also must go there first … Then, accordingly, you have the moral right to say to him: go there. If you've already been there yourself'.[18]

After the raid, Nikoliuk attempted to keep the Russians from advancing further east by establishing a defensive position opposite Yahidne on the junction of the E95 and M01 highways, but this was shelled and bombed so heavily that eventually he was forced to retreat. On 5 March, the Russians continued their push to envelop Chernihiv, attacking up the M01 toward the village of Ivanivka with a BTG of the 90th GTD. The settlement was held by just 50 Ukrainian infantry and five BMPs from the 15th Battalion. Approaching from all directions and supported by intensive artillery fire, the Russians were able to break into the village and knock out all five of the Ukrainian

A T-72B3 that fell into the Desna during the 28 February Tochka-U strike on the Russian pontoon bridge outside Shestovystya was recovered in the summer of 2023 by Ukraine's State Special Transport Service. Reportedly, it was restored and put into service with the ZSU. (State Special Transport Service of Ukraine)

BMPs. Overwhelmed, the surviving Ukrainian infantry managed to escape encirclement and retreat to friendly lines. Continuing up the highway, the 90th GTD's BTG then attempted to take the village of Kolychvika but was repulsed. The fighting had taken a heavy toll on the 15th Battalion: in one company just two of the original 10 BRDMs were left, whilst the battalion's mortars had worn out their barrels from constant firing. Despite this, the battalion continued resisting Russian attacks, including a few raids by Tiger MRAPs of the 55th MMRB against its positions in the villages of Skorinets' and Krasne, which blocked the way to Kyiv down the E95. Besides these raids however, Ryzhkov did not attempt an attack in this direction yet. Chernihiv's encirclement had to be completed first.

To accomplish this, Ryzhkov ordered the 90th GTD's BTG to attack Kolychivka again. Chernihiv's remaining supply route to the rest of Ukraine ran through this village, giving it a vital importance. Success here would complete the encirclement of the city, freeing up units of the 41st CAA to join the 2nd GCAA's advance on Kyiv. Trapped inside the ring meanwhile, the 1st Tank Brigade could be bled out and eventually destroyed. However, Kolychivka's significance was not lost on OC North either, and many Ukrainian units were in position to defend it, including elements of the 21st Separate Rifle Battalion, 2nd National Guard Regiment (having arrived in Chernihiv from Shostka in early March), and 58th Motorised Brigade, all supported by the artillery of the 1st Tank Brigade. Nikoliuk personally commanded the village's defence.

On 7 March, the Russian attack began with preparatory fire from artillery and tanks, but this proved largely ineffective against the dug-in Ukrainian infantry. The four Ukrainian tanks defending the village (T-64BVs from the 58th Motorised Brigade) also went unscathed by constantly changing their positions. Apparently confident the defenders had been suppressed, the Russian BTG drove in a column directly up Kolychivka's central street. Emerging from cover, the Ukrainian infantry opened fire with NLAWs and RPGs, knocking out several Russian vehicles and causing the rest to flee. At the column's head, a pair of T-72s continued straight through the ambush and drove northwards toward Chernihiv, but soon became immobilised on a minefield. The four Ukrainian tanks advanced to dispatch them. One Russian crew sensibly abandoned their tank, but the second crew continued to fight, firing their tank's main gun continuously. Major Maksym Khrebtov, commanding the Ukrainian tank group, held back in the hope this crew would surrender once they had exhausted their ammunition, but the Russians refused to go quietly and began shooting at Ukrainian infantry with their co-axial machine gun. Infuriated, Khrebtov ordered forward one of his T-64s. The Ukrainian tank's first armour-piercing fin-stabilised discarding sabot (APFSDS) round struck the T-72 in the turret ring, before a second shot with a high-explosive anti-tank (HEAT) round blew the turret off entirely. With these final shots, the battle of Kolychivka came to an end.[19]

Despite the defeat, the 41st CAA continued its efforts to isolate Chernihiv, aiming to instead create a wider encirclement through the villages of Lukashivka and Baklanova Muraviika. However, time was running out for Ryzhkov. The supply lines supporting his bridgehead on the Desna were still under constant fire. For instance, on 8 March, a convoy of 14 fuel and ammunition trucks was destroyed in a single Ukrainian strike on Shestovytsya, likely using an Uragan or a Tochka. Indeed, the shelling of this village became so severe that the Russians were forced to evacuate their HQ on Lan farm shortly afterwards, already littered as it was with burnt out equipment. Meanwhile, Ukrainian partisans continued to pick off supply columns deep in the army's rear areas. Nevertheless, Ryzhkov – having already kicked and dragged his units this far – remained intent on finishing the encirclement, setting his sights on Lukashivka.

The Battle of Lukashivka

Like Ivanivka, Lukashivka was defended by a comparatively small Ukrainian force: 100–200 infantry from the 21st Separate Rifle Battalion's 2nd Company and 58th Motorised Brigade's 16th Battalion, supported by four BRDMs and a pair of the brigade's T-64BVs.[20] Their defence was centred on a farm complex on the village's southern outskirts, which had already been subjected to constant artillery, Grad, and Uragan fire over the proceeding days.

A still from a video filmed during the battle of Kolychivka, showing an abandoned Russian BTR-82A(M) illuminated by burning housing. The vehicle was later pressed into Ukrainian service. (National Guard of Ukraine)

The wreckage of the stubborn Russian T-72 destroyed at the close of the battle. (ZSU)

Rescue workers examine the devastated remains of the Russian supply column destroyed in Shestovytsya on 8 March 2022. A rusted APFSDS round stands upright in the centre of the road. (Ukrainian government)

This bombardment was only a prelude though. At 0700hrs on 9 March, the Ukrainians heard the roar of tank engines approaching across the fields. Ryzhkov had tasked a BTG of the 74th GMRB for the attack, further reinforced with elements of the 90th GTD.[21] In total, the force numbered some 36 tanks and more than 70 other AFVs, dwarfing the Ukrainian defenders. Approaching from multiple directions, the Russian attack quickly overwhelmed the forward Ukrainian positions, forcing the survivors back toward the farm. Brothers Roman and Leonid Butusin, ethnic Russians but soldiers in the 58th Motorised Brigade, continued fighting within the village, destroying a BMP-2. *Viking*, another member of the brigade, recalled their fate: 'The brothers fought to their last. Their armour was a mess of rags and plates – broken plates. In each of their helmets there were several bullet holes. When we found them, the boys were lying one with the other, as if they had hugged in their last seconds'.[22]

Completely outnumbered, the two Ukrainian tanks were both destroyed, though their crews seemingly survived. At the farm, the Ukrainian infantry fought from the outbuildings and a small ditch circling its perimeter, but these offered little protection from the direct tank and autocannon fire. Volodymyr Haidaichuk, a soldier of the 21st Separate Rifle Battalion, was wounded by a tank round and dragged into the shelter of the farm's chicken coop by his comrades, where he was buried under falling rubble, dug up, and buried again as further tank rounds obliterated the concrete structure. Miraculously, Haidaichuk survived the ordeal and was carried away from Lukashivka by a tank crew. By now, the farm was almost entirely encircled and groups of Ukrainian infantry began attempting to breakout and escape. One group of 60 had barely made it beyond the farm when they encountered a column of Russian trucks driving through the middle of the battle in apparent confusion. Several were soon destroyed, though, in the process, the 2nd Company's commander was shot in the head by a machine gun and killed. The situation looked bleak for those trying escape: the farm was surrounded by open fields, easily dominated by the Russian tanks. Fortunately, at the critical moment a heavy snowfall began, allowing many Ukrainians to escape to Baklanova Muraviika and the village of Budy.

Not all were so fortunate, however. At least 20 Ukrainians had been killed, and several more were taken prisoner. Others were sheltered by the locals and eventually made it back to friendly lines, but a few were caught by Russian patrols in the process and shot. The Russian BTG commander, known only by his callsign *Titan*, tortured a group of nine Ukrainian POWs with a baseball bat before they were loaded into an MT-LB armoured personnel carrier and sent toward the Russian rear. Fortunately for them, the MT-LB hit a mine on its way to Ivanivka, allowing them to escape. When the Russian crew trapped inside the burning vehicle asked them for help, the Ukrainians closed the vehicle's hatches on them.

Whilst the Russians had won the battle of Lukashivka, they still had to take Baklanova Muraviika beyond to cut off the Ukrainian supply route into Chernihiv. Unfortunately for them, this village lay on raised ground, allowing its defenders to dominate the surrounding fields. Nikoliuk had concentrated numerous ATGM teams and MT-12 Rapira towed anti-tank guns from the 1st Tank Brigade and 58th Motorised Brigade for this exact purpose, and the initial Russian probes were quickly blunted. Aware that the encirclement effort was faltering, Ryzhkov tried to cut the supply route further south by taking Budy, directing repeated airstrikes and artillery barrages against the elements of the 16th Battalion defending the village. However, the Ukrainians held firm, and a final effort by the 74th GMRB ran aground when two of its T-72B3s hit mines on the road into the village. Exhausted, the 41st CAA had been fought to a standstill just kilometres from completing its encirclement of Chernihiv.

The Last Gasp

As the 41st CAA was finally halted, the 90th GTD's own attack toward Kyiv was disintegrating.[23] Following its rapid advance from the Udai basin, the division had begun encountering Ukrainian resistance on 5 March as it bypassed the city of Bobrovystya, lying some 60 kilometres north-east of Kyiv. The only Ukrainian unit in this area was a single company group detached from the 16th Battalion, but this alone was enough to inflict several casualties on the division's columns as they struggled through the soft ground either side of the city. Among the Russian losses were two completely intact Tor SAM systems, left abandoned after they had bogged down in the mud. This event can be seen as symbolic of the poor morale situation across the whole division. Indeed, the 16th Battalion's soldiers soon noticed a marked difference in the combat ability of the 90th GTD compared to the 2nd GCAA units they had faced at the war's outset, or those of the 41st CAA they'd been fighting around Chernihiv. Whilst these formations had been aggressive, the units of the 90th were skittish in their behaviour, rarely returning fire when attacked and often appearing to concern themselves more with looting than fighting. This poor performance of the division can be explained in part by its status as a second-rate formation, reflected by the presence of conscripts inside its BTGs and the dated equipment it possessed, including obsolescing T-72As.[24]

Despite these issues, the division's commander – Colonel Ramil Rakhmatulovich Ibattulin – continued pressing his units forward, possibly under pressure from Putin himself. On 6 March, the division crossed the border of the Kyiv Oblast in the vicinity of the Trubizh railway station and advanced toward the villages of Zavorychi and Mokrets on the Trubizh River. Here it again took losses when it was ambushed by a Ukrainian KORD team.[25] In the chaos, a group of vehicles from the division's 6th Tank Regiment sank into the soft ground along the riverbank, becoming sitting ducks for the KORD team's RPGs. A Tor SAM system and a T-72 were destroyed, whilst another seven T-72s were abandoned by their crews. Undeterred by this minor disaster, Ibattulin continued pressing westward toward the E95 highway, which offered a direct route to the heart of Kyiv. Though the division's advance was slowed by the maze of villages and woods it had to negotiate in this area, its appearance still caused great concern at Syrskyi's HQ, and elements of the 10th SSO "Shaman" Battalion, the Carpathian Sich Special Police Battalion, and the Kyiv Azov Regiment were rushed to reinforce Kyiv's north-eastern defences.[26] These units joined the positions of 3rd Mechanised Battalion, 72nd Mechanised Brigade, already entrenched around the suburb of Brovary in the path of any Russian advance down the E95.[27]

Attempting to slow down the 90th GTD's advance still further, on 8 March four helicopters from the 11th Army Aviation Brigade were dispatched to strike the division as it approached the village of Bohadanivka near the E95. Unfortunately, the otherwise routine sortie quickly became a tragedy after the flight ran into dense Russian air defences, losing two Mi-8s and an Mi-24. The remaining Mi-24 managed to limp back to base. Of the downed crews, only Major Ivan Papalyashkin and Captain Ivan Chich survived the crash of their Mi-8, becoming POWs. Having brushed aside the Ukrainian helicopters, the 90th GTD reached Bohadanivka around 1130hrs. After weeks of fighting and hundreds of losses, the stage was finally set for a Russian breakthrough attempt into Kyiv's east.

One of the Tor SAM systems operated by the 90th GTD's 288th Anti-Aircraft Battalion and subsequently abandoned, seen being inspected by civilians in northern Bobrovystya on 5 March 2022. (Bobrovystya Territorial Community)

The Battle of Brovary

Around midday on 9 March, the division began its attack down the E95. A BTG from the 6th Tank Regiment spearheaded the advance, led by the regiment's own commander – Colonel Andrey Zakharov.[28] Unfortunately for him, he was driving straight into a trap. The 3rd Mechanised Battalion had carefully organised a multi-layered ambush along the highway. Closest to the approaching Russians was an NLAW team concealed amongst woodland outside the village of Zalissya. Next were a pair of Stugna-P ATGM crews positioned on the flanks of the highway. Finally, there was the primary Ukrainian ambush position in the village of Skybyn, with RPG teams dug-in amongst the houses and a Corsair ATGM crew enfilading down the street. As a *coup de grace*, Ukrainian artillery was pre-sighted onto the expected kill zone.

The ambush went off almost exactly as planned. The NLAW team hit a T-72A, which continued rolling down the highway ablaze as Russian dismounts spilled out of their BMPs. Collecting themselves following this first loss, the BTG moved off again in a long column

One of the seven bogged T-72s abandoned by the 6th Tank Regiment in Zavorychi. This example is a T-72A, as distinguishable by the racks of smoke launchers mounted on the turret front. (16th Battalion, 58th Motorised Brigade)

Stills from a video taken by a Ukrainian UAV, showing the NLAW team's ambush against the 6th Tank Regiment BTG just south of Zalissya. In the first still, an NLAW missile detonates directly above a T-72A. The second still captures the Russian reaction to the ambush, with the bright white line on the left of the image marking the path of a 30mm tracer shell fired by one of the BMP-2s. (ZSU)

of vehicles. On cue, the Stugna teams opened fire, picking off more AFVs. It was at this point that Zakharov was wounded so severely he was initially thought dead by his own subordinates, possibly when an R-149MA1 command and staff vehicle accompanying the BTG was destroyed.[29] Leaderless, the Russian column continued in confusion toward Skybyn. Waiting for the right moment, the Ukrainians allowed the leading Russian tank platoon to pass well into the village before springing their ambush, catching the BTG as it crammed itself onto the main street in a four-lane-wide column. Artillery rounds from the 43rd Artillery Brigade and 72nd Mechanised Brigade exploded among the concentration of personnel and vehicles, whilst the Corsair picked off individual targets from the front. At this critical moment, the crew of a crippled T-72AV from the leading platoon had the presence of mind to begin deploying their smoke screen, which soon obscured much of the Russian column. Seizing this opportunity to escape, the BTG turned around under continued artillery and ATGM fire and fled back towards the north. At least six AFVs had been destroyed and another three abandoned. Zakharov was rushed back to Bohadanivka, but he died before he could be operated on. One Russian soldier lamented afterwards to an onlooking local civilian: 'We no longer have a commander. We don't know what to do: go forward or go back'.[30]

The defeat effectively paralysed the 90th GTD, and no attacks any larger than platoon-strength would be launched toward Brovary again. Demoralised and vengeful, soldiers from the division instead contented themselves with looting houses and terrorising the local population. At least two civilians were raped and another three killed during the occupation of Bohadanivka alone.[31] Putin's final hope for reaching Kyiv's east had ended only in depravity and failure.

Stills from another video filmed by a Ukrainian UAV of the Skybyn ambush itself. In the first still, the leading Russian tank platoon advances through the village. In the distance, a vehicle from the BTG's main body is already ablaze up the highway. The second still captures the BTG as it turns around and begins retreating. The explosion and distinctive wispy smoke trail beside the TOS-1A heavy flamethrower system is characteristic of the detonation of a HEAT warhead, which produces a high-speed 'jet' of deformed metal to penetrate its target. In this case, the vehicle was hit by a Corsair ATGM. (Azov)

11
THE TIDE TURNS IN THE EAST

The dual failures to reach Brovary and to complete the encirclement of Chernihiv marked the culmination point of the three combined armies arrayed to Kyiv's east. Though attacks continued at the tactical level in the hope of clawing some kind of result presentable to Putin, the Russians had lost the operational initiative. Several BTGs had been badly mauled, and others completely destroyed. By mid-March, the 1st GTA alone had endured at least 410 casualties and lost 312 vehicles, including 115 tanks.[1] Moreover, Nizhyn, Pryluky, and Sumy remained islands of Ukrainian resistance deep in the Russian rear, interdicting the supply columns and reinforcements heading west. For instance, during the night of 12 March, a column of vehicles from the 90th GTD's 6th Tank Regiment and 228th Motor Rifle Regiment was ambushed by the 250th Engineering Centre near Nizhyn and destroyed, with the Ukrainians capturing several vehicles.[2] Whilst the Russians grew weaker, the Ukrainian units east of Kyiv were only gaining strength as new reinforcements arrived. Significant among these was the 8th Mountain Assault Battalion, 10th Mountain Brigade, which had spent the previous days defending the Boryspil and Vasylkiv airfields,[3] and the famous 1st Assault Company 'Da Vinci Wolves', operating at the time as a joint UAV reconnaissance unit and D-20 howitzer battery.[4] Meanwhile, StarLink terminals, Stinger MANPADs, and a multitude of anti-tank systems were also beginning to arrive in significant numbers as Western aid reached the battlefield. With this new combat power, the Ukrainians prepared to counterattack.

The Battle of Rudnyt'ske
As with the initial counterattacks on the western side of Kyiv, the first Ukrainian counterattack in the east proved a difficult undertaking. The 8th Mountain Assault Battalion arrived in the vicinity of Rusaniv as the 72nd Mechanised Brigade's 1st Mechanised Battalion continued to hold off half-hearted attacks by the 2nd GCAA in this area. Instead of attacking the Russians directly in Peremoha, the 8th Battalion was ordered to attack into the Russian flank and storm the village of Rudynts'ke, located six kilometres south-east of Peremoha, below the H07. Preliminary reconnaissance established the settlement was defended by a Russian BTG comprised of a company of T-72B3s and a battalion of BMP-mounted infantry (likely from the 21st MRB), so the battalion commander decided to conduct a dismounted attack using infantry groups, rather than risk a tank battle in which his own BMPs would fare poorly against the Russian armour. The operation began early on 10 March, with the battalion using light vehicles to reach Rudynt'ske, then advancing on foot through the woods on the village's east. The Ukrainian infantry sections were festooned with a variety of Western and Soviet anti-tank launchers, and it was hoped the unexpected direction of approach would take the defenders by surprise. Unfortunately, the Russians were prepared, and the attack quickly began to falter as the advancing sections came under machine gun fire. Some soldiers made it inside the village, but they found that most of the Russian infantry was staying in cover whilst the Russian tanks shelled any Ukrainians caught in the open at close range. Having already sustained two killed and several wounded in this manner, the battalion commander decided not to press the attack further and gave the order to retreat. After returning to their staging point in the town of Baryshivka, the battalion came under fire again that night when an Iskander-M landed just 30 metres away from their base, wounding an accompanying journalist.[5]

The defeat at Rudynt'ske temporarily halted the Ukrainian counteroffensive in the H07 direction, but in the meantime their artillery continued to shell the Russian units arrayed along the highway, destroying them vehicle by vehicle. Particularly effective in this task were the D-20s of 1st Assault Company 'Da Vinci Wolves'. Operating against the villages of Nova Basan and Novyi Bykiv from around 12 March, the Wolves caught one Russian Msta-B howitzer

A still from a UAV video filming the assault on Rudynt'ske on 10 March 2022. Two Russian tanks are visible dominating the village's main street. Beside the church, infantry take cover. (Ukrainian Internet)

Ukrainian soldiers help carry one of their wounded away during the retreat from Rudynt'ske. (Marian Kushnir)

battery in the open and burned dozens more trucks and AFVs.[6] In another instance on 15 March, the company was observing Novyi Bykiv using a UAV when they saw a Russian Buk battery open fire on a Ukrainian MiG-29 passing overhead. The jet – Bort 15 White of the 40th Tactical Aviation Brigade – was hit, but the pilot managed to crash-land his stricken aircraft onto a field outside of Nova Basan and seemingly escaped alive. Seeking revenge, the Wolves quickly identified the position of the offending Buk and, within five minutes of it shooting down the MiG, began shelling it. The battery's fire control radar was destroyed, and the rest of its firing units badly damaged. By the time the D-20s had ceased firing, a further 10–15 Russian vehicles were wrecked.[7] The drone-spotted Ukrainian artillery fire eventually became so oppressive that the officers of the 2nd GCAA reportedly began issuing cigarette cartons as rewards to any soldier who downed a UAV.[8] Other Russian responses were less cheerful. Civilians suspected of spotting for the Ukrainian artillery were detained, abused, and frequently shot.[9] In Novyi Bykiv, 20 men were confined to a small boiler room and tortured, three of whom were eventually executed.[10] Nevertheless, the shelling continued. Slowly but surely, the 2nd GCAA was being bled out.

A still from a video showing the D-20 battery of the Da Vinci Wolves opening fire toward Novyi Bykiv, mid-March 2022. (Da Vinci Wolves)

The Siege of Chernihiv

As the fighting persisted along the H07, in the north, Chernihiv remained under a state of siege.[11] Humanitarian aid and war material still flowed into the city through the corridor held open by the 58th Motorised Brigade, but the Russian artillery bombardment and air raids continued in turn, devastating the city and inflicting hundreds of civilian casualties.[12] On 16 March, 18 people were killed and 26 wounded when a bread line on Dotsenka Street was hit by Russian artillery. A day later an Uragan cluster munition killed another 14 civilians and injured 24 when it fell on the Regional Children's Hospital on Pyrohova Street.[13] The arrival of Stinger MANPADs in mid-March helped alleviate the bombing, but there was no similar answer to the Russian shells and rockets. The Ukrainian artillery inside the city fought back as best they could, manoeuvring constantly to avoid counter-battery fire, but were outnumbered by their Russian counterparts at ratios as severe as 1:8. At least three 2S3s and two MT-LBu command vehicles from the 1st Tank Brigade's 2nd Artillery Battalion were hunted down and destroyed.[14] Nevertheless, the 41st CAA was unable to convert this superiority in artillery into any kind of operational success.

Indeed, rather than attempting again to cut the supply route south of Chernihiv, Ryzhkov instead began ordering assaults against the city itself, something he had previously gone lengths to avoid in the weeks before. This change in tactics can either be attributed to an intervention by Putin, or else to Ryzhkov deciding that the units in the Desna bridgehead were no longer capable of offensive action and that this was the only course of action left. With most of his army's BTGs either in the bridgehead or already depleted, Ryzhkov instead turned to the two Spetsnaz regiments subordinated to his command.[15] As special forces, these units were far better trained and motivated than the average motor rifleman, enjoying superior equipment such as advanced body armour, night vision optics, and suppressors. However, they numbered too few and lacked the AFVs necessary to have a hope of taking the city themselves, mounted as they were on Tiger MRAPs and Iveco LMVs. Indeed, earlier in the invasion, two companies of the 2nd Spetsnaz Brigade had attempted to storm Kharkiv alone and taken heavy casualties, with one company essentially destroyed and seven Tigers lost.[16] Unwilling to repeat this disaster, Ryzhkov instead employed the Spetsnaz as shock troops with attached support from the tanks, IFVs, and artillery of his army's regular brigades. Whilst this was arguably a waste of specialised reconnaissance troops, it at least gave the 41st CAA a new force to grind into Chernihiv with.

On the north-western flank of the city, in the Masany district, the Spetsnaz conducted raids supported by artillery and armour against the elements of the 105th Border Guard Detachment holding the line there, inflicting several casualties. However, their main blow fell against the village of Novoselivka on the north-eastern side of Chernihiv. Here a large ridge rises above the otherwise flat terrain, granting sweeping views over the surrounding area. Khoda outlined its strategic significance in a subsequent interview:

> If the Russians had occupied the hill near Novoselivka in the first days, they would have planted their own people there – observers – and would raze Chernihiv to the ground and destroy our artillery, which [was] already scarce. And there are not many places for tactical manoeuvring between houses. Taking this height in the early days, perhaps it would have driven us into a dead end.[17]

Fortunately for Chernihiv's defence, the Russians had not assaulted the height in the war's first weeks, instead subjecting it to intensive artillery fire and airstrikes. Defending the area, the 1st Tank Brigade's 1st Mechanised Battalion (reinforced with elements of the 21st Separate Rifle Battalion and 134th Security Battalion) had endured heavy casualties as a result, often losing two or three soldiers killed every day. Despite the cost, the crucial terrain feature had remained in Ukrainian hands. Now, however, the Spetsnaz were tasked with seizing it. The assault began at 0400hrs on 16 March with the usual preliminary bombardment. Two platoons of Russian tanks rushed

A still from a helmet camera video capturing the moment a convoy of Russian Spetsnaz passes a knocked out 1st Tank Brigade T-64BV north of Chernihiv, March 2022. (Russian Ministry of Defence)

onto the hill, followed by the Spetsnaz in their Tigers, leveraging their superior night vision capabilities in the pre-dawn darkness. Private Denys Kuzmenko, a soldier in the 1st Tank Brigade, remembered the scene:

> Bullets were flying. I thought we were breathing those bullets there. There was simply no free space in the air. RPGs are there, bullets are there, VOGs are there, AGS grenade launcher is there, everything is there. Tigers are sowing us with machine guns; machine gunners were on both sides. The plane is coming. It was altogether a horrible picture.[18]

Overwhelmed as the Spetsnaz began assaulting their trenches, the Ukrainian units were ordered to retreat. At least four soldiers were taken prisoner and many more were killed. The withdrawal also proved bloody. A 1st Mechanised Battalion BMP-1 rolled forward to provide covering fire only to be destroyed itself, killing two of its three crewmembers. Lieutenant Volodymyr Andriichenko, a medical officer in the 1st Tank Brigade, tried to evacuate casualties from the ridge in a civilian vehicle marked with red crosses, but was hit by machine gun and RPG fire in the attempt and mortally wounded.

Though the Russians had seized the height, there was no breakthrough into Chernihiv itself. The Ukrainians withdrew three kilometres and established a new defensive line running along the city limits, with the compound of a biathlete training centre – known locally as the ski base – becoming a strongpoint. An initial attack by the Spetsnaz there after the capture of Novoselivka was repulsed when a Tiger was knocked out by an SPG-9 73mm recoilless gun. This brought the day's fighting to an end and the lines resolidified with the Russians in control of the ridge and the Ukrainians arrayed below. As it happened, the loss of Novoselivka did not prove as devastating as Khoda had originally feared, and the Russian artillery proved insufficient to break the Ukrainian positions alone, even with spotters on the heights.

Likely under continued pressure from Putin for results, Ryzhkov ordered a new assault against the ski base. The goal of this operation can only be described as symbolic, since there was no hope of the Spetsnaz, few as they were, of being able to take much of Chernihiv, let alone secure the city. Instead, their objective was only to seize a foothold. Colonel Dmytro Bryzhynskyi, commanding the city's defence, later speculated that the Russians had aimed to break through the ski base and continue three kilometres south to the Chernihiv Radio Plant, whose robust construction and deep bunkers would provide a bulwark for further operations inside the city.

Rather than attacking under the cover of darkness again, the Spetsnaz began their assault during the mid-morning of 22 March. Having recently received quadcopter UAVs, the Ukrainians soon spotted the assault force of 10 Tigers and several BMPs approaching the ski base, and the 58 soldiers of the 21st Separate Rifle Battalion defending the position were able to hold the Russians off for several hours. Eventually, however, the Spetsnaz began to surround the complex and the Ukrainian group was forced to withdraw. Eight soldiers were cut off and took shelter in the complex's basement, responding to Russian demands they surrender with hand grenades. At this critical moment, the 1st Mechanised Battalion committed its 3rd Company to the battle, which drove the Spetsnaz back, saving the trapped soldiers and capturing a Tiger and a BMP in the process. The battles for Novoselivka and the ski base proven extremely costly for the Ukrainians, as many as 100 dead and 3–400 wounded according to official sources, but Ryzhkov's last ditch effort had been contained. Indeed, the battle for the ski base would prove the 41st CAA's final offensive operation against Chernihiv.

Following the defeat, the Russians turned to bombing and shelling the final supply route into Chernihiv, attempting to isolate the city through firepower alone. On 23 March, VKS fighter-bombers destroyed the highway bridge over the Desna, cutting the last road into the city. Shortly after, the nearby pedestrian bridge was also destroyed by shelling, removing the final land connection. Nevertheless, supplies continued flowing into the city via boat. Making matters worse for Ryzhkov, OC North was planning its own counteroffensive to relieve Chernihiv from the south. The 58th Motorised Brigade's 16th Battalion was ordered to take the village of

A still from footage recorded by UAV of the 1st Tank Brigade showing the battle of the ski base. The complex burns in the bottom left of the shot, whilst several Russian Tigers and BMPs manoeuvre closer to the shattered building. (Texty.org.ua)

Sloboda and so cut off the two Russian BTGs holding Lukashivka. However, preliminary reconnaissance revealed that Sloboda was heavily defended and so, rather than repeating the initial failed counterattacks of the 10th Mountain Brigade and 14th Mechanised Brigade, Major Logush decided to wait and degrade the Russian positions with artillery fire until his battalion faced better odds.[19] Over the following days, the Ukrainian artillery savaged the Desna bridgehead, with the attacks on the pontoon bridge at Shestovysya becoming so oppressive that the Russians struggled to keep their forces at Lukashivka supplied with fuel. As it happened, the failures of Russian forces elsewhere around Kyiv would prompt the 41st CAA to retreat before the 16th Battalion could even begin its attack.

Luk'yanivka, Nova Basan, and the Withdrawal of the 2nd GCAA

After its failure to take Rud'yntske on 10 March, the 8th Mountain Assault Battalion had regrouped whilst the Ukrainian artillery ground down the 2nd GCAA in the intervening weeks. Sensing the Russians were reaching their saturation point, the 8th Battalion was tasked to attack the southern flank of the 2nd GCAA again, this time toward the village of Luk'yanivka, located a kilometre further east of Rud'yntske. The settlement was comparatively lightly defended by a company-sized element from the 21st MRB, and it was hoped success here would isolate the larger Russian formations at Peremoha and Rud'yntske. For the operation, the 8th Battalion was heavily reinforced with elements of the volunteer Bratstvo Battalion, Carpathian Sich Special Police Battalion, and GUR SOF. Nevertheless, the initial assault force numbered only 120 strong, supported by two T-64BVs and two BMPs.

The attack commenced on 24 March, with 120mm mortar fire suppressing the Russian positions inside Luk'yanivka as the assault force approached. Upon entering the village, the Ukrainian tanks were engaged at close range by a platoon of Russian T-72B3s and several BMP-2s. After knocking out a T-72 and a BMP, one T-64 entered into a duel with another T-72. In the exchange of fire, the Ukrainian tank was hit in the tracks, whilst its return shot hit the T-72 in the turret face but failed to penetrate the tank's ERA. Nevertheless, the Russian crew, their optics shattered by the impact, hastily withdrew, later abandoning their tank after it became bogged. This action helped decide the battle, and the surviving Russians fled, reportedly leaving behind some 40 dead, along with 13 destroyed and damaged AFVs. In return, the Ukrainians had lost at least three soldiers,[20] though several more were wounded. Having secured the village, the 8th Battalion emplaced Stugna ATGMs and Rapira anti-tank guns in preparation for the Russian BTG in Rud'yntske to counterattack. As night fell, several tank platoons did sally out to shell the Ukrainian positions, and – lacking thermal optics – the Stugnas and Rapiras could do little in response. In the end, however, an artillery barrage from the 43rd Artillery Brigade silenced the Russian fire.[21]

The loss of Luk'yanivka left the already fragile position of the 2nd GCAA even more fraught. The BTGs of the 15th MRB, 21st MRB, and 90th GTD west of the settlement now had to run a gauntlet of Ukrainian fire along the H07 to escape east. Meanwhile, the supply lines of the army continued to suffer devastating artillery strikes, fixing units in place only for them to endure still more shelling. Gurov's forward logistics hub and HQ at the village of Velyka Doroga, located beside the centre of the Udai basin, was itself coming under fire, leaving dozens of vehicles destroyed and damaged.[22] Making matters worse, the 1st GTA on the 2nd GCAA's southern flank was also under pressure as the 93rd Mechanised Brigade's counteroffensive gathered pace against the 4th GTD in Trostianets. By 27 March, Ukrainian forces were approaching the international border south of Sumy, liberating the settlements of Slavhorod and Krasnopilia, as the 1st GTA began withdrawing into Russia.[23] The 2nd GCAA, if it had not already been ordered to retreat, now risked being turned from the flank. In the final days of March, the army's BTGs began streaming back through the Udai basin.

A 120mm mortar round explodes beside a Russian T-72B3 concealed within a backyard in Luk'yanivka prior to the 24 March assault. (Bratstvo Battalion)

Jubilant Ukrainian soldiers pose with the crew of the victorious T-64BV in the battle's aftermath, the damage to the vehicle's left track clearly visible in the photograph. The inscription on the barrel reads: 'Good evening, we are from Ukraine!' (Bratstvo Battalion)

Of all the armies on the Kyiv axes, Gurov's retreat proved the bloodiest. This was because the 2nd GCAA was closely pursued by Ukrainian units for the entirety of its withdrawal, unlike the 35th CAA. The 250th Engineering Centre and 54th Reconnaissance Battalion also posed significant obstacles across the army's avenue of retreat. On 29 March, one BTG from the 90th GTD was ambushed by the 250th as it passed the town of Dorohynka on its way through the basin. The Russians had by now become wary of the frequent mining of the roads around Nizhyn, and the Ukrainian's first effort to halt the BTG failed when their radio-controlled landmines were jammed by Russian EW systems. Undeterred, a wire-controlled mine was emplaced which blew up the squad of Russian sappers sweeping the road in front of the BTG's column. Now proceeding blindly, the BTG soon ran into a conventional minefield where, immobilised, it was shattered by artillery fire.[24] The retreat of the rest of the army was similarly chaotic, with Russian soldiers scrambling to pack what loot they could onto their vehicles before pulling out, abandoning countless pieces of equipment on the way. Outside of Brovary in Bohdanivka on 30 March, one villager came across a peculiar scene:

> We left to go to the village centre on the main road – and there were no Russian soldiers. The thing that made the biggest impression on me was one of the Russian soldiers riding a bicycle, with three or four of his subordinates following him on foot. One of them ran up to us and asked what side Russia was on. We pointed in the direction of the Russian Federation. Then he asked where the military vehicles had gone — we pointed him towards Shevchenkovo [a village five kilometres east of Bohdanivka], and they went that way. A little bit later, another soldier on a moped and another one on a bicycle went by, trying to catch up with the others.[25]

In a bid to cut off the retreating columns, the 8th Mountain Assault Battalion and its attached elements struck toward Nova Basan on the same day. The battalion was further bolstered for the operation with a few T-72s from the 3rd Tank Brigade, a Reserve Corps formation which had been fed into the fighting piecemeal as its sub-units reached readiness one by one.[26] Approaching Nova Basan from the south, the Ukrainian battlegroup held off its attack as it waited for a retreating Russian BTG to continue through the village. Once the threat had passed, the assault began, with each of the 8th Battalion's companies advancing along a separate street. Taken off guard, most of the Russian garrison fled. One group continued fighting from the Russian HQ, located inside a kindergarten, but were forced to surrender when a T-72B under the command of Lieutenant Nazar Vernihora began shelling the building at close range. Spreading out in the assault's aftermath, the Ukrainian infantry companies seized ambush positions, whilst Vernihora's T-72B concealed itself behind ruined houses with a key-hole view of the highway. The Ukrainians did not have long to wait, as another retreating Russian BTG, in this case from the 15th MRB, was already approaching from the west along the H07.

The Russian column came under fire as soon as it entered the village, immediately losing one T-72B outside an industrial compound. Reacting to the incoming fire, some of the Russian infantry dismounted to run alongside their BTR-82As, which continued at pace along the highway – desperate to escape eastwards. Inside Vernihora's T-72B, his gunner struggled to make out the passing Russian vehicles as his gunsight had depressurised and begun to fog. Nevertheless, Vernihora was able to direct the tank's fire using his own optics. Their first shot went high and several BTRs passed by unscathed, but their next round set one ablaze. As the following vehicles negotiated the burning wreckage and bodies, another BTR was knocked out. Though the ruined houses had sheltered his tank so far from return fire (including autocannon bursts from the BTRs and RPGs launched by the dismounts), Vernihora in a flash of intuition decided to remove the Ukrainian flag fixed to his tank's antenna. This was a prudent decision, as four Russian tanks appeared shortly after on his left flank. Vernihora recalled the scene:

> It was sleeting and raining at that moment. The armour was wet, so you couldn't see the [Ukrainian] pixellated pattern. The first tank that aimed at us didn't fire, maybe because it thought we were Russians – they had the same T-72B tank models. So, it didn't shoot. But the last one in the column shot for some reason. The round hit us. Our tank got a shake, but my gunner didn't get confused and started firing in the direction of the Russian tanks and fortunately hit the last one.[27]

The immediate aftermath of the Dorohynka ambush on 29 March 2022. The various smoke plumes mark the location of burning Russian vehicles. (ZSU)

Another still of the same event. On the right side of the road, a Ural-4320 truck lies flipped and shattered. Still on the road, a Tor SAM system stands abandoned. Left of the road, an MT-LB is also flipped over and ablaze. Close by, a pair of KamAZ 6x6 trucks are bogged in the mud. (ZSU)

This success proved enough to drive the other Russian tanks away. Still, Vernihora and his crew fought on for several more hours until they ran low on armour-piercing shells and had to withdraw, offloading their machine gun ammunition to friendly infantry on their way out. Though the Russian column was in some disarray after these losses, it continued to fight its way east, now under Ukrainian artillery fire. In the process, an 8th Battalion BMP-1 was ambushed by three BTR-82s and knocked out. The BMP's gunner, Junior Sergeant Nazar Nebozhynsky, was killed. At least two more Ukrainians would die before the village was secured that evening, and even then several groups of Russians were rooted out of basements the following morning in individual firefights. Russian casualties were heavier, at least 10 killed and several more taken prisoner. Additionally, 15 Russian vehicles were captured around Nova Basan and another 19 found destroyed, some during the battle, others by earlier artillery strikes.[28] Despite these losses, the 15th MRB's BTG had managed to escape relatively intact, though the brigade would later be marked by mass-resignations upon its return to Russia.[29]

In the aftermath of Nova Basan, the 8th Mountain Assault Battalion and the 1st Mechanised Battalion, 72nd Mechanised Brigade, pursued the retreating Russians towards the border despite

A still from the famous video of the stand of Lieutenant Nazar Vernihora and his crew during the battle of Nova Basan. Marked by flags edited over the footage, the T-72B watches from its key-hole position as the BTR-82s approach. One BTR is seen attempting to suppress the firing position in vain, the flash of a 30mm tracer shell clear to see. (Bratstvo Battalion)

their own exhaustion. A UAV operator within the 1st Mechanised Battalion's 3rd Company described the advance in his journal:

> 2 April 2022.
> We are raiding the enemy. First, we raid in the east, then the north, and then back again to the east.
> Our tasks keep changing as we move from place to place. We paint a picture for ourselves. The intel we receive is contradictory. The Moskali retreated very quickly. We see a lot of abandoned equipment. We are constantly ahead of the convoy – somehow it seems to just turn out that way. Gray villages, steep roads, local old men, people all offering food. Some are crying. It is raining and everyone is wet. We fly the drone low under the clouds. There is no front line, everything is a relative gray zone. Everyone acts with their own risks.
>
> The battalion is on a raid. We are driving in a jeep and get tired. How the boys in armoured vehicles can travel so much is a total mystery to me.[30]

By 4 April, the Chernihiv Oblast and most of the Sumy Oblast had been liberated, relieving the garrison of Sumy city.[31] Tractors flocked to drag away the hundreds of Russian vehicles and artillery pieces abandoned in the fields and along the roads. The final elements of the 2nd GCAA and 1st GTA withdrew from the Sumy oblast over 9–10 April, although small groups of Russian stragglers would continue to make their way across the border for some time afterwards.[32] In the end, both combined armies received only a temporary reprieve before being sent to join the fighting in the east of Ukraine.

The Escape of the 41st CAA

As the other combined armies arrayed around Kyiv withdrew, the 41st CAA also began its retreat to the border.[33] Unlike his counterparts, Ryzhkov had not been directly forced into a withdrawal, although the successful counteroffensives against the other armies now made his own position untenable. The writing was on the wall for the 41st CAA either way, as Ukrainian artillery strikes and partisan activity attrited its logistics and C2 hubs, extinguishing what little offensive capacity it had left. Ryzhkov's own HQ at the village of Vyshneve was attacked in late March, destroying at least one Pantsir-S SAM system assigned to its defence, along with several trucks. Meanwhile, on the frontline, the ammunition depot of the Russian BTGs holding Lukashivka blew up on 30 March, wiping out a command post, several vehicles, and an 120mm mortar battery along with it. Nikoliuk has remained ambivalent about OC North's involvement in this explosion because the depot was located inside a historic local church, but it seems likely it was hit by a Ukrainian Uragan strike. In the end, the detonation of the depot would pre-empt the beginning of the Russian withdrawal from the Desna bridgehead that same day.

Still occupied with staging their attack toward Sloboda at the time, the commanders of 16th Battalion, 58th Motorised Brigade, realised with alarm that the Russians were already evacuating the village. Major Logush rapidly directed the brigade's artillery onto the retreating Russian columns and organised a hasty attack. This quick reaction caught the Russian rearguard before it could escape, destroying at least one T-72B3 in the process and capturing two MT-LBs. Nevertheless, Logush's reaction had still been too slow to catch most of the Russian elements defending Sloboda, and the two BTGs holding Lukashivka also managed to slip away under the cover of nightfall, ending Nikoliuk's hopes of creating the 'Lukashivka cauldron'. These Russian units joined the stream of personnel and vehicles fleeing over the Shestovtysa pontoon bridge. The number of casualties the 41st CAA sustained during this crossing remains unknown, though Nikoliuk's claim that the Russians lost 70 percent of their equipment in the process remains to be confirmed by visual evidence.[34] Indeed, overall, the 41st CAA's retreat was conducted with efficiency and success, the army falling back on the many

A photo taken after the liberation of Lukashivka showing the scorched remains of the Church of the Ascension. (National Police of Ukraine)

pre-war rehearsals of fighting withdrawals. Any notions of the withdrawal being a 'goodwill measure' are undermined by the fact that the Russian artillery fired off all their stockpiled ammunition towards the Ukrainian lines before pulling out. By 3 April, the last elements of the 41st CAA had left the Chernihiv Oblast.

Clearing the villages of Yahidne, Luksahivka, and Ivanivka, the soldiers of the 58th Motorised Brigade were horrified by what they found. As with seemingly everywhere else the Russians passed around Kyiv, the occupation of these villages was marked with wanton violence and cruelty. In Yahidne, 368 civilians had been confined to a school basement by soldiers of the 55th MMRB, ostensibly to protect them from the Ukrainian shelling, though the Russians used the building above as a HQ and frequently harassed and humiliated those trapped inside. At least 10 died during the ordeal.[35] In Ivanivka, a civilian was executed by Russian soldiers after he refused to leave his house,[36] whilst in Lukashivka, the 58th Motorised Brigade soldiers discovered the bodies of their comrades executed in the aftermath of the battle on 9 March, alongside those of several civilians who had apparently been tortured before they were killed.[37]

In the end, the 58th Motorised Brigade would not have long to wait before it had its revenge. Fighting on the eastern front in May, the brigade destroyed two of the 41st CAA's BTGs outside the village of Bilohorivka when they tried to cross the Donets River, killing hundreds of Russian soldiers. From the sea of wrecked AFVs, many half-submerged in the river, the Ukrainians discovered possessions stolen from Chernihiv and its surroundings two months prior.[38] The story of that battle, however, remains to be covered in the future volumes of this sub-series, along with the hundred other dramas of the following months and years of the war.

APPENDIX: KNOWN UKRAINIAN ARMY, AIR FORCE, TERRITORIAL DEFENCE & NATIONAL GUARD UNITS INVOLVED IN THE DEFENCE OF KYIV AND SURROUNDING AREAS, FEBRUARY–APRIL 2022

Unit	Equipment	Notes
Air Command Centre; CO: Lieutenant General Anatoily Kryvonozkho		
31st Communications Regiment		Garrisoned in Kyiv
19th Special Purpose Radio Intercept Brigade		Garrisoned in Halytsynov
2204th Electronic Warfare Battalion		Garrisoned in Vasylkiv
138th Radio Technical Brigade		Garrisoned in Vasylkiv
96th Anti-Aircraft Missile Brigade	S-300PS	Garrisoned in Danylivka
210th Anti-Aircraft Regiment	S-300V1	Garrisoned in Uman
156th Anti-Aircraft Regiment	Buk M1	Garrisoned in Zolotonosha. Deployed around Kyiv pre-war
160th Anti-Aircraft Brigade	S-300PM/PS	From AC South. One S-300PS battalion engaged at Kyiv
7th Tactical Aviation Brigade	18 Su-24M, 9 Su-24MR	From AC West. Some aircraft detached for sorties under AC North
39th Tactical Aviation Brigade	23 Su-27S/P/P1M/UB, L-39M1	Garrisoned in Ozerne AB. Some aircraft detached elsewhere.
40th Tactical Aviation Brigade	9 MiG-29S, 11 MiG-29MU1, 4 MiG-29UB, L-39M1	Garrisoned in Vasylkiv AB
299th Tactical Aviation Brigade	24 Su-25/25M1/M1K, 7 Su-25UB/UBM1/UBM1K	From AC South. Some aircraft detached for sorties under AC North
831st Tactical Aviation Brigade	22 Su-27P/M1/UB/UM (2 squadrons), L-39M1	Garrisoned in Myrhorod AB. Some aircraft detached elsewhere
15th Transport Aviation Brigade	5 An-26, 3 An-30, 4 Mi-8, 1 Tu-134	Garrisoned in Boryspil IAP
456th Transport Aviation Brigade	9 An-26, 7 Mi-8	Garrisoned between Vinnytsia/Havryshivka AB
383rd Regiment of Remotely Controlled Aircraft	30 TB2, Tu-141, Tu-143	From AC West. Some aircraft detached for sorties under AC North
Operational Command North; COs Major General Viktor Nikoliuk and Colonel General Oleksandr Syrskyi		
Army Aviation		
16th Army Aviation Brigade	Mi-24P/PU1, Mi-8MT/MTV/MSB-V	Garrisoned in Brody. Some aircraft detached under OC North
18th Army Aviation Brigade	Mi-24P/PU1, Mi-8MT/MTV/MSB-V, Mi-2MSB-V	Garrisoned in Poltava AB
Special Operations Forces		
10th SSO "Shaman" Battalion		Formed from GUR operators. Closer to platoon-strength on Kyiv axes. Fought at Hostomel, Brovary, Moschun and Irpin
8th SSO Regiment		At least one team present at Kyiv
3rd SSO Regiment	Humvee and Kozak MRAP	
Kyiv Azov Regiment		Formed during the battle originally as a TDF unit, but joined the SSO around 9 March 2022
Air Assault Forces		
199th Training Centre		Garrisoned in Zhytomyr. Dispatched team of 50 for the retaking of Antonov IAP
80th Air Assault Brigade	Three battalions mounted on Humvee and BTR-80, company of T-80BV, artillery group consisting of a battalion each of D-30, 2S1, BM-21	The brigade's 2nd BTG fought under OC North at war's outset, rest of brigade fought under OC South
81st Airmobile Brigade	Four battalions mounted on BMP-1, BTR-80, and Kozak-2 MRAP, company of T-80BV, artillery group consisting of 2S1 and BM-21	The brigade's 5th BTG fought briefly in the defence of Sumy city before being dispatched to the Zaporizhzhia Oblast

95th Air Assault Brigade	Three battalions mounted on at least 1 BMP-1TS, BTR-80, BTR-3, Kozak-2 and Dozor-B MRAP, company of T-80BV, artillery group of D-30 and 2S1	1st and 3rd battalions fought in Makariv area
Land Forces		
1st Assault Company "Da Vince Wolves"	D-20 battery and assorted UAV	Arrived on eastern side of Kyiv around mid-March 2022
1st Tank Brigade	Three tank battalions with T-64BV/BM, one mechanised battalion on BMP-1/2, artillery group consisting of a battalion each of 2S1, 2S3, BM-21	
3rd (Reserve) Tank Brigade	Three tank battalions with T-72AV/B/AMT, one mechanised battalion on BMP-1, artillery group consisting of 2S1, 2S3, and Verba MRLS system	At least one tank company dispatched to south-western Kyiv on 28 February 2022, more fought on eastern axes
10th Mountain Assault Brigade	8th, 108th, and 109th Mountain Battalions, mounted on BMP-1/2, one tank battalion with T-72AV/B, artillery group consisting of D-30, 2S1, BM-21	From OC West
14th Mechanised Brigade	1st, 2nd, and 3rd Mechanised Battalions mounted on BMP-1/2, 1st Motorised Infantry Battalion, one tank battalion with T-64BV and 5 T-84 Oplot, artillery group consisting of 2S1 and BM-21	From OC West
19th Rocket Artillery Brigade	12 Tochka-U, 7th Guard Battalion attached	Partially assigned to OC North
21st Separate Rifle Battalion		
24th Separate Assault Battalion Aidar		Elements fought in defence of Irpin
26th Artillery Brigade	1st and 2nd Artillery Battalions with 2S19, 3rd Artillery Battalion with 2S5, anti-tank battalion with MT-12, 14th Guard Battalion attached	
27th Rocket Artillery Brigade	Four battalions of BM-27, 41st Guard Battalion attached	1st Battalion assigned to OC North
43rd Artillery Brigade	Four battalions of 2S7	At least one battalion assigned to OC North
44th Artillery Brigade	1st Artillery Battalion with Msta-B, 2nd and 3rd Artillery Battalions with Giantsint-B, 4th Artillery Battalion with 2S7, 5th Anti-Tank Battalion with MT-12, 6th Guard Battalion attached	From OC West. 1st Artillery Battalion supported defence of Chernihiv; remainder of brigade deployed around Kyiv
45th (Reserve) Artillery Brigade	57th and 59th Artillery Battalion with 32 Msta-B, 62nd Artillery Battalion with 16 Giantsint-B, 87th Anti-Tank Battalion with MT-12 and assorted ATGMs	87th Anti-Tank Battalion deployed to Kyiv around 4 March 2022, followed by 57th Artillery Battalion
54th Reconnaissance Battalion		
58th Motorised Brigade	13th, 14th and 15th Motorised Infantry Battalions mounted on BMP-1, BRDM-2, MT-LB and light vehicles, one tank battalion with T-64BV, one artillery battalion with D-20, one anti-tank battalion with MT-12 and assorted ATGM	
72nd Mechanised Brigade	1st, 2nd, and 3rd Mechanised Battalions mounted on BMP-2, one tank battalion with T-64BV, artillery group consisting of 1st Artillery Battalion with 2S1, 2nd Artillery Battalion with 12 2S3, 3rd Artillery Battalion with BM-21, and 4th Artillery Battalion with MT-12	
91st Operational Support Regiment	Three battalions mounted on BRDM-2, PTS amphibious vehicles, and BTR	
93rd Mechanised Brigade	1st, 2nd, and 3rd Mechanised Battalions on BMP-2, one tank battalion with T-64BV, artillery group of 2S1, 2S3, BM-21 and MT-12	From OC East
101st Guard Brigade of the General Staff	BTR-80, BRDM-2, Varta MRAP	
128th Mountain Assault Brigade	Three mechanised battalions, one tank battalion with T-72AV/B, artillery group of D-20, 2S1, 2S3, BM-21 and MT-12	From OC West. At least one artillery battalion deployed to Kyiv around 26 February 2022, rest of the brigade fought in Zaporizhzhia Oblast

Unit	Equipment	Notes
134th Security Battalion		
169th Training Centre		
184th Training Centre		Deployed at least one CTG
214th Special Battalion OPFOR	Mounted on BRDM-2 and BMP	From OC West. ZSU's single opposing force (OPFOR) training unit, deployed in the defence of Kyiv
250th Engineering Centre		
1129th Anti-Aircraft Missile Regiment	Five batteries of Osa-AKM	Garrisoned in Bila Tserkva
Territorial Defence Forces		
112th TDF Brigade		Garrisoned in Kyiv
114th TDF Brigade		Garrisoned in Kyiv
115th TDF Brigade		Garrisoned in Zhytomyr Oblast
116th TDF Brigade		Garrisoned in Poltava Oblast. Defeated elements of 4th GTD near Hadyach
117th TDF Brigade	Accumulated several BTR and BMP over the course of the initial fighting	Garrisoned in Sumy
Bratstvo Battalion		Formed after war's outbreak as volunteer formation. Fought initially on western side of Kyiv, then east along the H07
Irpin Company Tactical Group	3 BTR-80, 1 Kozak MRAP	Formed after war's outbreak as a volunteer formation, later inducted into the 114th TDF Brigade
International Legion		Originally subordinated to the TDF, the International Legion was an umbrella for several sub-units, including the Georgian and Belarussian Legions, and the Chechen Dzhokhar Dudayev Battalion
Aerorozvidka	Assorted UAV, including R18 Hexacopter bombers and A1-CM Furia	Volunteer group operating as a joint UAV and SOF team
National Guard		
1st Battalion of State Facilities Protection		Surrendered holding the Chernobyl NPP
1st Presidential Operational Brigade	Three infantry battalions on Kozak-2 and Varta MRAP, artillery and anti-aircraft battalion	
2nd Shostka Regiment	Varta MRAP	Elements fighting in Moschun, Brovary, and Chernihiv
4th Rapid Reaction Brigade	Two infantry battalions on BTR-3 and Varta MRAP, tank battalion with T-64BV, artillery group with D-30	Sent to OC East, reserve CTG remained at Antonov IAP
8th Operational Regiment	Included an artillery and anti-aircraft group	Deployed to Kyiv on 26 February 2022 and fought in E40 direction
22nd Battalion	3 BTR-70	
25th Public Security Protection Brigade	Kozak MRAP	Provided rear-area security inside Kyiv
27th Pechersk Brigade		Provided rear-area security and fought in Bucha and Vyshhorod
Omega Special Forces Squadron of the National Guard's Northern Regional Command	Kozak and Varta MRAP	Fought throughout Kyiv Oblast
National Guard Aviation Base	15 Mi-8MT/MSB-V, Mi-2MSB and Airbus H225, 1 squadron operating assorted UAVs, including Fly Eye, RQ-11 Raven, A1-CM Furia, MARA-2	Detachments from the UAV squadron fought in Kyiv and Sumy oblasts

SELECT BIBLIOGRAPHY

Chung, W. J., *War In Ukraine Volume 4: Main Battle Tanks of Russia and Ukraine, 2014-2023: Soviet Legacy and Post-Soviet Russian MBTs* (Warwick: Helion & Company Publishing, 2023)

Chung, W. J., *War In Ukraine Volume 5: Main Battle Tanks of Russia and Ukraine, 2014-2023: Post-Soviet Ukrainian MBTs and Combat Experience* (Warwick: Helion & Company Publishing, 2023)

Cooper, T., Fontanellaz, A. and Sipos, M., *War In Ukraine Volume 6: The Air War February-March 2022* (Warwick: Helion & Company Publishing, 2024)

Cooper, T., Fontanellaz, A., Crowther, E. and Sipos, M., *War In Ukraine Volume 2: Russian Invasion, February 2022* (Warwick: Helion & Company Publishing, 2023)

Galeotti, M., *Putin's Wars: From Chechnya to Ukraine* (Revised electronic edition, London: Bloomsbury, 2024)

Grau, L. W. and Bartles, C. K., *The Russian Way of War; Force Structure, Tactics, and Modernization of the Russian Ground Forces* (Fort Leavenworth: Foreign Military Studies Office, 2017)

Harding, L., *Invasion: Russia's Bloody War and Ukraine's Fight for Survival* (London: Guardian Faber, 2022)

Holcomb, F., *The order of Battle of the Ukrainian Armed Forces: A key component in European Security* (Washington: Institute for the Study of War, 2016)

Laidlaw, N. *What War Did To Us Volume 2: Ukraine: The First 150 Days of Combat February 24-July 24* (Amazon, 2022)

Lawrence, C. A., *The Battle of Kyiv: The Fight for Ukraine's Capital* (Barnsley, Pen & Sword, 2023, e-book edition)

Matthews, O., *Overreach: The Inside Story of Putin's War Against Ukraine* (Revised edition, London: Mudlark, 2023)

National Guard of Ukraine, *The military formations and units of the National Guard of Ukraine honorary titles*, volume 22 of the Data and Analytic Brochure Series (Kyiv: National Guard of Ukraine Public Affairs Publishing Centre, 2023)

Nikoliuk, V., *In Defence of the Sumy Region: The Defence and Liberation of the Sumy Region, February-April 2022* (In Ukrainian) (ZSU Centre for Military History Research, 2023)

Ramani, S., *Putin's War on Ukraine: Russia's Campaign for Global Counter-Revolution* (London: Hurst & Co, 2023)

Shuster, S., *The Showman: The Inside Story of the Invasion That Shook the World and Made a Leader of Volodymyr Zelenksy* (London: William Collins, 2024)

Trofimov, Y., *Our Enemies Will Vanish: The Russian Invasion and Ukraine's War of Independence* (London: Penguin, 2024)

US Army, *ATP 7-100.1 Russian tactics* (Fort Belvoir: US Army Publishing Directorate, 2024)

Watling, J., *The Arms of the Future* (Reprint, London, Bloomsbury, 2024)

ENDNOTES

Introduction

1. For example: Luke Harding, *Invasion: Russia's Bloody War and Ukraine's Fight for Survival* (London: Guardian Faber, 2022); Yaroslav Trofimov, *Our Enemies Will Vanish: The Russian Invasion and Ukraine's War of Independence* (London: Penguin, 2024); Owen Matthews, *Overreach: The Inside Story of Putin's War Against Ukraine* (Revised edition, London: Mudlark, 2023).
2. Prominent examples include: 'Preliminary Lessons in Conventional Warfighting from Russia's Invasion of Ukraine: February-July 2022', RUSI, Special Report, 30 November 2022; 'Preliminary Lessons from Russia's Unconventional Operations During the Russo-Ukrainian War, February 2022-2023', RUSI, Special Report, 29 March 2023; Ronald Ti and Christopher Kinsey, 'Lessons from the Russo-Ukrainian conflict: the primacy of logistics over strategy', *Defence Studies*, 23:3 (2023), pp.381–398.
3. Tom Cooper, Adrien Fontanellaz, Edward Crowther, Milos Sipos, *War In Ukraine Volume 2: Russian Invasion, February 2022* (Warwick: Helion & Company Publishing, 2023); Wen Jian Chung, *War In Ukraine Volume 5: Main Battle Tanks of Russia and Ukraine, 2014–2023: Post-Soviet Ukrainian MBTs and Combat Experience* (Warwick: Helion & Company Publishing, 2023); Tom Cooper, Adrien Fontanellaz, Milos Sipos, *War In Ukraine Volume 6: The Air War February–March 2022* (Warwick: Helion & Company Publishing, 2024).
4. James Sladden, Liam Collins, Ben Connable, 'The Battle of Irpin River', *The British Army Review*, 187 (2024), pp.1–54; Christopher A. Lawrence, *The Battle of Kyiv: The Fight for Ukraine's Capital* (Barnsley, Pen & Sword, 2023, e-book edition).

Chapter 1

1. Mark F. Cancian, 'Putin's Invasion Was Immoral but Not Irrational', CSIS, 10 May 2022; Dale Copeland, 'Is Vladimir Putin a Rational Actor?', *Miller Centre*, 10 March 2022; John Mearsheimer and Sebastian Rosato, 'The Russian invasion was a rational act: It is in the West's interest to take Putin seriously', *UnHerd*, 14 September 2023.
2. Huw Dylan, David V. Gioe, Elena Grossfeld, 'The autocrat's intelligence paradox: Vladimir Putin's (mis)management of Russian strategic assessment in the Ukraine War', *The British Journal of Politics and International Relations*, 25:3 (2023), pp.385–404.
3. Gideon Rachman, 'Vladimir Putin has created his own worst nightmare', *Financial Times*, 24 June 2023; Robert Person and Michael McFaul, 'What Putin Fears Most', *Journal of Democracy*, 33:2 (2022), pp.18–27.
4. Dylan, Gioe, Grossfeld, 'The autocrat's intelligence paradox', p.390.
5. Dylan, Gioe, Grossfeld, 'The autocrat's intelligence paradox', pp.394–395.
6. Nick Reynolds and Jack Watling, 'Ukraine Through Russia's Eyes', *RUSI.org*, 25 February 2022.
7. 'Preliminary Lessons from Russia's Unconventional Operations During the Russo-Ukrainian War, February 2022-2023', RUSI, Special Report, 29 March 2023, p.12.
8. Luke Harding, Andrew Roth, Shaun Walker, 'Dumb and Lazy': the flawed films of Ukrainian 'attacks' made by Russia's 'fake factory', *The Guardian*, 21 February 2022.
9. Unless stated otherwise, this sub-chapter is based on 'The Russian General Staff: Understanding the Military's Decisionmaking Role in a "Besieged Fortress"', RAND, Research Report, 22 March 2023, pp.vi, 12, 20–21, 83–85; 'Preliminary Lessons in Conventional

9. Warfighting from Russia's Invasion of Ukraine: February-July 2022', RUSI, Special Report, 30 November 2022, p.12.
10. Mark Galeotti, *Putin's Wars: From Chechnya to Ukraine* (Revised electronic edition, London: Bloomsbury, 2024) p.346.
11. Matthews, *Overreach*, pp.12–13.
12. Cooper et al., *War In Ukraine Volume 6*, p.37
13. Alberto Nardelli and Jennifer Jacobs, 'U.S. Intel Shows Russia Plans for Potential Ukraine Invasion', *Bloomberg UK*, 21 November 2021.
14. Cooper et al., *War In Ukraine Volume 2*, pp.53–61.
15. Unless stated otherwise, this sub-chapter is based on 'Preliminary Lessons in Conventional Warfighting from Russia's Invasion of Ukraine: February-July 2022', RUSI, Special Report, 30 November 2022, p.11; 'Preliminary Lessons from Russia's Unconventional Operations During the Russo-Ukrainian War, February 2022-2023', RUSI, Special Report, 29 March 2023, pp.18–19.
16. Carl Von Clausewitz, *On War* (Peter Paret and Michael Howard translation, London: David Campbell Publishers, 1993) p.241–243.
17. An airhead is an area seized by airborne landing and subsequently used for bringing in supplies and reinforcements by air.
18. Cooper et al., *War In Ukraine Volume 2*, p.39.
19. Michael Schwirtz, Anton Troianovski, Yousur Al-Hlou, Masha Froliak, Adam Entous, Thomas Gibbons-Neff, 'Putin's War', *The New York Times* (NYT), 18 December 2022.
20. Harold Chambers, 'One month on in the Ukraine war: what role for the kadyrovsty?', *Fondation pour la recherche stratégique*, 6 April 2022.
21. 'Preliminary Lessons in Conventional Warfighting from Russia's Invasion of Ukraine: February-July 2022', RUSI, Special Report, 30 November 2022, p.9; Erina Kinetz, 'Takeaways from investigation of Russian general in Ukraine', *AP News*, 27 October 2022.
22. Cooper et al., *War In Ukraine Volume 2*, p.36.
23. 'Russian Military Strategy: Core Tenets and Operational Concepts', CNA, Research Report, 19 October 2022, pp.10–14; Alex Vershinin, 'Feeding the Bear: A Closer Look at Russian Army Logistics and the Fait Accompli', *War on the Rocks*, 23 November 2021; Ti and Kinsey, 'Lessons from the Russo-Ukrainian conflict', pp.387–388.
24. 'Russian Logistics and Sustainment Failures in the Ukraine Conflict', RAND, Research Report, 11 July 2023, pp.5–6.
25. Suspilne Chernihiv, '*Russian Invasion of Ukraine and the first battles in Chernihiv region | Battle for Chernihiv Episode 1*', YouTube, 6 May 2023.
26. Michael Kofman and Rob Lee, 'Not Built for Purpose: The Russian Military's Ill-Fated Force Design', *War on the Rocks*, 2 June 2022. The number of conscripts to contract personnel could vary widely depending on the unit. For instance, VDV formations typically had much higher ratios of contract personnel compared to SV formations.
27. Matthews, *Overreach*, pp.306–307.
28. 'Russian Defence Ministry Confirms Presence of Conscripts In Ukraine War For First Time', *Radio Free Europe*, 9 March 2022.
29. Lester W. Grau and Charles K. Bartles, 'Getting to Know the Russian Battalion Tactical Group', *RUSI.org*, 14 April 2022; Galeotti, *Putin's Wars*, pp.242–243; Cooper et al., *War In Ukraine Volume 2*, p.17.
30. Gonzalo Báez, 'At First Sight: Russian Armour/Mechanised Battalion Tactical Groups in Ukraine War', *Armour Magazine*, No. CXXXIV, Summer 2022; Charles Dick, 'Russian Ground Forces Posture Towards the West', Chatham House, Research Report, 4 April 2019, p.10.
31. Amos C. Fox, 'Reflections on Russia's 2022 Invasion of Ukraine: Combined Arms Warfare, the Battalion Tactical Group and Wars in a Fishbowl', *AUSA*, 29 September 2022.
32. Michael Kofman and Rob Lee, 'Not Built for Purpose: The Russian Military's Ill-Fated Force Design', *War on the Rocks*, 2 June 2022.
33. Michael Kofman and Rob Lee, 'Not Built for Purpose: The Russian Military's Ill-Fated Force Design', *War on the Rocks*, 2 June 2022. Janes provides evidence that the 55th MMRB deployed with all three of its manoeuvre battalions (see 'Russia builds up forces on Ukrainian border', *Janes*, 9 December 2021). Max Schönhausen describes the 155th NIB as deploying as a complete brigade (see 'Wounded Tiger 3 – Staging in Belarus: The story about the Russian 155th Marine Brigade in the war in Ukraine', *Medium*, 8 March 2023).
34. Schönhausen, 'Wounded Tiger 3', *Medium*, 8 March 2023.
35. Unless stated otherwise, sub-chapter based on Jörgen Elfving, 'An Assessment of the Russian Airborne Forces and Their Role on Tomorrow's Battlefield', The Jamestown Foundation, April 2021; Michael Kofman, 'Rethinking the Structure and Role of Russia's Airborne Forces, *Russian Military Analysis blog*, 30 January 2019; Roger N. McDermott, 'General Shamanov and the Russian Airborne Forces', *The Journal of Slavic Military Studies*, 23:3 (2010), pp.412–437; Rod Thornton, 'Organisational Change in the Russian Airborne Forces: The Lessons of the Georgian Conflict', *Current Politics and Economics of Russia, Eastern and Central Europe*, 32:3 (2017), pp.267–315; Battle Order, '*The Weakness of Russian VDV Airborne Force Structure*', YouTube, 10 May 2022.
36. Presence and purposes of these units synthesised from following sources: *Russo-Ukrainian WarSpotting*, <https://ukr.warspotting.net/search/>, accessed 30 October 2024; Vladimir D, 'Начало СВО: битва за пригороды Киева' [Načalo SVO: bitva za prigorody Kieva], *Lostarmour.info*, no date; Cooper et al., *War In Ukraine Volume 2*, pp.39–41.
37. Unless stated otherwise, sub-chapter based on Cooper et al., *War In Ukraine Volume* 2, p.13; Cooper et al., *War In Ukraine Volume 6*, pp.6–9, 22, 33, 35, 41; 'The Russian Air War and Ukrainian Requirements for Air Defence', RUSI, Special Report, 7 November 2022, pp.1, 27–29.
38. Matthew S. Galamison and Michael B. Petersen, 'Failures of the Russian Aerospace Forces in Ukraine', *Air & Space Operations Review*, 2:3 (2023), pp.4–19 (6–7).

Chapter 2

1. Erin Banco, Garrett M. Graff, Lara Seligman, Nahal Toosi, Alexander Ward, 'Something Was Badly Wrong': When Washington Realized Russia Was Actually Invading Ukraine', *Politico*, 24 February 2023.
2. Giangiuseppe Pili and Fabrizio Minniti, 'Understanding Russia's Great Games: From Zapad 2013 to Zapad 2021', *RUSI.org*, 7 June 2022.
3. 'Russian troops now number 90,000 near Ukraine border after drills, Kyiv says', *Reuters*, 3 November 2021.
4. Simon Shuster, *The Showman: The Inside Story of the Invasion That Shook the World and Made a Leader of Volodymyr Zelenksy* (London: William Collins, 2024), p.209.
5. Banco et al., 'Something Was Badly Wrong…', *Politico*, 24 February 2023.
6. Shuster, *The Showman*, pp.208–209; Samuel M. Seitz, 'Letting sleeping bears lie: Ukraine's cautious approach to uncertainty before the war', *Contemporary Security Policy*, 44:4 (2023), pp.530–543 (534–536); Matthews, *Overreach*, pp.202–203.
7. It is important to note the VSRF also maintained a reserve system, seeing most active brigades and divisions staffed at 70–90 percent of their paper strength (these percentages including both serving contract personnel and conscripts). However, as there was no mobilisation until September 2022, this structure was of little relevance to Russian unit strengths during the invasion, BTGs being drawn from serving contract personnel.
8. Cooper et al., *War In Ukraine Volume 2*, pp.6–10.
9. Cooper et al., *War In Ukraine Volume 2*, p.37.
10. Sladden et al., 'The Battle of Irpin River', pp.10, 25–26.
11. Paragraph compiled from: Cooper, Fontanellaz, Crowther, Sipos, *War In Ukraine Volume 2*, pp.11–12; Mykola Bielieskov, 'Ukraine's Territorial Defence Forces: The War So Far and Future Prospects', *RUSI.org*, 11 May 2023.
12. Paragraph compiled from: Sladden et al., 'The Battle of Irpin River', p.17; Oksana Torop and Svyatoslav Khomeko, 'The fight for Hostomel airfield. How the gates to Kyiv stayed locked', *BBC News Russian*, 29 February 2024; National Guard of Ukraine, *The military formations and units of the National Guard of Ukraine honorary titles*, volume 22 of the Data and Analytic Brochure Series (Kyiv: National Guard of Ukraine Public Affairs Publishing Centre, 2023).
13. Unless stated otherwise, sub-chapter based on Cooper et al., *War In Ukraine Volume 2*, pp.37–39, 47; Trofimov, *Our Enemies Will Vanish*, pp.30, 105; Shuster, *The Showman*, pp.214–217; Cooper et al., *War In Ukraine Volume 6*, pp.38–40; Paul Sonne, Isabelle Khurshudyan, Serhiy Morgunov, Kostiantyn Khudov, 'Battle for

Kyiv: Ukrainian Valor, Russian Blunders combined to save the Capital', *The Washington Post* (WP), 24 August 2022.
14 Banco et al., 'Something Was Badly Wrong...', *Politico*, 24 February 2023.
15 This figure includes the 35th and 41st CAAs alone as it appears Ukrainian intelligence had not recognised the threat the 2nd GCAA and 1st GTA also posed to the capital at the time. The exact manning figures of the two armies remain hazy, and the figure given by the author should be treated as rough estimate. Sladden et al. give a figure of 7–10,000 personnel for the 35th CAA (see 'The Battle of the Irpin River', p.9), but this seems too small given the additional VDV and SV units attached to it. By contrast, Jian Chung describes the 41st CAA as 13–15,000 strong, although this army had half as many units as the 35th CAA (see *War in Ukraine Volume 5*, p.42).
16 The 4th Rapid Reaction Brigade was actually on exercise in the Yavoriv training ground in the Lviv Oblast when the order was given and went east without stopping over at Antonov (see Torop and Khomeko, 'The fight for Hostomel airfield...').
17 Unless otherwise stated, compiled from Jack Watling and Nick Reynolds, 'Russian Military Objectives and Capacity in Ukraine Through 2024', RUSI.org, 13 February 2024; US Army, *ATP 7-100.1 Russian tactics* (Fort Belvoir: US Army Publishing Directorate, 2024), Chapter 3, pp.11–12; Lester W. Grau and Charles K. Bartles, *The Russian Way of War; Force Structure, Tactics, and Modernization of the Russian Ground Forces* (Fort Leavenworth: Foreign Military Studies Office, 2017), p.94.
18 'Найден документ, раскрывающий боевой состав тактической группы 36-й отдельной мотострелковой бригады ВС РФ' [Najden dokument, raskryvajušij boevoj sostav taktičeskoj gruppy 36-j otdel'noj motostrelkovoj brigady VS RF], InformNapalm, 11 October 2016.
19 Denis Yadov, *Начало войны. Орки передвигаются по территории Зоны Отчуждения* [Načalo vojny. Orki peredvigajutsja po territorii Zony Otčuždenija], YouTube, 24 April 2022.
20 Sladden et al., 'The Battle of the Irpin River', pp.14–16.
21 Violetta Kirkota, 'Десантник Віталій Возіян: "Бойове завдання – штурмувати аеродром у Гостомелі. Росіяни вже були там"' ['Desantnik Vitalij Vozijan: "Bojove zavdannja – šturmuvati aerodrom u Gostomeli. Rosijani vže buli tam"'], Censor.net, 31 July 2023.
22 Ukraine Today – 'Money', *Битва за Киев — документальный фильм про войну в Украине* ['Bitva za Kiev — dokumental'nyj fil'm pro vojnu v Ukraine'], YouTube, 10 December 2022; Lesya Pinyak, '"If you hesitate a split second or feel sorry for the enemy, you're gone." Hero of Ukraine Ihor Dykun', *Hromadske*, 15 March 2023.
23 Elena Removskaya, '"Жити в мріях — не вихід для нації, що має вижити» — Герой України Межевікін про мобілізацію, фронт і переваги дронів' ['"Žiti v mrijah — ne vihid dlja naciï, šo maє vižiti» — Geroj Ukraïni Meževikin pro mobilizaciju, front i perevagi droniv'], *Suspilne*, 8 February 2024.
24 Viktor Nikoliuk, *In Defence of the Sumy Region: The Defence and Liberation of the Sumy Region, February-April 2022* (In Ukrainian) (ZSU Centre for Military History Research, 2023), p.3.
25 Violetta Kirkota, 'Заступник командира 93-ої бригади полковник Олександр Сліпко: "За п'ять місяців біля Барвінкового на Харківщині ми знищили близько ста танків противника. І це тільки танків"' ['Zastupnik komandira 93-oï brigadi polkovnik Oleksandr Slipko: "Za p'jat' misjaciv bilja Barvinkovogo na Harkivšini mi znišili bliz'ko sta tankiv protivnika. I ce til'ki tankiv"'], Censor.net, 20 April 2023.
26 This sub-chapter is based on Cooper et al., *War In Ukraine Volume 6*, pp.35, 38–40; 'The Russian Air War and Ukrainian Requirements for Air Defence', RUSI, Special Report, 7 November 2022, p.26; Sonne et al., 'Battle for Kyiv: Ukrainian Valor...', WP, 24 August 2022.
27 Unless stated otherwise, this sub-chapter is based on Matthews, *Overreach*, pp.16–18; Shuster, *The Showman*, pp.224–226; Trofimov, *Our Enemies Will Vanish*, pp.1–5.
28 'Preliminary Lessons in Conventional Warfighting from Russia's Invasion of Ukraine: February-July 2022', RUSI, Special Report, 30 November 2022, p.26.

Chapter 3

1 Cynthia Brumfield, 'Incident response lessons learned from the Russian attack on Viasat', *CSO*, 16 August 2023.
2 Aside from the CSO article, this account of the opening Russian cyber attacks is based on Cooper et al., *War In Ukraine Volume 6*, p.37; Christian Vasquez and Elias Groll, 'Satellite hack on eve of Ukraine war was a coordinated, multi-pronged assault: The satellite hack that took the world by storm was more complex than initially thought, according to a Viasat executive', *CyberScoop*, 10 August 2023; Patrick Howell O'Neill, 'Russia hacked an American satellite company one hour before the Ukraine invasion: the attack on Viasat showcases cyber's emerging role in modern warfare', *MIT Technology Review*, 10 May 2022; Mayuresh Dani, 'Ukrainian Targets Hit by HermeticWiper, New Datawiper Malware, blog.quays.com, 1 March 2022; David E. Sanger, Julian E. Barnes, Kate Conger, 'As Tanks Rolled Into Ukraine, So Did Malware. Then Microsoft Entered the War', *The New York Times* (NYT), 28 February 2022.
3 Unless stated otherwise, this sub-chapter is based on Cooper et al., *War In Ukraine Volume 6*, pp.9, 22, 37–38, 40; 'The Russian Air War and Ukrainian Requirements for Air Defence', RUSI, Special Report, 7 November 2022, pp.6, 13–14, 17, 26-27; 'Preliminary Lessons in Conventional Warfighting from Russia's Invasion of Ukraine: February-July 2022', RUSI, Special Report, 30 November 2022, pp.24–26.
4 'Operation Z: The Death Throes of an Imperial Delusion', RUSI, Special Report, 22 April 2022, p.2.
5 Early reporting claimed the PSZSU's units had dispersed well before the strikes began. For example, see Schwirtz et al., 'Putin's War', *NYT*, 18 December 2022.
6 Yuriy Butusov, 'Трагічні питання 24 лютого ціною у тисячі життів Джерело' ['Tragični pitannja 24 ljutogo cinoju u tisjači žittiv Džerelo'], *Censor.net*, 26 February 2023.
7 The loss of the battery is clear in subsequent satellite imagery. 'ID40295 5P851 launcher', *Lostarmour.info*, <https://lostarmour.info/pvo/40295>, accessed 30 October 2024.
8 Vladislav Nazarkevich, '"Ми знищили понад сорок ворожих літаків та гвинтокрилів"— Герой України Андрій Круглов' ['"Mi znišili ponad sorok vorožih litakiv ta gvintokriliv"— Geroj Ukraïni Andrij Kruglov'], *ArmyInform.com.ua*, 8 July 2022.
9 It is worth highlighting this reconstruction of the RUK cycle is heavily based off 'The Russian Air War and Ukrainian Requirements for Air Defence', RUSI, Special Report, 7 November 2022, pp.27–28.
10 Justin Bronk, 'Russian Combat Air Strengths and Limitations: Lessons from Ukraine', CNA Occasional Paper, 17 April 2023, p.4. Cooper et al. describe the total VSRF strike campaign on 24 February 2022 as consisting of 160+ ballistic and cruise missiles (see *War In Ukraine Volume 6*, p.38). By comparison, the US Navy launched 100+ cruise missiles in the first two hours of Operation Desert Storm alone (see Steve Froggett, 'Tomahawk in the Desert', *US Naval Institute Magazine*, vol. 118 (1992)).
11 Sladden et al., 'The Battle of Irpin River', p.18; Tatyana Popova, 'How Kyiv was Defended in the First Days of The Russian Full-Scale Invasion: The story of Oleksandr Vdovychenko – Commander of the 72nd Separate Mechanized Brigade', *KyivPost*, 24 February 2023.
12 Artem Linkov, quoted in Suspilne Chernihiv, '*Russian Invasion of Ukraine and the first battles in Chernihiv region | Battle for Chernihiv Episode 1*', YouTube, 6 May 2023.
13 Sladden et al., 'The Battle of Irpin River', p.18; Torop and Khomeko, 'The fight for Hostomel airfield...', *BBC News Russian*, 29 February 2024.
14 Philip Wasielewski, 'The Roots of Russian Military Disfunction', *Foreign Policy Research Institute*, Eurasia Program Report, 31 March 2023, pp.12–13.
15 First among them was the 72nd Mechanised Brigade's 2nd Mechanised Battalion, on its way north from Bila Tservka by rail (see Sladden et al., 'The Battle of Irpin River', p.16).

Chapter 4

1 Vladyslav, quoted in Claire Press and Svitlana Libet, 'How Russia's 35-mile armoured convoy ended in failure', *BBC News*, 22 February 2023.

2 'How Russia Spread a Secret Web of Agents Across Ukraine', *voanews.com*, 30 July 2022.
3 Justin Bronk, 'Russian Combat Air Strengths and Limitations: Lessons from Ukraine', CNA Occasional Paper, 17 April 2023, p.13.
4 Unless otherwise stated, this reconstruction of the 35th CAA's advance through the Chernobyl Zone is based off the captured 76th GAAD synchronisation table reproduced in Schwirtz et al., 'Putin's War', NYT, 18 December 2022 and the other following sources: Kirkota, 'Десантник Віталій Возіян…' ['Desantnik Vitalij Vozijan…'], Censor.net, 31 July 2023; Press and Libet, 'How Russia's 35-mile armoured convoy ended in failure', *BBC News*, 22 February 2023; Yann, 'Defending the Kyiv Region: Interview with Omega Special Unit Operator', *Militarnyi*, 10 June 2023; Olga Golovka, '"We Blew Up The Last of the Three Bridges on the Uzh River Along With The Occupiers"' (In Ukrainian), *savelife.in.ua*, 27 December 2023; Suspile, '"Видимий ворог" — документальний проєкт Суспільного про окупацію Чорнобильської зони військами РФ' ['"Vidimij vorog" — dokumental'nij proєkt Suspil'nogo pro okupaciju Čornobil's'koї zoni vijs'kami RF'], YouTube, 26 April 2023; 'How Russia seized the ChNPP: the reconstruction of events and names responsible', The Media Initiative for Human Rights, 22 November 2023; Maxim Kamenev, 'How Russia Took Over Chernobyl', *openDemocracy*, 22 June 2022; Max Schönhausen: 'Wounded Tiger 4-Invasion', *Medium*, 8 March 2023.
5 Unless stated otherwise, following sub-chapter is based firstly on open-source aircraft loss information compiled by Milos Sipos for War in Ukraine Volumes 6 and 7. All Russian losses are cross-referenced with *Russo-Ukrainian WarSpotting*. Literature and media sources referenced include Cooper et al., *War In Ukraine Volume 6*, pp.25, 41–47; Sladden et al., 'The Battle of Irpin River', pp.18–20; Yann, 'Defending the Kyiv Region…', *Militarnyi*, 10 June 2023; Torop and Khomeko, 'The fight for Hostomel airfield….', *BBC News Russian*, 29 February 2024; Operator Starsky, 'What happened in Hostomel | Day 365', YouTube, 23 February 2023.
6 There is some difficulty in determining the exact number of helicopters employed because they came in two waves.
7 The Russian Air War and Ukrainian Requirements for Air Defence', RUSI, Special Report, 7 November 2022, pp.9–10.
8 Ponomarov, quoted in Conflict Camera, *Survivor: Russian VDV Airborne Soldier Talks About Their Initial Invasion of Hostomel Airport'*, YouTube, 21 April 2022.
9 Mark Mackinnon, 'The Fearless: An elite squad of fighters has been on the front lines of every major battle for Ukraine's independence. This is the story of their war', *The Globe and Mail*, 6 June 2024.
10 Sources range between two ZU-23-2s (see Yann, 'Defending the Kyiv Region…') and three ZU-23-2s (see Yuriy Butusov, 'Трагічні питання 24 лютого ціною у тисячі життів Джерело' ['Tragični pitannja 24 ljutogo cinoju u tisjači žittiv Džerelo'], Censor.net, 26 February 2023).
11 This change in tactics and the lost Omega vehicles are specifically described in Yann, 'Defending the Kyiv Region…', *Militarnyi*, 10 June 2023'. The loss of the BTR-3 is confirmed by 'BTR-3E', *Lostarmour.info*, <https://lostarmour.info/armour/37348>, accessed 30 October 2024.
12 Vitaly Rudenko, quoted in Torop and Khomeko, 'The fight for Hostomel airfield….', BBC News Russian, 29 February 2024.
13 Paul Sims and James Somper, 'British Lion: I'm one of the first Brits to join Ukraine – they fight like lions and I'm proud to take on Putin with them', *The Sun*, 9 March 2022.
14 The activities of the second wave prior to and after landing have been shown in footage released on Russian media: Pill Time, *'Russia Published The Footage Of First Day Of Invasion Of Ukraine'*, YouTube, 16 August 2022.
15 Unless stated otherwise, this sub-chapter is cross-referenced from the following sources: Sladden et al., 'The Battle of Irpin River', pp.20–21, 47; Sonne et al., 'Battle for Kyiv: Ukrainian Valor…', *WP*, 24 August 2022; Cooper et al., *War In Ukraine Volume 2*, p.41; Cooper et al., *War In Ukraine Volume 6*, pp.49–50; Ashleigh Stewart, 'The Battle of Hostomel: How Ukraine's unlikely victory changed the course of the war', *Global News*, 18 February 2023; Kirkota, 'Десантник Віталій Возіян…' 'Десантник Віталій Возіян…' ['Desantnik Vitalij Vozijan…'], Censor.net, 31 July 2023; ArmyTV- Ukrainian military channel, *'ZEUS. A MAN WHO BEAT THE RUSSIANS HARD AT HOSTOMEL'*, YouTube, 15 August 2023; Sergiy Lemekha, 'Снайпер Марк: "Коли робиш влучний постріл — ворог панікує, покладається не на розум, а на інстинкти"' ['Snajper Mark: "Koli robiš vlučnij postril — vorog panikuє, pokladaєt'sja ne na rozum, a na instinkti"'], *ArmyInform. com.ua*, 15 July 2023; Valentyn Stolyarchuk and Mykhailo Chubay, 'Війна очима десантника Юрія' ['Vijna očima desantnika Jurija'], *ArmyInform.com.ua*, 22 August 2022; Shuster, *The Showman*, pp.31–32, 75.
16 Mykhailo Podolyak, quoted in Shuster, *The Showman*, p.31.
17 Christo Grozev, '!!! Ukrainian government sources tell me 18 Il-76 planes have left Pskov direction Kyiv, will arrive in about an hour' [Twitter post], 3:41 p.m., 24 February 2022, <https://x.com/christogrozev/status/1496873022229073924>, accessed 31 October 2024.
18 See Sladden et al., 'The Battle of Irpin River', pp.19–20.
19 Zeus, quoted in ArmyTV- Ukrainian military channel, *'ZEUS. A MAN WHO BEAT THE RUSSIANS HARD AT HOSTOMEL'*, YouTube, 15 August 2023.
20 Volodymyr Zelensky, quoted in Shuster, *The Showman*, p.32.
21 Unless stated otherwise, this sub-chapter's account is cross-referenced from Sladden et al., 'The Battle of Irpin River', pp.15, 23; Tim McMillan, 'Know No Mercy: The Russian Cops Who Tried To Storm Kyiv By Themselves', *The Debrief*, 20 May 2022; Yann, 'Defending the Kyiv Region…', *Militarnyi*, 10 June 2023; Shuster, *The Showman*, pp.28–29; Office of the Prosecutor General, *'Five Russian servicemen were notified of suspicion of shooting cars with civilians in Hostomel'*, YouTube, 28 September 2022. Captured documents from the 19th Operational Brigade were also referenced, see Militarnyi, 'Документи , яких українські силовики розбили під Гостомелем…' ['Dokumenti , jakih ukraïns'ki siloviki rozbili pid Gostomelem…'][Twitter post], 8:10 a.m., 27 February 2022, <https://x.com/mil_in_ua/status/1497846512604360709/photo/2>, accessed 31 October 2024.
22 Dmitry Astakhov, quoted in Zolkin Volodymyr, *'WHAT DO THE RUSSIAN POLICE FORGET IN UKRAINE? | Police Lieutenant Colonel SOBR'*, YouTube, 29 June 2022.
23 This diagram and accompanying account are sourced from the following sources: Militarnyi, 'Документи , яких українські силовики розбили під Гостомелем…' ['Dokumenti , jakih ukraïns'ki siloviki rozbili pid Gostomelem…']; McMillan, 'Know No Mercy'; Office of the Prosecutor General, *'Five Russian servicemen were notified of suspicion of shooting cars with civilians in Hostomel'*; Volodymyr, *'WHAT DO THE RUSSIAN POLICE FORGET'*; Zolkin Volodymyr, *'Captain of the POLICE Spiridonov Yevgeny | "Twenty people fell DEAD"'*, YouTube, 19 June 2022; Russo-Ukrainian WarSpotting, <https://ukr.warspotting.net/search/?belligerent=2&division=221&location=16>, accessed 2 February 2025; ' "In the area of the Maidan or Khreshchatyk, we will prepare dances." What was reported to the person with Kadyrov's voice on the eve of Russia's invasion of Ukraine', *BBC News Russian Service*, 26 February 2022.
24 There is only limited evidence for actual Russian casualties. One Kyiv surgeon reported operating on wounded Russian infiltrators (see Christopher Miller, '"Our Duty": Ukrainian Surgeons Are Operating On Russian Soldiers Wounded In Ukraine', *BuzzFeed News*, 7 March 2022).
25 The number of friendly fire casualties is attested to widely (see Trofimov, *Our Enemies Will Vanish*, p.59; Sladden et al., 'The Battle of Irpin River', p.23).
26 'Ukraine Invasion: Kyiv imposes curfew amid sabotage fears', *BBC News*, 26 February 2022.
27 Unless stated otherwise, this sub-chapter's account is synthesised from Oksana Ivanets, 'Рік на чолі бригади і нелегкі місяці на шести напрямках фронту. Інтерв'ю з комбригом 14-ї ОМБр Олександром Охріменком' ['Rik na čoli brigadi i nelegki misjaci na šesti naprjamkah frontu. Interv'ju z kombrigom 14-ї OMBr Oleksandrom Ohrimenkom'], *slovopravdy.com.ua*, 19 October 2022; 'У Львівській області попрощалися з Віталієм Сапіло танкістом, якого атакував російський Су-25' ['U L'vivs'kij oblasti poprošalisja z Vitaliєm Sapilo tankistom, jakogo atakuvav rosijs'kij Su-25'], *Ukraine Live*, 28 February 2022; Oksana Ivanytska and Mariana Pietsukh, 'Heroes who died in the first days of the full-scale war', *Hromadske*, 29 February 2024. ZSU vehicle losses are confirmed around 'ID 30584 T-64BV Model 2017', *Lostarmour. info*, <https://lostarmour.info/armour/30584>, accessed 30 October 2024.

28 Oleksandr Ohrimenko, quoted in Oksana Ivanets, 'Рік на чолі бригади…' ['Rik na čoli brigadi…'], *slovopravdy.com.ua*, 19 October 2022.
29 Alexander Fedorchak, 'Ярость Ареса: как "древнегреческий" танк громит боевиков на полях сражений СВО' ['Jarost' Aresa: kak "drevnegrečeskij" tank gromit boevikov na poljah sraženij SVO'], *Zvezda*, 12 September 2022.
30 Compiled from Sladden et al.,'The Battle of Irpin River', pp.22–24; 'A bridge blown up on the Kyiv-Zhytomyr highway. One child dead, several people wounded', *Ukrainska Pravda*, 26 February 2022; Lawrence, *The Battle of Kyiv*, p.161.
31 Eugene Simonov and Oleksii Vasyliuk, 'Plans to rebuild Ukraine shaped by solutions for Irpin', *Ukraine War Environmental Consequences Work Group*, 9 September 2022.
32 The Irpin's flow was originally north-easterly, but the flooding reversed this to a south-western flow. It is according to the latter direction that downriver and upriver are used throughout the book.
33 Compiled from Cooper et al., *War In Ukraine Volume 6*, pp.50–51; Carlotta Gall, 'When the Russians Picked the Wrong Town to Invade', *NYT*, 2 April 2022; Anna Gudz, 'Як у перші дні вторгнення рф наші військові обороняли аеродром у Василькові' ['Jak u perši dni vtorgnennja rf naši vijs'kovi oboronjali aerodrom u Vasil'kovi'], *ArmyInform.com.ua*, 7 July 2022; Anatoly Gaevsky and Olga Golovka, 'Навчити оператора FPV складніше, ніж навідника БМП: керівник Школи «Ятаган» Сергій Матвійчук' ['Navčiti operatora FPV skladniše, niž navidnika BMP: kerivnik Školi «Jatagan» Sergij Matvijčuk'], *savelife.in.ua*, 22 April 2024; 'Heroes of Ukraine: Vasyl Boyechko, former history teacher, stops Russia breaking through to Kyiv', *Espreso*, 10 June 2022.
34 The 8th Battalion had arrived by rail from the Starychi training ground early on 25 Feb. Its elements were distributed between the various airfields south of Kyiv. (see Gaevsky and Golovka, 'Навчити оператора FPV складніше…' ['Navčiti operatora FPV skladniše…'], *savelife.in.ua*, 22 April 2024).

Chapter 5

1 This paragraph is based on 'The Russian Air War and Ukrainian Requirements for Air Defence', RUSI, Special Report, 7 November 2022, p.13; Radio Liberty, *How Russian commanders gained the trust of locals in Kyiv region | Investigation*, YouTube, 5 July 2023; Erika Kinetz, 'Kill everyone': Russian brutality in occupied Ukraine was strategic, organized and linked to high-ranking officer', *Anchorage Daily News*, 26 October 2022.
2 Anti-Terrorist Operation was a Ukrainian term used to describe the initial war against the Russian separatists in the east of the country)
3 This name was apparently chosen as a pun on battalion tactical group.
4 This paragraph is synthesised from Shuster, *The Showman*, p.75; Sladden et al., 'The Battle of Irpin River', pp.10, 29, 32; Kirkota, 'Десантник Віталій Возіян…' ['Desantnik Vitalij Vozijan…'], *Censor.net*, 31 July 2023; War in Ukraine with English Subtitles, *'Red Dawn near "Giraffe" (Battle of the Irpin Bridge)'*, YouTube, 15 February 2023.
5 Cooper et al., *War in Ukraine Volume 2*, pp.47, 62–63; Oksana Chmilenko, 'Коли на фронті нема і хвилини спокою, вдома найбільше лякає тиша, — тернопільський артилерист' ['Koli na fronti nema i hvilini spokoju, vdoma najbil'še ljakaje tiša, — ternopil's'kij artilerist'], *Ternopil*, 22 November 2023.
6 Unless stated otherwise, this reconstruction of the 27 February fighting in Hostomel, Bucha, and Irpin is based off a cross-examination of the following accounts: Conflict Camera, *'Survivor: Russian VDV Airborne Soldier Talks…'*, YouTube, 21 April 2022; Cooper et al., *War in Ukraine Volume 2*, pp.43-44; Yevheniia Mazur, 'The battle of Vokzalna Street, or How defenders of Bucha foiled Russia's Kyiv offensive', *LIGA.net*, 31 March 2023; War in Ukraine with English Subtitles, *'Red Dawn near "Giraffe"…'*, YouTube, 15 February 2023; War in Ukraine with English Subtitles, *'The defiant duo from Bucha'*, YouTube, 26 October 2022; Press and Libet, 'How Russia's 35-mile armoured convoy ended in failure', *BBC News*, 22 February 2023; Olha Kyrylenko and Dmytro Larin, 'It was necessary to see how the "Pions" weighing 47 tons were moving under their own power along Peremohy Avenue – Brigade Commander of the 43rd Brigade Oleh Shevchuk', *Ukrainska Pravda*, 22 February 2023; Pete Shmigel, 'Partisan Pensioners Versus Russian Tanks: Tales From Bucha One Year Later', *Kyiv Post*, 31 March 2023; Aleksandr Vizgin, '"Били їх на досвіді": як ветерани АТО перетнули ворогу шлях до Ірпеня' ['"Bili ïh na dosvidi": jak veterani ATO peretnuli vorogu šljah do Irpenja'], *ArmyInform.com.ua*, 20 May 2022; Schönhausen, 'Wounded Tiger 6'; Schönhausen, 'Wounded Tiger 7'.
7 For confirmation of the presence of the 104th Regiment, 76 GAAD, see '#1076 1V119 'Reostat' artillery command vehicle', *Russo-Ukrainian WarSpotting*, <https://ukr.warspotting.net/view/1076/>, accessed 31 October 2024.
8 "Zeus" attests to downing a Ka-52 (see ArmyTV- Ukrainian military channel, *'ZEUS. A MAN WHO BEAT THE RUSSIANS…'*, YouTube, 15 August 2023), but this is likely a misidentification as the only helicopter shot down matching the dates is an Mi-28UM (see '#3109 Mi-28N attack helicopter', *Russo-Ukrainian WarSpotting*, <https://ukr.warspotting.net/view/3109/10440/>, accessed 31 October 2024.
9 Ponomarov, quoted in Conflict Camera, *'Survivor: Russian VDV Airborne Soldier Talks…'*, YouTube (21 April 2022).
10 See Mazur, 'The battle of Vokzalna Street…', *LIGA.net*, 31 March 2023.
11 Losses confirmed around '#1372 BMP-2(K)', *Russo-Ukrainian WarSpotting*, <https://ukr.warspotting.net/view/1372/5909/>, accessed 31 October 2024.
12 Valentyn Didkovskiy, quoted in] Radio Liberty, 'Ukrainian Pensioner Who Took On Russian Column Shares Phone Video Of Destruction', YouTube, 3 August 2022.
13 The Su-24 bombing run was witnessed by those on the ground (see Mazur, 'The battle of Vokzalna Street…', *LIGA.net*, 31 March 2023). Loss of the aircraft and crew confirmed by 'ID 31071 Su-24M', *Lostarmour.info*, <https://lostarmour.info/avia/31071>, accessed 31 October 2024.
14 Ukraine Weapons Tracker, '#Ukraine: A Barnaul-T 9S932-1 command post…'[Twitter post], 12:12 p.m., 3 March 2022, <https://x.com/UAWeapons/status/1499357110378938370/>, accessed 31 October 2024.
15 This sub-chapter is based on Radio Liberty, *'The battle for Kyiv | How did elite Russian troops fail? | Unknown details (ENG SUB)'*, YouTube, 25 February 2023; Sonne et al., 'Battle for Kyiv: Ukrainian Valor…', *WP*, 24 August 2022; Sladden et al., 'The Battle of Irpin River', pp.32-33; Anastasia Bogach, 'Ми тицьнули пикою "другу армію світу" у її реальний статус'— сержант Денис' ['"Mi tic'nuli pikoju 'drugu armiju svitu' u ïï real'nij statuc"— seržant Denis'], *armyinform.com.ua*, 18 November 2022.
16 Unless otherwise stated, this sub-chapter is compiled from the following sources: Apostrophe TV, *'ПЕРША битва за Київщину. З рушницями проти танків. Як росіяни нищили Макарів з авіації'* ['PERŠA bitva za Kiïvšinu. Z rušnicjami proti tankiv. Jak rosijani nišili Makariv z aviaciï'], YouTube, 25 February 2024; Alexey Slavin, Sasha Sivtsova, and Gleb Golod, 'Worse than Bucha: Meduza speaks to Borodyanka residents about how they survived under Russian occupation', *Meduza*, 8 April 2022; Alexey Slavin, ''Stolen lives, stolen hopes' Borodyanka Mayor Georgiy Yerko on how Russian forces occupied his town and left it in ruins', *Meduza*, 11 April 2022; 'Бородянка. Як все було' ['Borodjanka. Jak vse bulo'], *Espreso*, 1 April 2023; III_regiment_SOF, *'3 полк ССО: бій під Бородянкою 27 лютого 2022'* ['3 polk SSO: bij pid Borodjankoju 27 ljutogo 2022'], YouTube, 2 May 2024; ArmyTV- Ukrainian military channel, *'MAKARIV WAS NEVER UNDER OCCUPATION'*, YouTube, 6 May 2022; NYT, *'Russia Struggled to Capture a Ukrainian Town. Intercepted Radio Messages Show Why.'*, YouTube, 24 March 2022; 'Фельдшер Марія Захарченко про активні бойові дії у Макарівській громаді: "28 лютого обстріляли автівки цивільних, пораненого в живіт вдалося врятувати"' ['Fel'dšer Marija Zaharčenko pro aktivni bojovi diï u Makarivs'kij gromadi: "28 ljutogo obstriljali avtivki civil'nih, poranenogo v živit vdalosja vrjatuvati"'], *makariv.media*, 3 August 2023; Ashleigh Stewart, 'Propaganda or Providence: one Ukrainian's Wild Story of Survival', *Global News*, 20 June 2022.
17 These captured documents are referred to here: Apostrophe TV, *'ПЕРША битва за Київщину. З рушницями проти танків. Як росіяни нищили Макарів з авіації'* ['PERŠA bitva za Kiïvšinu. Z rušnicjami proti tankiv. Jak rosijani nišili Makariv z aviaciï'], YouTube, 25 February 2024.
18 People's Voice of Ukraine, 'Центр Бородянки Київської області, біля Фори та АТБ. Обстріл російської колони вночі…' ['Centr

Borodjanki Kiïvs′koï oblasti, bilja Fori ta ATB. Obstril rosijs′koï koloni vnoči…'], *Facebook.com*, 1 March 2022.

19 Ghanna Mamonova and Yuliana Skibitska, '"It's not the pilots' fault — they purposefully dropped bombs." In March, the Russian occupiers launched dozens of airstrikes on Borodyanka. The story of a ruined house and the people who lived there', *Babel*, 13 May 2022.

20 Ekaterina Foma, '"Dispose of Them," the Commander Ordered', *Pulitzer Centre*, 18 August 2022.

21 Johnny O'Reilly, 'Before the Russian Retreat, A Rescue Mission And A Reunion in Ukraine', *Radio Liberty*, 15 April 2022.

22 The splitting of the 37th GMRB's BTGs in western and south-eastern directions may have come about as an accident. Ukrainian villagers attest to switching local road signs, causing the first BTG to turn onto the E40 and drive west, whilst the one behind continued southeast through Kopyliv (see Sarah Rainsford, 'Ukraine war: Bodies of dead Russian soldiers abandoned near Kyiv', *BBC News*, 25 May 2022). Certainly, one BTG sized column was filmed by CCTV driving in the 'correct' direction (see MVA78UA, '*Копилів 2022-02-27 колона техніки. Kopyliv -column of rus armored vehicles, from the Zhytomyr highway*', YouTube, 13 March 2023).

Chapter 6

1 This paragraph is cross-referenced between Apostrophe TV, '*ПЕРША битва за Київщину…*' ['PERŠA bitva za Kiïvŝinu…'], YouTube, 25 February 2024, and United 24, 'Myla, 40B/1 Komarova St.', Rebuild Ukraine Program (2023) <https://u24.gov.ua/rebuild/Mila_str_Komarova_40B_1>, accessed 31 October 2024. The latter article suggests the 5th GTB was halted before the Irpin, but the presence of a knocked-out T-72B from the brigade on the outskirts of Stoyanka suggests it got as far as the river, if only briefly (see #57 T-72B, *Russo-Ukrainian WarSpotting*, <https://ukr.warspotting.net/view/57/7329/>, accessed 31 October 2024).

2 Rainsford, 'Ukraine war: Bodies of dead Russian soldiers…', BBC News, 25 May 2022

3 Aside from Rainsford's article, this paragraph is cross-referenced between Apostrophe TV, '*ПЕРША битва за Київщину…*' ['PERŠA bitva za Kiïvŝinu…'], YouTube, 25 February 2024; Cooper et al, *War In Ukraine Volume 6*, p.53; Schönhausen, 'Wounded Tiger 8', *Medium*, 8 March 2023; NYT, '*Russia Struggled to Capture a Ukrainian Town….*', YouTube, 24 March 2022; Nabih Bulos, 'Raining rockets, scattered corpses, an existential battle: A 500-mile journey across a week of war', *LA Times*, 5 March 2022.

4 "Yug-95", quoted in NYT, '*Russia Struggled to Capture a Ukrainian Town….*', YouTube, 24 March 2022.

5 Unless stated otherwise, this sub-chapter's reconstruction of the March 3 fighting in Kyiv's suburbs is based on the following sources: Vizgin, '"Били їх на досвіді"…', ArmyInform.com.ua, 20 May 2022; III_regiment_SOF, '*Гостомель 3 березня 2022 року. ПОДРОБИЦІ*' ['Gostomel' 3 bereznja 2022 roku. PODROBICÍ'], YouTube, 15 April 2024; Kirkota, 'Десантник Віталій Возіян…' ['Desantnik Vitalij Vozijan…'], *Censor.net*, 31 July 2023; '"Для беларусского народа он должен быть героем!": эмоциональная история беларуса, воющего за Украину' ['"Dlja belarusskogo naroda on dolžen byt′ geroem!": èmocional′naja istorija belarusa, vojušego za Ukrainu' 'Gostomel' 3 bereznja 2022 roku. PODROBICÍ'], *Charter 97*, 7 March 2022, <https://telegra.ph/Belarusskie-geroi-na-vojne-za-Ukrainu-03-07>, accessed 31 October 2024; NYT, '*Exposing the Russian Military Unit Behind a Massacre in Bucha | Visual Investigations*', YouTube, 22 December 2022; Ukraine Today- 'Money', '*Битва за Киев…*' ['Bitva za Kiev…'], YouTube, 10 December 2022; Mark Sirovoy, 'Гостомель. Спецназ ГУР знищив 20 бойових машин російського десанту, йде бій – відео' ['Gostomel'. Specnaz GUR zniŝiv 20 bojovih mašin rosijs′kogo desantu, jde bij – video'], *Liga.net*, 3 March 2022. All Russian vehicle losses confirmed via *Russo-Ukrainian WarSpotting*.

6 Cooper et al., *War in Ukraine Volume 6*, p.52.

7 A variety of captured 37th GMRB documentation was filmed by a French TV crew of Complementary Investigation: Louis Milano-Dupont, Julien Cholin, Guillaume Couderc and Olivier Broutin, *War crimes: the face of the executioners*, France 2 (2023), <https://www.francetvinfo.fr/replay-magazine/france-2/complement-d-enquete/video-crimes-de-guerre-le-visage-des-bourreaux_5658782.html>, accessed 2 January 2025.

8 Unfortunately, the original GUR web page detailing the roster has since been scrubbed, although translated copies exist in the possession of researchers Christopher Lawrence and Sasho Todorov, who generously shared them with the author.

9 ASLAN, 'Новые российские эшелоны прибыли в Беларусь.' ['Novye rossijskie èšelony pribyli v Belarus′.'] [Twitter post], 5:42 p.m., 26 January 2022, <https://x.com/antiputler_news/status/1486394194314895361>, accessed 2 January 2025; MVA78UA, '*Копилів 2022-02-27 колона техніки. Kopyliv -column of rus armored vehicles, from the Zhytomyr highway*', YouTube, 13 March 2023.

10 *Russo-Ukrainian WarSpotting*, <https://ukr.warspotting.net/search/?belligerent=2&division=16>, accessed 2 January 2025.

11 The exact day the signallers were encircled is unknown (see Liliya Dvoretska, '"Російська тюрма — це табір із виховання українських націоналістів"' ['"Rosijs′ka tjurma — ce tabir iz vihovannja ukraïns′kih nacionalistiv"'], *savelife.in.ua*, 22 March 2023).

12 Denis, quoted in '"Для беларусского народа он должен быть героем!": эмоциональная история беларуса, воющего за Украину' ['"Dlja belarusskogo naroda on dolžen byt′ geroem!": èmocional′naja istorija belarusa, vojušego za Ukrainu'], *Charter 97*, 7 March 2022, <https://telegra.ph/Belarusskie-geroi-na-vojne-za-Ukrainu-03-07>, accessed 31 October 2024.

13 This route of the 106th GAD is recounted in Vladimir D, 'Начало СВО: битва за пригороды Киева' [Načalo SVO: bitva za prigorody Kieva], *Lostarmour.info*, no date, and confirmed by Anhelina Sheremet, 'Ukraine identified Russian soldiers who shot 10 cars of civilians leaving Irpin last March. Then 9 people died', *Babel*, 6 March 2023.

14 "Shaman", quoted in Conflict Camera, '*"And So They Rode In Zinc"- Ukrainian Commander 'Shaman' On The Battle Of #Hostomel Glass Factory*', YouTube, 3 April 2022.

15 '*Alexey Osokin*', *topcargo.200.com*, <https://topcargo200.com/17/>, accessed 31 October 2024; 'Insur Kinyakaev', *topcargo.200.com*, <https://topcargo200.com/130/>.

16 Unless stated otherwise, this sub-chapter is drawn from the following sources: 'Here's how weeks of heavy Russian shelling has changed Yasnohorodka, once a cozy village north of Kyiv', *The New Voice of Ukraine*, 1 April 2022; Viktoriia Zhuhan, 'Ukraine war: The priest shot at checkpoint', *BBC News*, 25 March 2022; War in Ukraine with English Subtitles, '*Three little villages that could – The unconquerable Dmytrivka, Buzova, Yasnogorodka*', YouTube, 17 March 2023; Cooper et al, *War In Ukraine Volume 6*, p.53; Dvoretska, '"Російська тюрма…"' ['"Rosijs′ka tjurma…"'], *savelife.in.ua*, 22 March 2023.

17 "Nimble", quoted in War in Ukraine with English Subtitles, '*Three little villages that could – The unconquerable Dmytrivka, Buzova, Yasnogorodka*', YouTube, 17 March 2023.

18 'Yuri Medvedev', *topcargo.200*, <https://topcargo200.com/42/>, accessed 31 October 2024.

19 The story of the R-330Zh and the elderly woman is synthesised from 'A pensioner from Motyzhyn helped the Ukrainian military destroy about a hundred units of Russian equipment: the occupiers killed her' (in Ukrainian), *ZMINA*, 4 May 2022; '#4087 R-330Zh 'Zhytel' electronic warfare station', *Russo-Ukrainian WarSpotting*, <https://ukr.warspotting.net/view/4087/>, accessed 31 October 2024; 'Attacks on Civilians in Motzhyn, Kopyliv, and Severynivka, Ukraine', IPHR, Truth Hounds, Global Dilligence LLP, joint report, 30 January 2023, pp.9–10.

20 For just some of the many detailed reports on war crimes committed by 5th GTB and 37th GMRB see 'Attacks on Civilians in Motzhyn, Kopyliv, and Severynivka, Ukraine', IPHR, Truth Hounds, Global Dilligence LLP, joint report, 30 January 2023; Taras Lazer and Nadja Kelm, 'Mass murder on the Zhytomyr highway: map, chronology and investigation of Russian war crimes', *texty.org.ua*, 6 October 2023.

21 War in Ukraine with English Subtitles, '*Three little villages that could – The unconquerable Dmytrivka, Buzova, Yasnogorodka*', YouTube, 17 March 2023.

22 Unless stated otherwise, this sub-chapter on the Battle of Makariv is based on the following sources: Apostrophe TV, '*ПЕРША битва за Київщину. З рушницями проти танків. Як росіяни нищили*

Макарів з авіації', ['PERŠA bitva za Kiïvŝinu. Z rušnicjami proti tankiv. Jak rosijani nišili Makariv z aviaciï'] YouTube, 25 February 2024; ArmyTV- Ukrainian military channel, *'MAKARIV WAS NEVER UNDER OCCUPATION'*, YouTube, 6 May 2022; Olga Musafirova, 'Starry Skies and Minefields: How Nalyvaikivka, a fearless village in Ukraine's Kyiv region, lived through four months of war and what its residents think of the so-called "grain ceasefire"', *Novaya Gazeta Europe*, 24 July 2022; Guy Agam Fusfus, Benjamin den Braber, Sofia Santos, 'Documenting Rubble: How Russia Destroyed More Than 300 Buildings in Ukraine's Makariv', CFIR, Report, no date; Mansur Mirovalev, 'Resistance, calamity and looting in a Kyiv suburb', *Al Jazeera*, 27 June 2022.

23 May have specifically been the 95th Air Assault Brigade's 2nd BTG, as indicated by the following obituary 'Marchenko Alexander Vasilievich', warterars.org, <https://warterars.org/record/213808>, accessed 31 October 2024. Unintuitively, the 2nd BTG was seemingly not based on the brigade's 2nd Battalion, which was fighting in the Donetsk Oblast at the time. Instead, the brigade's 1st and 3rd Battalions fought at Makariv (see 10th Mountain Assault Brigade, 'Зі щитом!UA' ['Zi ŝitom!UA'] [Facebook post], 1 October 2022, <https://www.facebook.com/watch/?v=926793554947966&t=82>).

24 Based on research conducted by Milos Sipos for *War in Ukraine Volume 6*. Loss of the Su-25 confirmed at '#3055 Su-25SM close air support aircraft', *Russo-Ukrainian WarSpotting*, <https://ukr.warspotting.net/view/3055/6189/>, accessed 31 October 2024. Loss of the Mi-8 confirmed at: '#3089 Mi-8AMTSh transport helicopter', *Russo-Ukrainian WarSpotting*, <https://ukr.warspotting.net/view/3089/61028/>.

25 Maryana, quoted in Musafirova, 'Starry Skies and Minefield...', *Novaya Gazeta Europe*, 24 July 2022.

26 Natalia Mazina, '"How is my child intact if she was killed?" In memory of Heroine of Ukraine Kateryna Stupnytska', *Hromadske*, 9 March 2023.

27 "Poltava", quoted in Kateryna Farbar, 'Face-to-face with killers: how a Ukrainian village endured occupation', *openDemocracy*, 16 June 2022.

28 This reconstruction of the 9th Company's counterattack is based off Mazina, '"How is my child intact if she was killed?"...', *Hromadske*, 9 March 2023, and 'Vasich Serhii Viktorovych', *Ukrainian Memorial*, <https://ukraine-memorial.org/ua/biography/vasich-sergiy-viktorovich/>, accessed 31 October 2024.

29 Vasyl Shvets, quoted in Mazina, '"How is my child intact if she was killed?"...', Hromadske, 9 March 2023.

30 This reconstruction of the 5th Company's counterattack is based off 'Yurii Kindratyshyn', www.victims.memorial, <https://www.victims.memorial/people/yurii-kindratyshyn>, accessed 31 October 2024; Ruslana Bogdan, 'На Київщині встановили пам'ятник загиблим в бою за село Липівка бійцям' ['Na Kiïvŝini vstanovili pam'jatnik zagiblim v boju za selo Lipivka bijcjam'], *ArmyInform.com.ua*, 7 April 2023; 'Втрачені захисники. Євген Федосов – захищав Липівку, похований на Алеї Слави у Харкові' ['Vtračeni zahisniki. Êvgen Fedosov – zahišav Lipivku, pohovanij na Aleï Slavi u Harkovi'], *makariv.media*, 22 December 2023.

31 Kim Sengupta, 'Welcome to hell': Inside Makariv, the town Ukrainians took back from Russian troops', *The Independent*, 24 March 2022.

32 Reports on March 25 2022 still describe the town as fiercely contested (see 'Kyiv Regional Military Administration: Bucha, Irpin, Hostomel, Makariv are the fiercest points, the enemy has come close to Slavutych' (In Ukrainian), *interfax.com.ua*, 25 March 2022.

Chapter 7

1 Chapter introduction based off Cooper et al, *War in Ukraine Volume 6*, p.55; Schönhausen, 'Wounded Tiger 8', *Medium*, 8 March 2023; Schönhausen, 'Wounded Tiger 9'; Sladden et al., 'The Battle of Irpin River', p.24.

2 Unless stated otherwise, this sub-chapter's reconstruction of the 5–11 March fighting in Moschun is based on a cross-reference of the following sources: Cooper et al, *War in Ukraine Volume 6*, p.55; Schönhausen, 'Wounded Tiger 9', *Medium*, 8 March 2023; Schönhausen, 'Wounded Tiger 10'; Sladden et al., 'The Battle of Irpin River', pp.35–37, 39–41; Vladimir D, 'Битва за Мощун (часть 1)' ['Bitva za Moŝun (čast' 1)'], *Lostarmour.info*, no date; Radio Liberty, *'The battle for Kyiv | How did elite Russian troops fail?...'*, YouTube, 25 February 2023; Nicholas Laidlaw, *What War Did To Us Volume 2: Ukraine: The First 150 Days of Combat February 24-July 24* (Amazon, 2022), pp.97–134; Sonne et al., 'Battle for Kyiv: Ukrainian Valor...', *WP*, 24 August 2022.

3 Sladden et al. describe the Russian assault meeting fierce Ukrainian resistance and containing a mechanised component and pontoon bridge from the outset (see 'The Battle of Irpin River', pp.35–36). This contrasts with the account of a Russian marine from the 155th NIB who describes meeting no initial resistance during their crossing, which was conducted on foot without a pontoon bridge nor vehicles (see Alexei Sukonkin, 'Реку мы перешли, где вброд...' ['Reku my perešli, gde vbrod...'], [Telegram message], 3:38 a.m., 20 April 2023, <https://t.me/A_S_Sukonkin/4089>, accessed 31 October 2024).

4 For examination of issues with Soviet IFVs' amphibious capabilities see Military History Visualized, *'BMP: Amphibious or a Watery Grave?'*, YouTube, 21 March 2023.

5 Anon., quoted in Alexei Sukonkin, 'Реку мы перешли, где вброд...' ['Reku my perešli, gde vbrod...'], [Telegram message], 3:38 a.m., 20 April 2023, <https://t.me/A_S_Sukonkin/4089>, accessed 31 October 2024.

6 'Andrey Ivanov', *mptaifun.ru*, <https://mptaifun.ru/blog/nekrolog/2022-05-11-1180>, accessed 31 October 2024.

7 There is considerable divergence between accounts regarding which bridges were placed first and which were first destroyed. It is possible the Russians moved bridges during the period, deepening the confusion. Accordingly, the author's account should be treated as an estimate.

8 Roman Kovalenko, quoted in Sonne et al., 'Battle for Kyiv: Ukrainian Valor...', WP, 24 August 2022.

9 Schönhausen, 'Wounded Tiger 10'

10 Laidlaw, *What War Did To Us Volume 2*, pp.104, 118, 125, 131.

11 Ryan, quoted in Laidlaw, p.122.

12 Anon., quoted in Sladden et al., 'The Battle of Irpin River', p.41.

13 '"Скотившись на подвір'я, дістаю „ефку" й кидаю за паркан. Вибух! А далі — тиша" — спогади розвідника-диверсанта ГУР МОУ' ['"Skotivšis' na podvir'ja, distaju „efku" j kidaju za parkan. Vibuh! A dali — tiša» — spogadi rozvidnika-diversanta GUR MOU'], *ArmyInform.com.ua*, 2 April 2023.

14 Unless stated otherwise, this sub-chapter's reconstruction of the 12–21 March fighting in Moschun and aftermath is based off the following sources: Cooper et al, *War in Ukraine Volume 6*, p.55; Schönhausen, 'Wounded Tiger 11', *Medium*, 8 March 2023; Radio Liberty, *'The battle for Kyiv | How did elite Russian troops fail?...'*, YouTube, 25 February 2023; Trofimov, *Our Enemies Will Vanish*, p.139; '"Скотившись на подвір'я, дістаю „ефку" й кидаю за паркан. Вибух! А далі — тиша" — спогади розвідника-диверсанта ГУР МОУ' ['"Skotivšis' na podvir'ja, distaju „efku" j kidaju za parkan. Vibuh! A dali — tiša» — spogadi rozvidnika-diversanta GUR MOU'], *ArmyInform.com.ua*, 2 April 2023; 'The fate of Ukraine and the capital was decided in the battles for the towns and villages of Kyiv region – Volodymyr Zelenskyy honored the memory of the warriors fallen in the battle for Moshchun', *www.president.gov.ua*, 21 March 2024.

15 Oleksandr Vdovychenko, quoted in Radio Liberty, *'The battle for Kyiv | How did elite Russian troops fail?...'*, YouTube, 25 February 2023.

16 Rob Lee, 'Eastern Military District commander Colonel-General Alexander Chayko...' [Twitter post], 11:29 a.m., 24 March 2024, <https://x.com/RALee85/status/1506956474546851854>, accessed 1 November 2024; 'Preliminary Lessons in Conventional Warfighting from Russia's Invasion of Ukraine: February-July 2022', RUSI, Special Report, 30 November 2022, p.32.

Chapter 8

1 Unless stated otherwise, this sub-chapter's reconstruction of the 10th Mountain Brigade's counterattack and subsequent Ukrainian raiding is synthesised from the following sources: 10th Mountain Assault Brigade, 'Зі щитом!UA' [Facebook post], 1 October 2022, <https://www.facebook.com/watch/?v=926793554947966&t=82>, accessed 1 November 2024; Violetta Kirkota, 'Артилерист 10-ї гірсько-штурмової бригади "Едельвейс" Тарас Горпиняк:

"Росіяни жалілися: "Один танк и 15 "укропов" положили два с половиной наших батальйона"" ['Artilerist 10-ï girs′ko-šturmovoï brigadi "Edel′vejs" Taras Gorpinjak: "Rosijani žalilisja: "Odin tank i 15 "ukropov" položili dva s polovinoj našix batal′jona""], *Censor.net*, 29 January 2024; Lawrence, *The Battle of Kyiv*, pp.296, 311; '"Наши дроны не мажут": спецы из "Аэроразведки" рассказали, как уничтожают ВС РФ (видео)' ['"Naši drony ne mažut": specy iz "Aèrorazvedki" rasskazali, kak uničtožajut VS RF (video)'], *focus.ua*, 18 June 2022; James Marson, 'The Ragtag Army That Won the Battle of Kyiv and Saved Ukraine', *The Wall Street Journal* (WSJ), 20 September 2022; Radio Liberty, '*How Russian commanders gained the trust of locals in Kyiv region…*', YouTube, 5 July 2023; Schönhausen, 'Wounded Tiger 12', *Medium*, 8 March 2023; Schönhausen, 'Wounded Tiger 13'; 'Senior Sailor Kiril Cherepakhin', www.36thdivisionarchive.com, no date; Radio Liberty, '*Ukrainian Troops Hold A Defensive Line In The Kyiv Region*', YouTube, 2 April 2022. All Russian vehicle losses confirmed using *Russo-Ukrainian WarSpotting*.

2. 'Residents of the village of Obukhovychi near Kyiv: "The Russian military used us as a human shield"' (In Russian), *BBC News Russian*, 8 April 2022. Note that there is some discrepancy regarding the exact date of the Battle of Obukhovychi. The author has followed Schönhausen on placing it on 21 March (see Schönhausen, 'Wounded Tiger 12').

3. Sladden et al., 'The Battle of Irpin River', p.41; John Spencer and Liam Collins, 'Waterworld: How Ukraine Flooded Three Rivers To Help Save Kyiv', Modern War Institute, 1 July 2022.

4. Unless stated otherwise, this sub-chapter is based on Lesya Medvedenko; "Mars" – in memory of the Hero of the Defence of Irpin' (In Ukrainian), *ArmyInform.com.ua*, 14 September 2022; Lesya Pinyak, '"If you hesitate a split second…", *Hromadske*, 15 March 2023; Aleksandr Shulman, 'Junior Lieutenant Ihor Dykun destroyed eleven ruscists in battle and burned an enemy BMD' (In Ukrainian), *ArmyInform.com.ua*, 31 March 2022; Valentyna Rozumenko, 'Deputy Commander of the 133rd Battalion of the Territorial Defense on Bucha: "The Rashists understood: either they will be finished off there, or they must flee"' (In Ukrainian), *Ukraina Moloda*, 9 June 2022.

5. Presence of all these formations evidenced via confirmed vehicle losses in area, as seen on *Russo-Ukrainian WarSpotting*.

6. Trofimov, *Our Enemies Will Vanish*, pp.154–155.

7. 'Putin explains Russia's spring 2022 retreat from Kyiv. His account differs from expert opinion', *Meduza*, 29 July 2023.

8. Alexander Fomin, quoted in Guardian News, *'Russia says it will 'radically reduce military activity around Kyiv and Chernihiv'*, YouTube, 29 March 2022.

9. 'The operation in Ukraine is going according to plan, the tasks of the first stage have been solved. The Ministry of Defense of the Russian Federation summed up the results of the month', *TASS*, 25 March 2022.

10. Mason Clark, 'Russian Offensive Campaign Assessment, March 27', ISW, 27 March 2022.

11. Mason Clark, George Barros, Kateryna Stepanenko, 'Russian Offensive Campaign Assessment, March 30', ISW, 30 March 2022.

12. Jake Epstein and John Haltiwanger, 'The Pentagon doesn't buy Russia's claim that it's withdrawing troops around Kyiv', *Business Insider*, 29 March 2022; Steven Erlanger, 'NATO sees evidence that Russian troops are regrouping, not withdrawing from around Kyiv', *NYT*, 31 March 2022.

13. Mason Clark, 'Russian Offensive Campaign Assessment, March 27', ISW, 27 March 2022.

14. Pili and Minniti, 'Understanding Russia's Great Games: From Zapad 2013 to Zapad 2021', *RUSI.org*, 7 June 2022.

15. Schönhausen, 'Wounded Tiger 13', *Medium*, 8 March 2023.

16. Anon., quoted in Sladden et al., 'The Battle of Irpin River', p.48.

17. Unless stated otherwise, this reconstruction of the Battle of Dmytrivka is based off Aleksandr Shulman, 'A company of Galician lions in the battles for Dmytrivka', *ArmyInform.com.ua*, 4 April 2022; War in Ukraine with English Subtitles, *'My tank is called "Fury" -- (Battle of Dmytrivka)'*, YouTube, 28 October 2022; War in Ukraine with English Subtitles, *'Showdown in little Dmytrivka'*, YouTube, 4 October 2022; War in Ukraine with English Subtitles, *'Aftermath of the tank battle in Dmytrivka'*, YouTube, 28 October 2022; War in Ukraine with English Subtitles, *'Three little villages that could…'*, YouTube, 17 March 2023; BlueSauron, ''Special military Operation'.. well…' [Twitter post], 9:35 a.m., 1 April 2022, <https://x.com/Blue_Sauron/status/1509811578442596352>, accessed 1 November 2024.

18. This is based off Security Service of Ukraine (SBU) information provided to openDemocracy for their article on the village also named Dmytrivka in the Borodyanka region. Apparently, the SBU, confused between the two villages, provided them with information regarding Dmytrivka in the Bucha region, as opposed to Dmytrivka in the Borodyanka region. This is made evident by the SBU's reference to the 76th GAAD, which did not fight in the Borodyanka region. (See Farbar, 'Face-to-face with killers…', *openDemocracy*, 16 June 2022).

19. 'Verified video appears to show Ukrainian troops killing Russian captives. Here's what we know about it.', *Meduza*, 8 April 2022.

Chapter 9

1. Unless stated otherwise, this sub-chapter uses a cross-reference of the following sources: Sonne et al., 'Battle for Kyiv: Ukrainian Valor…', *WP*, 24 August 2022; Suspilne Chernihiv, *'Russian Invasion of Ukraine and the first battles…'*, YouTube, 6 May 2023; Jiang Chung, *War In Ukraine Volume 5*, pp.42–44; Cooper et al., *War In Ukraine Volume 2*, pp.45–46; Cooper et al., *War In Ukraine Volume 6*, p.57; National Guard of Ukraine, *'Defense of Chernihiv: a pain in invaders' neck'*, YouTube, 14 February 2023. Russian losses and relevant units confirmed via *Russo-Ukrainian WarSpotting*.

2. 'Oleksandr', quoted in Suspilne Chernihiv, *'Russian Invasion of Ukraine and the first battles…'* YouTube, 6 May 2023.

3. Mikhail Kulikov, quoted in Anton Gerashchenko, '8. Куликов Михаил Игоревич| Пленный из рф| #Ищисвоих' ['8. Kulikov Mihail Igorevič| Plennyj iz rf| #Iśisvoih'], YouTube, 26 March 2022.

4. See Jiang Chung, *War in Ukraine Volume 5*, pp.5–6 for detail regarding lack of modern radios and SNS systems in T-72A/AV/B/B3.

5. Stephen Bryen, 'The fatal failure of Russia's ERA cryptophone system', *Asia Times*, 26 May 2022; Cathal McDaid, 'The Mobile Network Battlefield in Ukraine- Part 2', *ENEA*, 31 March 2022. It is certain that the 41st CAA's ERA was specifically compromised (see Alexander Martin, 'Russians reportedly take out own secure communications system during Kharkiv assault', *Sky News*, 8 March 2022), although other CAAs may have also been affected.

6. 'The entire platoon of the Russian occupiers surrendered to the Ukrainian Armed Forces', *Lviv Now*, 24 February 2022.

7. 'ID 31117 T-64BV', *Lostarmour.info*, <https://lostarmour.info/armour/31117>, accessed 1 November 2024. Lostarmour lists two T-64BVs lost here, but one is misplaced from near the *Epitsentr* supermarket.

8. The presence of the 35th MRB is indicated by this BMP from the brigade abandoned nearby on the same day: '#14372 BMP-1(P)', *Russo-Ukrainian WarSpotting*, <https://ukr.warspotting.net/view/14372/56821/>, accessed 1 November 2024.

9. Viktor Nikoliuk, quoted in 'Командувач ОК "Північ" Віктор Ніколюк: У російського командування працює принцип Жукова "баби ще нарожають"' ['Komanduvač OK "Pivnič" Viktor Nikoljuk: U rosijs′kogo komanduvannja pracjuje princip Žukova "baby eše narožajut"'], *Censor.net*, 14 October 2022.

10. Anon., quoted in National Guard of Ukraine, *'Defense of Chernihiv: a pain in invaders' neck'*, YouTube, 14 February 2023.

11. 'Nikolai Pirozhkov', *topcargo200.com*, <https://topcargo200.com/89/>, accessed 1 November 2024.

12. This sub-chapter is based a cross-reference of the following sources: Violetta Kirtoka, 'Майор Богдан Гарнага, позивний Бахмат: "Ми палили броню ворога, а колони навіть не зупинялися – у них було завдання якомога швидше дістатися Києва"' ['Major Bogdan Garnaga, pozivnij Bahmat: "Mi palili bronju voroga, a koloni navit′ ne zupinjalisja – u nih bulo zavdannja jakomoga švidše distatisja Kieva"'], *Censor.net*, 15 May 2022; Violetta Kirkota, 'Герой України, командир 58-ої бригади Дмитро Кащенко: "Армія росії – не друга армія світу, а найдовша армія світу"' ['Geroj Ukraïni, komandir 58-oï brigadi Dmitro Kaśenko: "Armija rosii – ne druga armija svitu, a najdovša armija svitu"'], *Censor.net*, 23 May 2022; Violetta Kirtoka, 'Командир 16-го батальйону 58-ої бригади Володимир Логуш: "Як вони заходили через кордон? Ішла фура, за нею впритул три-чотири БТРи. В темряві незрозуміло було, що то кацапська техніка"' ['Komandir 16-

go batal'jonu 58-oï brigadi Volodimir Loguš: "Jak voni zahodili čerez kordon? Išla fura, za neju vpritul tri-čotiri BTRi. V temrjavi nezrozumilo bulo, ŝo to kacaps'ka tehnika"'], *Censor.net*, 8 June 2022; Nikoliuk, *In Defence of the Sumy Region* (In Ukrainian), p.4.
13 The identification of the 15th MRB is based on the presence of BTR-82s. The 2nd GCAA's 30th Motor Rifle Brigade was also equipped with BTRs, but it appears to have been travelling in the van of the army.
14 Vitaliy Derevyanko, quoted in Kirtoka, 'Командир 16-го батальйону 58-ої бригади...' ['Komandir 16-go batal'jonu 58-oï brigadi...'], *Censor.net*, 8 June 2022.
15 Volodymyr Logush, quoted in Kirtoka, 'Командир 16-го батальйону 58-ої бригади...' ['Komandir 16-go batal'jonu 58-oï brigadi...'], *Censor.net*, 8 June 2022.
16 This following reconstruction of the 90th GTD's crossing of the Desna is based firstly on evidence that a large VSRF armoured formation was moving in a Semenivka-Sosnytsya direction (see Elena Safarova, 'Іван Ващенко: про чернігівські "Чорнобаївки", рух опору та героїв оборони міста' ['Ivan Vašenko: pro černigivs'ki "Čornobaïvki", ruh oporu ta geroïv oborona mista'], *Suspilne Chernihiv*, 24 March 2022). Secondly, wrecked vehicles from the division are confirmed on the road to Sosntysa (see '#1090 TZM-T reloader vehicle (for TOS-1A 'Solntsepek')', *Russo-Ukrainian WarSpotting*, <https://ukr.warspotting.net/view/1090/131823/>, accessed 1 November 2024). Thirdly, the crossing of the division over the Desna is confirmed by *Russo-Ukrainian WarSpotting* and the testimonies in Kirtoka, 'Командир 16-го батальйону 58-ої бригади...' ['Komandir 16-go batal'jonu 58-oï brigadi...'], *Censor.net*, 8 June 2022. Further references used include Trofimov, *Our Enemies Will Vanish*, pp.104–106, and Suspilne Chernihiv, 'The encirclement of Chernihiv and the battle near the "Epicentre" | Battle for Chernihiv episode 2', YouTube, 30 May 2022. Table 4 contents synthesised from *WarSpotting* information and Sirdo, '90th Guards Tank Division', sirdo.substack.com, 15 April 2024.
17 Unless otherwise stated, the following sub-chapter is based on Cooper et al., *War in Ukraine Volume 6*, p.59; Schwirtz et al., 'Putin's War', *NYT*, 18 December 2022; Lawrence, *The Battle for Kyiv*, p.301; Nikoliuk, *In Defence of the Sumy Region* (In Ukrainian), pp.3, 6, 12; Joe Barnes, 'Vladimir Putin's elite 'bodyguards of Moscow' unit pulverized in Ukraine', *The Telegraph*, 13 September 2022; Lidi Ya Films, *'Good Morning we are from Okhtyrka! (real war documentary from Ukraine)'*, 21 May 2023; Kirkota, 'Заступник командира 93-ої бригади полковник Олександр Сліпко...' ['Zastupnik komandira 93-oï brigadi polkovnik Oleksandr Slipko...'], *Censor.net*, 20 April 2023; War Diary, *'SUMY. THE GUT PUNCH [Incredible bravery of civilians]'*, 17 February 2023; Golovka, '"We Blew Up The Last of the Three Bridges on the Uzh River..." (In Ukrainian), *savelife.in.ua*, 27 December 2023; Suspilne Chernihiv, *Знищення "Іскандерів", дзвінок Валерія Залужного, бої навколо міста│#Лютий #Опір #Прилуки*' ['Znišennja "Iskanderiv", dzvinok Valerija Zalužnogo, boï navkolo mista│#Ljutyj #Opir #Priluki'], YouTube, 5 March 2023. Locations and losses of Russian units confirmed via *Russo-Ukrainian WarSpotting*.
18 Konrad Muzyka, 'Russian Forces in the Western Military District', CNA, Occasional Paper, 28 June 2021, pp.9–12.
19 Based on captured documentation, see Rob Lee, 'Regarding the 4th Tank Division, it says the 12th Tank Regiment lost 18 T-80U and 13th Tank Regiment lost 47 T-80UE tanks...' [Twitter post], 12:50 p.m., 16 May 2022, <https://x.com/RALee85/status/1526168105835278337>, accessed 1 November 2024.
20 Andrea Rosa and Felipe Dana, 'Inside a Ukrainian town that warded off Russian troops', *PBS News*, 29 March 2022.
21 Militaryland.net, *'Destroyed convoy of Ukrainian Air Assault troops in Sumy (February 24, 2022)'*, YouTube, 24 February 2024.
22 This reconstruction of the 2nd GMRD's attack on Pryluky is based on *Russo-Ukrainian WarSpotting* loss data and Suspilne Chernihiv, 'Знищення "Іскандерів", дзвінок Валерія Залужного...' ['Znišennja "Iskanderiv", dzvinok Valerija Zalužnogo...'], YouTube, 5 March 2023.
23 At least some supporting elements of the 2nd GRMD would later cross the Udai basin with the 2nd GCAA but were not committed to the fighting outside Kyiv. (see '#10380 9S931-1 command post (for 'Barnaul-T' air defense command and control system)', *Russo-Ukrainian WarSpotting*, <https://ukr.warspotting.net/view/10380/58632/>, accessed 1 November 2024.

Chapter 10

1 Julia Semenets, 'The Battle of Kruty 100 years later. On February 28, 2022, the Russians were defeated there' (in Ukrainian), *texty.org.ua*, 28 February 2023.
2 Unless stated otherwise, this paragraph and following section describing the breakthrough of the 2nd GCAA are evidenced via the following sources: Suspilne Chernihiv, *'Знищення "Іскандерів", дзвінок Валерія Залужного...'* ['Znišennja "Iskanderiv", dzvinok Valerija Zalužnogo...'], YouTube, 5 March 2023; Golovka, '"We Blew Up The Last of the Three Bridges on the Uzh River..." (In Ukrainian), *savelife.in.ua*, 27 December 2022; 'Diary of a Scout: First 100 Days of War', *The New Voice of Ukraine*, no date; Carlotta Gall, 'At the Edge of Kyiv, Ukrainians Show Off Their Counteroffensive, *NYT*, 28 March 2022. Russian vehicle losses and units are confirmed via *Russo-Ukrainian WarSpotting*.
3 Dmytro Dzhulay, "'Shot In The Head': Beloved Son, Son-In-Law Among Victims Of 'Deliberate Cruelty' In Russian War On Ukraine', *Radio Liberty*, 4 May 2022.
4 Kira Tolstyakova, 'Post Office Massacre: Russian Soldiers Shot Five Ukrainian Civilians Seeking to Defend Their Village, Investigation Finds', *Radio Liberty*, 26 July 2022.
5 'Ukraine: Executions, Torture During Russian Occupation Apparent War Crimes in Kyiv, Chernihiv Regions', *Human Rights Watch*, 18 May 2022.
6 Andriy Verkhohliad was commander of 3rd Company, 1st Mechanised Battalion and was later credited for the defence of Rusaniv (see 'Verkhohliad, Andrey Leonidovich', vue.gov.ua.)
7 Anon., quoted in 'Diary of a Scout: First 100 Days of War', *The New Voice of Ukraine*, no date.
8 Alina Basenko, 'Мало хто усвідомлює, що знаковим для нашої громади стало 2 березня...' ['Malo hto usvidomljuje, ŝo znakovim dlja našoï gromadi stalo 2 bereznja...'] [Facebook post], 2 March 2023.
9 Serhii Burkovskyi, quoted in Golovka, '"We Blew Up the Last of the Three Bridges on the Uzh River..." (In Ukrainian), *savelife.in.ua*, 27 December 2022.
10 Confirmed by '#160 T-72A', *Russo-Ukrainian WarSpotting*, <https://ukr.warspotting.net/view/160/32620/>, accessed 1 November 2024.
11 Unless stated otherwise, the following sub-chapter is based off a synthesis of the following sources: Suspilne Chernihiv, 'The encirclement of Chernihiv...', YouTube, 30 May 2022; Suspilne Chernihiv, 'Russian SRG in Chernihiv and russian pilot in captivity/Battle for Chernihiv Episode 3', YouTube, 11 June 2023; Jian Chung, *War In Ukraine Volume 5*, p.44; Cooper et al, *War in Ukraine Volume 6*, p.58; 'The Russian Air War and Ukrainian Requirements for Air Defence', RUSI, Special Report, 7 November 2022, p.15; 'Attack on a school, abduction, captivity. How residents of Mykhailo-Kotsiubynske in Chernihiv Region survived the occupation', *Media Initiative for Human Rights*, 29 December 2023; Kirtoka, 'Майор Богдан Гарнага...' ['Major Bogdan Garnaga...'], *Censor.net*, 15 May 2022; 'Командувач ОК "Північ" Віктор Ніколюк...' ['Komanduvač OK "Pivnič" Viktor Nikoljuk...'], *Censor.net*, 14 October 2022.
12 Artem Linkov, quoted in Suspilne Chernihiv, 'The encirclement of Chernihiv...', YouTube, 30 May 2022.
13 Inna Gadzynska, Yevhenia Drozdova, Nadja Kelm, Petro Bodnar, Olha Makukha, Yuliia Semenets, 'Bombs, Death and a Downed Pilot. Three Days of Air Raids on Chernihiv in March 2022', *texty.org.ua*, no date.
14 Cooper et al. point to the kill being secured by an Osa-AKM SAM system of the 58th Motorised Brigade (see *War in Ukraine Volume 6*, p.48) but this separates from the account given in Suspilne Chernihiv, 'Russian SRG in Chernihiv...', YouTube, 11 June 2023.
15 Russia began the war with less than 100 fully trained and combat ready pilots (see 'Preliminary Lessons in Conventional Warfighting from Russia's Invasion of Ukraine: February-July 2022', RUSI, Special Report, 30 November 2022, p.47).
16 Oleksiy Luhina, quoted in 'Attack on a school, abduction, captivity...', *Media Initiative for Human Rights*, 29 December 2023.
17 Jiang Chung, *War In Ukraine Volume 5*, p.44.

18 Viktor Nikoliuk, quoted in 'Командувач ОК "Північ" Віктор Ніколюк…"' ['Komanduvač OK "Pivnič" Viktor Nikoljuk…'], *Censor.net*, 14 October 2022.
19 This description of the battle of Kolychikva is based off Suspilne Chernihiv, 'The encirclement of Chernihiv…', YouTube, 30 May 2022, and Aleksandr Shulman, 'Батальйон «виговців» за місяць затрофеїв 10 танків росії' ['Batal'jon «vigovciv» za misjac' zatrofeїv 10 tankiv rosiї'], *ArmyInform.com.ua*, 18 May 2022.
20 Unless stated otherwise, this reconstruction of the Battle of Lukashivka is based off the following sources: Suspilne Chernihiv, *'The encirclement of Chernihiv…'*, YouTube, 30 May 2022; Natalia Naidiuk, 'Lukashivka near Chernihiv year on after liberation: 32 houses completely destroyed, every single one damaged', *Hromadske*, 6 April 2023; Mariana Petsukh, '"The blood of my sons was not shed in vain." The story of two Russian brothers who died for Ukraine', *Homadske*, 7 April 2022; 'Командувач ОК "Північ" Віктор Ніколюк…"' ['Komanduvač OK "Pivnič" Viktor Nikoljuk…"'], *Censor.net*, 14 October 2022; Kirtoka, 'Командир 16-го батальйону 58-ої бригади…' ['Komandir 16-go batal'jonu 58-oї brigadi…'], *Censor.net*, 8 June 2022; Max Bearak and Siobhán O' Grady, 'In shattered Chernihiv, Russian siege leaves a city asking, 'Why?', *WP*, 5 April 2022. Ukrainian and Russian vehicle losses confirmed via *Lostarmour.info* and *Russo-Ukrainian WarSpotting* respectively.
21 Presence of 74th GMRB confirmed by Iryna Domashchenko, 'Russian Soldier Convicted of Brutal Treatment', *Institute for War & Peace Reporting*, 5 September 2023. Attachment of 90th GTD indicated by '#6443 T-72A', *Russo-Ukrainian WarSpotting*, <https://ukr.warspotting.net/view/6443/>, accessed 1 November 2024.
22 "Viking", quoted in Suspilne Chernihiv, *'The encirclement of Chernihiv…'*, YouTube, 30 May 2022.
23 Unless otherwise stated this account of the 90th GTD's advance on Brovary is reconstructed from *Russo-Ukrainian WarSpotting*; Kirtoka, 'Командир 16-го батальйону 58-ої бригади…' ['Komandir 16-go batal'jonu 58-oї brigadi…'], *Censor.net*, 8 June 2022; Cooper et al., *War In Ukraine Volume 6*, p.61; Anatasia Chumakova, Damir Nigmatullin, Liliya Yapparova, Alexey Kovalev, 'I can do whatever I want to you' Russian soldiers raped and murdered Ukrainian civilians in the village of Bohdanivka', *Meduza*, 18 April 2022.
24 Presence of conscripts confirmed by Chumakova et al., ''I can do whatever I want to you…', *Meduza*, 18 April 2022. For status as second wave formation see Petri Mäkelä, 'Yikes: Russia Just Concluded a War Game with 200 Tanks', *The National Interest*, 13 July 2019.
25 Paul P. Murphy and Josh Pennington, 'Ukrainian police special unit takes out tanks in outskirts of Kyiv', *CNN*, 7 March 2022.
26 Mackinnon, 'The Fearless: An elite squad of fighters…', *The Globe and Mail*, 6 June 2024; Sergiy Nuzhnenko, 'У Києві на Майдані Незалежності попрощались із командиром батальйону "Карпатська Січ" Олегом Куциним' ['U Kiєvi na Majdani Nezaležnosti poprošalis' iz komandirom batal'jonu "Karpats'ka Sič" Olegom Kucinim'], *Radio Liberty*, 22 June 2022; Artem Gorovenko, 'Бої під Броварами. Рештка розбитої "Азовом" БТГр розповіла про великі втрати' ['Boї pid Brovarami. Reštka rozbitoї "Azovom" BTGr rozpovila pro veliki vtrati'], *RBC Ukraine*, 11 March 2022.
27 Violetta Kirkota, 'Герой України Роман Дармограй про бої під Броварами: "Хотіли легенько коцнути їхній "Тигр", щоб залишити собі. Не пощастило. Йшли танки. Тому довелося забирати танки"' ['Geroj Ukraїni Roman Darmograj pro boї pid Brovarami: "Hotili legen'ko kocnuti їhnij "Tigr", šob zališiti sobi. Ne pošastilo. Išli tanki. Tomu dovelosja zabirati tanki"'], *Censor.net*, 13 April 2022.
28 Unless stated otherwise, the following reconstruction of the Battle of Brovary is based off firstly videos of the event itself: The Sun, *'Another Russian convoy is ambushed by brave Ukrainians using chillingly lethal anti-tank missiles'*, YouTube, 13 March 2022, and In The Trenches, *'Battle of Brovary- Russian Armoured Column Ambushed'*, YouTube, 10 March 2022. Also referenced were the following media sources: Kirtoka, 'Герой України Роман Дармограй…"' ['Geroj Ukraїni Roman Darmograj…"'], *Censor.net*, 13 April 2022; Tatyana Nikolaenko, 'Тетяна Чорновол: "В тому знаменитому бою, де на відео розлітаються танки, насправді працювали не байрактари, а наші дві "Стугни" і "Корсар"' ['Tetjana Čornovol: "V tomu znamenitomu boju, de na video rozlitajut'sja tanki, naspravdi pracjuvali ne bajraktari, a naši dvi "Stugni" i "Korsar"'], *Censor.net*, 6 April 2022; Marson, 'The Ragtag Army…', *WSJ*, 20 September 2022; Kyrylenko and Larin, 'It was necessary to see how…', *Ukrainska Pravda*, 22 February 2023.
29 Wire-tapped audio of the Russian radio net reveals as such (see The Trenches, 'Battle of Brovary- Russian Armoured Column Ambushed', YouTube, 13 March 2022). Zakharov was only wounded however (see Marson, 'The Ragtag Army…', *WSJ*, 20 September 2022). Confirmation of R-149MA1 loss: '#2393 R-149MA1 command and staff vehicle', *Russo-Ukrainian WarSpotting*, <https://ukr.warspotting.net/view/2393/10093/>, accessed 1 November 2024.
30 Anon., quoted in Marson, 'The Ragtag Army…', *WSJ*, 20 September 2022.
31 As confirmed by multiple corroborating accounts: Chumakova et al., ''I can do whatever I want to you…', *Meduza*, 18 April 2022; Olena Mukhina, 'She hid her daughters in the cellar for a month: how a village near Kyiv survived Russian occupation', *Euromaidan Press*, 19 June 2022; Catherine Philip, 'Russian soldiers raped me as my terrified son cried', *The Times*, 28 March 2022.

Chapter 11

1 Based on captured documentation, see Rob Lee, 'Ukraine published documents reportedly from Russia's 1st Tank Army showing its losses through March 15…' [Twitter post], 12:36 p.m., 16 May 2022, <https://x.com/RALee85/status/1526164608238624769>, accessed 1 November 2024.
2 Golovka, '"We Blew Up the Last of the Three Bridges on the Uzh River…' (In Ukrainian), *savelife.in.ua*, 27 December 2022.
3 Gaevsky and Golovka, 'Навчити оператора FPV складніше…' ['Navčiti operatora FPV skladniše…'], *savelife.in.ua*, 22 April 2024.
4 Violetta Kirkota, 'The last interview of the Hero of Ukraine Dmytro Kotsiubailo (Da Vinci)', *ukrainefrontlines.com*, 10 March 2023. For proof the company was in theatre as early as 13 March see Serhiy Prytula, 'Друг Да Вінчі вміє зробити все красиво' ['Drug Da Vinči vmiє zrobiti vse krasivo'] [Telegram message], 14:35 p.m., 13 March 2022, <https://t.me/serhiyprytula/501>.
5 This reconstruction of the Battle of Rudnyts'ke is drawn from Gaevsky and Golovka, 'Навчити оператора FPV складніше…', *savelife.in.ua*, 22 April 2024; Radio Liberty, 'Ukrainian Troops Attempt To Drive Russian Forces From Village Near Kyiv', YouTube, 10 March 2022; 'Maryan Kushnir: Journalist of the Ukrainian service of RFERl', *journalistsatwar.gongadzeprize.com.ua*; Author conversation with Maryan Kushnir.
6 Cross-referenced between *Russo-Ukrainian WarSpotting* and Serhiy Prytula, 'Друг Да Вінчі вміє зробити все красиво' ['Drug Da Vinči vmiє zrobiti vse krasivo'] [Telegram message], 14:35 p.m., 13 March 2022, <https://t.me/serhiyprytula/501>.
7 Cross-referenced between *Russo-Ukrainian WarSpotting*; Research by Milos Sipos for *War in Ukraine Volume 6*; Kirtoka, 'The last interview of the Hero of Ukraine Dmytro Kotsiubailo…', *ukrainefrontlines.com*, 10 March 2023; "Da Vinci Wolves" separate 108th battalion, На відео ви бачите, як наша пташка зафіксувала роботу ворожого ЗРК "Бук"…' [Na video vi bačite, jak naša ptaška zafiksuvala robotu vorožogo ZRK "Buk"…'] [Telegram message], 4:28 a.m., 21 March 2022, <https://t.me/smertvorogy/30>.
8 CNN, *'See how gamers are outwitting and helping to kill Russian soldiers'*, YouTube, 13 May 2022.
9 'Ukraine: Executions, Torture During Russian Occupation Apparent War Crimes in Kyiv, Chernihiv Regions', *Human Rights Watch*, 18 May 2022.
10 Olena Gobanova, 'Tamara and Mykola's tale of a week in hell', *voxeurop.eu*, 22 December 2023.
11 Unless otherwise stated, this sub-chapter is drawn from a cross-reference of the following sources: Jian Chung, *War In Ukraine Volume 5*, p.46; Suspilne Chernihiv, *'Russian SRG in Chernihiv…'*, YouTube, 11 June 2023; Olha Makukha, Yuliia Semenets, Margarita Hogun, Yevheniia Drozdova, Nadia Kelm, Inna Gadzynska, 'Height: How Ukrainian fighters stopped the Russians near Chernihiv' (In Ukrainian), *texty.org.ua*, no date.

12 Denys Karlovskyi, 'Chernihiv: About 700 people were killed during the blockade of the city by Russian troops – the mayor', *Ukrainska Pravda*, 8 April 2022.
13 'Ukraine: Russian Strikes Killed Scores of Civilians in Chernihiv', *Human Rights Watch*, 10 June 2022.
14 Confirmed via *Lostarmour.info*.
15 Major General Viktor Nikoliuk describes the Russian SOF formations as 'regiments.' Unfortunately, there is lack of information as to which Spetsnaz Brigades these were drawn from.
16 Informer, '"Tigers" in the snow. The sad story of the assault on Kharkov on February 27 by the forces of the 2nd Special Forces Brigade of the RF Armed Forces' (In Russian), *VK*, <https://vk.com/@milinfolive-tigry-v-snegu-pechalnaya-istoriya-shturma-harkova-27-fevraly>, accessed 1 November 2024.
17 Leonid Khoda, quoted in Makukha et al., 'Height: How Ukrainian fighters stopped the Russians near Chernihiv' (In Ukrainian), texty.org.ua, no date.
18 Denys Kuzmenko, quoted in Suspilne Chernihiv, *'Russian SRG in Chernihiv...'*, YouTube, 11 June 2023.
19 Kirtoka, 'Командир 16-го батальйону 58-ої бригади…' ['Komandir 16-go batal'jonu 58-oï brigadi…'], Censor.net, 8 June 2022.
20 'Dmitriy Kirichenko', www.victims.memorial, <https://www.victims.memorial/people/dmytro-kyrychenko>; 'Denis Kotenko', www.victims.memorial, <https://www.victims.memorial/people/denis-kotenko>; 'Serhii Zaikovskyi', www.victims.memorial, <https://www.victims.memorial/people/sergey-zaikovskiy> [all accessed 1 November 2024].
21 This account of the Battle of Luk'yanivka is reconstructed from Gaevsky and Golovka, 'Навчити оператора FPV складніше…', *savelife.in.ua*, 22 April 2024; War in Ukraine with English Subtitles, *'Tank Battle in Luk'yanivka'*, YouTube, 27 October 2022; Radio Liberty, *'Ukrainians Seize Russian Tanks After Retaking Village'*, YouTube, 28 March 2022; Josh Layton, 'Web designer now fighting for Ukraine tells of coming within 100 metres of Russian tank', *Metro*, 13 April 2022; Danspiun, '115-6. Luk'yanivka cont. (tweet 104–114). Atmospheric film from Volunteer 'Brotherhood Battalion…' [Twitter post], 2:24 a.m., 25 March 2022, <https://x.com/Danspiun/status/1507181526382952459>, accessed 1 November 2024.
22 The presence of a large HQ and logistics hub is confirmed by the following articles: 'Російські загарбники у Великій Дорозі: як ідентифікували підрозділи й окремих військових' ['Rosijs'ki zagarbniki u Velikij Dorozi: jak identifikuvali pidrozdili j okremih vijs'kovih'], *dostup.org.ua*, 26 September 2023; Pavlo Lisnychenko, '"They Drove Into the Yard and Shot the House at Close Range": Tragedy in Chernihiv Region', *bihus.info*, 11 October 2024. Losses confirmed via *Russo-Ukrainian WarSpotting*.
23 Nikoliuk, *In Defence of the Sumy Region* (In Ukrainian), p.12.
24 Golovka, '"We Blew Up The Last of the Three Bridges on the Uzh River…" (In Ukrainian), *savelife.in.ua*, 27 December 2023; corroborated by *Russo-Ukrainian WarSpotting* data.
25 Dmitry, quoted in Chumakova et al., '"I can do whatever I want to you…", *Meduza*, 18 April 2022.
26 Oksana Ivanets, 'Під час боїв на Харківщині на один наш танк приходилося п'ять ворожих — командир танкової Залізної бригади' ['Pid čas boïv na Harkivšini na odin naš tank prihodilosja p'jat' vorožih — komandir tankovoï Zaliznoï brigadi'], *ArmyInform.com.ua*, 13 October 2022.
27 Nazar Vernihora, quoted in Vĩnh San, *'Nazar Vernyhora, 21, led his tank crew in battle with four Russian tanks in March/2022'*, YouTube, 5 August 2022.
28 This reconstruction of the Battle of Nova Basan is based on a cross-reference of the following sources: Gaevsky and Golovka, 'Навчити оператора FPV складніше…' ['Navčiti operatora FPV skladniše…'], *savelife.in.ua*, 22 April 2024; 3rd Separate Iron Tank Brigade, 'Це вражаюче відео з дрону — бій одного українського танку з броньованою армадою рашистів — давно гуляє інтернетом…' ['Ce vražajuče video z dronu — bij odnogo ukraïns'kogo tanku z bron'ovanoju armadoju rašistiv — davno guljae internetom…'] [Facebook post], 1 July 2024, <https://www.facebook.com/watch/?v=449005833353421>, accessed 1 November 2024; Kateryna Prystupa and Daria Yanushkevich, 'Паніка росіян, залишені БТРи з награбованим та люди, що несли їжу військовим ЗСУ: спогади про визволення Нової Басані' ['Panika rosijan, zališeni BTRi z nagrabovanim ta ljudi, ŝo nesli ïžu vijs'kovim ZSU: spogadi pro vizvolennja Novoï Basani'], *Suspilne Chernihiv*, 3 April 2024; 'We are Honoring People who Deserve the All-Ukrainian Gratitude – The President during the Presentation of the Order of the Golden Star and the Cross of Military Merit Awards', www.president.gov.ua, 22 April 2024.
29 Alexandra Sivtsova, '"I'm sure of mine." "He could not give such an order" The story of two Russian soldiers whom their wives tried to find in the war. Both served in the "peacekeeping" brigade that killed civilians near Kyiv', *Meduza*, 19 October 2022.
30 Anon., quoted in 'Diary of a Scout: First 100 Days of War', The New Voice of Ukraine, no date.
31 'Russian troops no longer hold any settlements in Ukraine's Sumy region, says governor', *Reuters*, 4 April 2022.
32 Nikoliuk, In Defence of the Sumy Region (In Ukrainian), p.13.
33 Unless stated otherwise, the following sub-chapter is based on Jian Chung, *Volume 6*, p.47; 'Командувач ОК "Північ" Віктор Ніколюк…"' ['Komanduvač OK "Pivnič" Viktor Nikoljuk…"'], *Censor.net*, 14 October 2022; Kirtoka, 'Командир 16-го батальйону 58-ої бригади…', *Censor.net*, 8 June 2022. Russian losses corroborated with *Russo-Ukrainian WarSpotting*.
34 There are no vehicle losses listed around the pontoon crossing on WarSpotting. See '#2588 River link pontoon (for PMP(-M) floating bridge system)', *Russo-Ukrainain WarSpotting*, <https://ukr.warspotting.net/view/2588/>, accessed 1 November 2024.
35 Svitlana Oslavska, 'The hunt for Russian war criminals. The year-long investigation to uncover Russian war crimes in Yahidne', *Ukrainska Pravda*, 12 May 2023; Iryna Domashchenko, 'Defence claims that the convicted soldiers were not proven guilty in the nearly one year-long trial prove unsuccessful.', *Institute for War & Peace Reporting*, 19 June 2024.
36 Yuliana Skibitska and Yevheniya Mazur, '"That suitcase is where we buried him." In March, the Russians occupied Ivanivka in the Chernihiv region. They burned Afghanistan war veteran Ihor Zuyuk in his own house. This is his story', *babel.ua*, 8 November 2022.
37 Sean Rubinsztein-Dunlop and Phil Hemingway, 'Russia's unspeakable horrors in northern Ukraine: Torture, murder and cluster bombs', *ABC News*, 17 April 2024.
38 'Командувач ОК «Північ» Віктор Ніколюк…»' ['Komanduvač OK "Pivnič" Viktor Nikoljuk…"'], *Censor.net*, 14 October 2022.

ABOUT THE AUTHOR

Joseph Mathers is a Politics and International Relations graduate from the University of Exeter with a specific interest in modern warfare. He is currently pursuing an MA in War Studies at King's College London. This is his first book for Helion.